Ozark Voices

Ozark Voices
Oral Histories from the Heartland

ALEX SANDY PRIMM

Foreword by C. Ray Brassieur

McFarland & Company, Inc., Publishers
Jefferson, North Carolina

Portion of transcript from *Late Night with David Letterman* used by permission of Worldwide Pants Inc.

ISBN (print) 978-1-4766-8617-2
ISBN (ebook) 978-1-4766-4532-2

LIBRARY OF CONGRESS AND BRITISH LIBRARY
CATALOGUING DATA ARE AVAILABLE

Library of Congress Control Number 2022001005

© 2022 Alex Sandy Primm. All rights reserved

No part of this book may be reproduced or transmitted in any form or by any means, electronic or mechanical, including photocopying or recording, or by any information storage and retrieval system, without permission in writing from the publisher.

Front cover: *background photograph* Hawksbill Crag, Upper Buffalo Wilderness Area, Ozark National Forest, Arkansas (Shutterstock/Glenn W. Wheeler); *inset drawing of a man turning hardwood timber into railroad ties, a major industry in the Ozarks after the Civil War into the Great Depression and beyond (drawing by Anna Bolt)*

Printed in the United States of America

*McFarland & Company, Inc., Publishers
Box 611, Jefferson, North Carolina 28640
www.mcfarlandpub.com*

For my partner, Cathy Kovarik Primm.
In memory of my parents,
A. Timon and Nancy Russell Primm,
and my foster grandson,
Tristen Briar Christopher Russ,
and with appreciation for Ozarkers everywhere.

This map of the Ozarks gives a bird's eye view of select communities, streams and special places in a region as big and almost as varied as modern-day Greece (map by Patsy McDowell).

"Dust devils dance in the noonday heat
There's rats in the alley and trash in the street
Gang graffiti on a boxcar door
We can't make it here anymore."
—From "We Can't Make It Here,"
ballad by James McMurtry.

"In the ideal collaborative process everybody contributes knowledge and everybody learns something."
—From *Recording Oral History*,
guide by Valerie Raleigh Yow, 2005

"None of the essays in this book requires elucidation, other than to say, as in everything I write, they are meant to serve as antidotes to despair. Despair leads to boredom, electronic games, computer hacking, poetry and other bad habits."
—From *Down the River*,
essays by Edward Abbey, 1982

Table of Contents

Acknowledgments	xiii
Foreword: Collecting Recollections by C. Ray Brassieur	1
Preface: A Wagonload of Fire	5
Introduction: Backwoods Interviewing	7

**Part I: My First Ozark River Oral Histories:
Headwaters—Setting Forth in Oral History**   11

  1. King of the Ozark Rivers: Ralph "Treehouse" Brown   15
  2. Taking Care of His Creek: George Langenberg   24
  3. Highlights of Ozark Rivers Oral History   32
  Memoir: At Trails End Camp   38

**Part II: Working with the U.S. Forest Service:
Techniques—Beginning in Oral History**   43

  4. Palmer, Missouri: In the Valley of the Ghosts   46
  5. Grasshopper Hollow: Fieldwork in the Ozark's Largest Fen   53
  6. Establishing a Farm and Hunting Fox: Amel Martin   60
  Sidebar: Alford Forest Wins New Lease on Life   62
  Memoir: Adirondack and Ozark Ancient Forests   65

**Part III: U.S. Geological Survey of Gravel and the River:
Fieldwork—Researching Downstream and Up**   69

  7. Gardening for a Life of Abundance: Ted and Kay Berger   73
  8. Gravelbars and a Thief at the Corn Crib: Rev. Cecil King   79

Table of Contents

    9. "We are losing this river...": Jack Toll 82

    Memoir: Almost a Great Job for an Oral Historian 87

Part IV: Marching with the Military Again: Enlistment—Public Service Interviewing in the Ozarks 94

    10. Hogs and Midwives: Interviews with Ft. Wood's Early Settlers 96

    11. The Lady with the Bull Dick Cane on TV: Aileen Hatch 101

    12. Missouri Moonshining Days: George Lane, Waynesville, MO 107

    Sidebar: Ambrosia on the Piney 109

    13. The Cadillac Mayor of Crocker, Missouri: Norma Lea Mihalevich 112

    Memoir: Dancing with the Spirit of Vietnam, May 2014 115

Part V: Journalism into History: Deadline—Every Day a New Story 122

    14. Two Special Parents for Special Children: The Earl Adamses 123

    15. Bass Fishing Tournament: Basil Bacon 126

    16. Area Inventor Looking for Business Partner: Louis Moore 130

    Sidebar: Fine Art from White Oak Forests 134

    17. Local Prophet Carves Wide Swath: Rev. Joseph Jeffers 136

    18. From Birch Tree to the Battle of the Bulge and Back: Bill and Trudy Reed 139

    19. Exposé from a Newbie Election Judge 143

    20. A Day with the Rainbow Family: Ted Berger and Ronnie Jones 145

    Memoir: Holding the Feather: Reflections on the Rainbow Family 152

Table of Contents   xi

Part VI: Making It as a Freelancer:
Gigging—Community Culture from Diverse Angles   154

21. *La Guignolée*—Fiddling in the New Year: Kent Beaulne   157
22. Good Sports: A Burnham Sunday Tradition: Gini Webb Scudder   160
23. A Visit with Bob Holt and Venae Heier   163
24. View to the East: Country Folks Will Wave   165
25. Route 66: African American History Along the Mother Road   167
Sidebar: Hard Traveling in the Ozarks   172
26. Celebrating the Ozark Highlands Viticulture: Mary Codemo   174
27. Visit with an Ozark Swamp Queen: The Nature Conservancy   177
28. Video with Ralph "Treehouse" Brown and Others   179
29. Voice as Fast as a Fiddle: Dancing at a Country Music Club   184
30. Deliberate Lives: A Celebration of Three Missouri Masters   187
Memoir: Hillbillies and Black Helicopters   190

Part VII: Profiles, Portraits and Champions:
Likeness—Capturing an Essence   196

31. Healing the Waters on an Ozark Frontier   198
32. Organic More Than a Century: Frances "Nana" Yeary   205
Sidebar: Is It True?   210
33. Visiting Moondog in Manhattan   211
34. Magic Quartz Near Mount Ida   213
35. Selling Ties in an Early Blizzard   215
36. A Man Who Loved Copperheads: Ken Carey   219
37. An Ozarker in His New Kentucky Home: George Marshall Smith   227
38. Clyde and the Recycled Chairs   230

39. Woodcarvers: Harold and Elaine Enlow — 232
Memoir: Portrait of my Father as an Eminent Hillbilly: A Cautionary Tale — 235

**Part VIII: Ethics, Activists and Timber:
Hillbilly Ethics—Truth-tellin' and Rural Rapport** — 243

40. The Sweetest Fiddler in All of Arkansas: Violet Hensley — 252
41. This Is the Ozark Earth: A Conversation with a River Conservationist — 254
Sidebar: Rex Harrel's Best Story — 260
42. In Search of Commonwealth: In Memory of Doug Wixson — 262
43. Plonked in Nowheresville: Tristen Russ — 265
Memoir: From China's Skuzziest City—Teaching Oral History — 267

Epilogue: Bedrock, Paradox and Petroforms — 277
Appendix 1: A Brief Guide to Doing Oral History Interviews — 281
Appendix 2: Oral History Projects and Related Contributions — 283
Appendix 3: Oral and Community History Bibliography — 286
Appendix 4: Schedule of Questions: Oral History of Land Use in the Ozarks — 292
Notes — 295
Index — 299

Acknowledgments

My first appreciation goes to all whose interviews and stories appear here. My gratitude also to their families, my editors and project sponsors. I seek to carry forward the spirit of those dedicated to strong communities in our gently changing region.

I've tried to contact all involved or their families to tell each about this publication. All signed releases when I did initial interviews. A copy of the basic release form is in the appendix. I explained that their stories would be preserved, mainly at the State Historical Society of Missouri or sponsoring agencies, and further publication might be possible.

Many stories didn't fit here. I will search for opportunities to share more. My hope is this book will add to a dialog among people in the Ozarks and beyond on rural oral history.

Some wondered whether this project would ever finish. It has been underway over a decade during which I moved from Rolla to Mountain View and several Springfield locations, all thoroughly Ozarky. My mom died during this time, not understanding why I never landed a regular job, like my father who worked for Pulitzer Publishing Co. for forty years.

Both mom and Cathy found many ways to be querulous yet supportive and patient, as have my sisters, family and friends. Since my days as a reporter, I have enjoyed exploring diverse scenes. Initially, I felt a lack of technical expertise to pass along, so resisted a book. Finally, Cathy suggested, why not join my personal perspective on doing community and oral history along with short pieces? That could be worthwhile, I agreed. I'm not an expert on current methodology but have seen the field grow and change. This is one pilgrim's progress.

Special thanks for permission to use lines from the song "We Can't Make It Here Anymore" courtesy of James McMurtry, Short Trip Music & BMI.

Thanks also to the patience and skill of illustrator Anna Bolt, Springfield, who grew up in the mountains of Douglas County while living in a bread truck on the side of a river as a hippie baby, inspiring her love of art and nature; to map maker Patsy McDowell, an illustrator from Northern

Ireland, currently living in Berlin, Germany, specializing in book and role-playing game illustration. His work can be found at https://patsymcd.artstation.com/ or on Twitter @anyonespatsy.

For perseverance, advice, skepticism, leads, rereading, and general joy, thanks especially Brooks Blevins, Elizabeth Akiya Chestnut, Robb and Anne Jacobson, Peter Morrin and Carolyn Brooks, Linda Palmisano, Ross Payton, Molly Bess Rector, Tianna Snyder, and Susan Thel.

Among persevering friends who must know how much I appreciate their diverse inspiration: Tom Ashcraft, Jeff Bentley, Jim Bogan, Kent Brown and Louise Wienckowski, Loring Bullard, Jean Carnahan, Rita and Ron Chaskelson, Andy Cline and Lola Butcher, Jeff Corrigan, Hank and Katie Dorst, Bill and Nancy Echols, John Fernie, Jacqui Froelich, Sam Gifford, Mac and Pinky Gum, Lanny Jones, Janet McKean, Jim Merritt, Mark and Cay Miller, Lynn Morrow, Justin and MaryAnn Mutrux, Chris and Susan Pantaleoni, Jim and JudyJo Protiva, Bob Ranney, Peter Raven, Chris and Tim Roehl, Neil and DeAnna Rosenbaum, Mike and Karen Schneider, Howard and Tsila Schwartz, Nancy Shelton, Jay Shoemaker and Teresa Mears, Betsy Van Dyke, and Denise Vaughn. Also, radio KZGM, Cabool, and neighbors on Windy Ridge Road and the Greenwood Forest.

Finally in memory of a few special Ozarkers and inspirations: Leon Cambre, Michael Castro, Kenny Fiebelman, Leonard and Virginia Hall, Richard Jouharian, Norma Kraus, George McPherson, Jr., James Neal Primm, Lynda Richards, and Jerry Vineyard.

Foreword

Collecting Recollections

BY C. RAY BRASSIEUR

Recollections may be the greatest of human treasures—so precious we spend our days reflecting upon them and sharing them with others. But the great mass of recollections is never permanently recorded. For such a precious cache of treasures, most recollections remain transitory and in danger of permanent loss were it not for the methods of oral history, and the devotion of oral historians like Alex Primm.

When Alex invited me to write this foreword to his terrific collection of Ozark oral histories, I remembered the doctoral dissertation (University of Chicago) of Carl Ortwin Sauer, the dean of American historical geography. Sauer's dissertation, *The Geography of the Ozark Highland of Missouri*, was published 100 years ago, as *Bulletin No. 7*, of *The Geographic Society of Chicago*, 1920. Half of Sauer's work details the physiographical dynamics of the Ozarks; the other half wades deeply into the culture history and human development of this region. I recommend Professor Sauer's work to all interested in the Ozarks, especially those faced with recording the transformations that occurred during the 20th century. How do we square these great changes with the popular promotions of the Ozarks as the home of old-time folk tradition?

Many of Sauer's century-old ideas stand out to me as entirely relevant today. In contrast to the conventional thoughts of his day, Sauer insisted that landscapes do not determine the culture of people who inhabit them. Instead, Sauer insisted that humans create cultural landscapes through their work and play. I would add that memories are essential in that creative process. Recollections of the "good old ways" are continuously recalled and redirected into renewed forms of tradition. Such "recursions" of tradition, as folklorist Henry Glassie called them, have always been part of the living culture process. As Alex demonstrates in his Ozark oral histories, the important stories are not always those orated by classic exemplars of antiquity. Folks and folk regions are mutable and dynamic.

Carl Sauer recognized that landscapes should not be thought of as unchanging. He insisted that all landscapes on earth are the products of human manipulation. This idea influenced the development of the current field of historical ecology. Sauer directed researchers toward holistic views of humans as persistent actors within ecological processes, and he encouraged the documentation of massive environmental changes wrought by humans. In this collection of oral histories, Alex often addresses historical ecological concerns.

I was delighted to read, for example, about Alex's collaborations with Dr. Robb Jacobson in the study of "Historical Land-Use Changes and Potential Effects on Stream Disturbance in the Ozark Plateaus, Missouri," a report published by the USGS in 1994. For good reason, we admire the glory of Ozark rivers like the Current, Jacks Fork, and Little Piney. But our contemporary understandings too often overlook the massive timber cutting, farming, livestock production, and gravel mining that transformed those land and waterscapes into their current forms.

Demonstrations of oral history method and techniques are masterfully presented throughout this book. Still, the field application of oral history can be tricky—especially if you don't expect the unexpected. As a folklorist, and especially while working in the Ozarks, I learned to anticipate the likelihood of collecting in varied genres. For example, I have recorded interviews that broke out in rhyme, song, tall tales, proverbs, poems, harangues, sayings, sermons, and so forth. And quite a range of jokes.... Are such items oral history? They certainly contribute mightily to creative communication in the Ozarks.

During the 1990s, Alex and I shared many delightful experiences working together in the northeastern Ozarks among descendants of French miners. I am thus inspired to share a piece of lore. I collected this item from an Anglo-American English speaker who perceived it as a joke. I believe it is an ancient instance of crude humor that marks the ethnic boundary between French and Anglo settlers of the Ozarks. It goes like this:

The Poor Mountain Lion and the Frenchman

One day two mountain lions met on a hill in the Ozarks. One of the lions was fat and healthy and the other was poor and skinny. The fat lion looked at his skinny friend and remarked, "Hey, you look feeble, are you eating well these days?" The skinny lion replied, "Well, I hunt and eat every day, but I stay poor and skinny. I don't know what's wrong." The fat lion said, "Tomorrow I'll go hunting with you and try to find out your problem." The next morning the two mountain lions climbed on a cliff overhanging a well-worn trail. Before long here comes a French miner just a whistling a lively tune and pushing his wheelbarrow to the mine. When the Frenchman arrived at the base of cliff below the mountain lions, the skinny lion let out a terrible roar, pounced down on the Frenchman, and quickly gobbled him down—belt buckle and all. The fat lion climbed down off the cliff and said, "Now I see your problem, my friend. First, you roared so loud that you scared the crap out of that Frenchman. Then you pounced on him hard enough to squeeze all of the hot air from him. Now, when you remove the crap and hot air from a Frenchman there is not much left—no wonder you're starving to death."

This old gag, far too crude for public repetition, undoubtedly was retold for many generations. The sense of the jest reveals that mountain lions (Anglo Americans) are aware of the typical *joie de vivre* of the jovial Frenchmen, but they fail to place much value (nutritive or otherwise) in this cultural feature. As such, we have here a symbolic kernel of the relationship between French and Anglo settlers of the Ozarks—an uneasy relationship shaped by episodes of war, changes of governmental authority, and ultimate Anglo-American domination. With this tale I'm merely suggesting that oral historians should expect the unexpected—you may collect far more than you plan for.

I am honored to contribute these few words in praise of Alex's fine collection of oral histories. Primm describes his own writing as a combination of memory and memoir. The author shares the wisdom and voices of fascinating characters, but he places himself as a character in these stories. We learn as much about Alex Primm as we do about his collaborating informants. We are not left wondering about the author's positionality or role in this literary production. Creativity is generously shared among all characters and participants in these stories, producing a superior collection of oral histories, and a model for the discipline of oral history.

Specializing in the culture of Mississippi Valley, C. Ray Brassieur earned his PhD at the University of Missouri, Columbia, where his dissertation focused on Ozark "PawPaw" French traditions. He served as program coordinator for the university's Cultural Heritage Center, then as director of the state historical society's oral history program. He wrote Inherit the Atchafalaya, *a history at the heart of Louisiana culture.*

Preface

A Wagonload of Fire

> This story from Aileen Hatch, at her farm near Plato, Missouri, stands out as one of the greatest oral histories I have ever heard.

"My grandfather was a professional hunter. By that, I mean he had dogs and horses and guns. He would go to a farmer's house, and the family would keep him, feed his dogs, and him and his horses until he killed their winter's meat. Killed and cured—they salted it—killed their winter's meat. This was my grandfather—James Meadows. Whenever they had all they wanted, then he'd go to the next farm. And he would kill and cure their meat for the winter.

"I think he started in about October and went all through the winter. What he got out of it was his room and his board and the furs, the skins and the furs.

"By spring he would have a wagonload of furs and skins and he would take them to St. Louis and sell them. This would be his money for that year.

"Evidently, they were a pretty good price, the furs were this particular year. My grandfather had come on to all the other houses and got their winter's meat. And then came spring and it was time for him to go to St. Louis, sell his furs.

"So he started to St. Louis with his wagonload of furs piled up, you know, and skins and so on his way, just about to Rolla the first day. He camped that night and he slept under his wagon. He built a fire and evidently he got too much fire too close to the hides and you know—I don't know what you know about skins, but they're very—they'll burn quick—a lot of suet on them, dried suet, that's like grease.

"So the wagon and the furs caught on fire and burnt up. Well, that burned up all my grandfather's property. He didn't have anything else. That's all he had, that wagon and his horses and his dogs and his guns and the furs. And so that fire put him out of business. So after that he didn't go back into the business anymore. He decided he was too old for that. He went to California and stayed with my aunts, that was his daughters, and lived out there until he died."

> This story shows what it takes to make a living in the Ozarks. Not only a century ago but still. This is a rough place to live. You got to be clever, never give up, laugh and have some good friends, if not family in California.
>
> Mrs. Hatch tells more stories in Parts IV & VIII. Sometimes I wish I could put a recording in this book of the many folks I've interviewed over the years. But our technology changes so fast you can probably find a lot out about her, and others in these pages, on the Internet.
>
> Her words as written themselves are enough.

Introduction

Backwoods Interviewing

Loading up gear to do an interview, my mind often wanders toward special folks and places visited over 40 years of work. I love these times so much I constantly replay certain special visits in my mind. Interviewing has become a skill and an inspiration I want to share. Isn't this something basic we love and need?

Once I spent time along Roubidoux Creek in the northern Ozarks where I met a woman who lived as her Cherokee ancestors taught her. Daniel Boone weathered several months of a long hunt nearby shortly before the War of 1812. Many people escaped from the Trail of Tears during the hard winter of 1838–39 into these welcoming Ozark forests. They hunkered down in the tangle of streams south of what is now known as Fort Leonard Wood, a.k.a. Fort Lost in the Woods. This huge military base has become a massive economic engine. We take it for granted; war seems almost good for us. I worked briefly on the base and had my share of flashbacks inspired by PTSD from a year in Vietnam long ago.

Many of the Cherokee who settled here during their traumatic forced march West had to hide their true identities for decades. Generations of PTSD! The Ozarks have historically harbored a variety of folks on the run, from the Jesse James era all the way to *Winter's Bone*. I settled here after being drafted into the Army and sent to Vietnam as an editor for a newspaper affiliated with the *Stars and Stripes*. I've met many Vietnam veterans in the backcountry. Certain kinds of people like these remote hills. They don't mind the rough, rocky ground, ticks and chiggers, boiling summers and unpredictable winters. Actually, the variety of people surviving in these five states (Arkansas, Kansas, Missouri and Oklahoma plus, some say, southern Illinois), which contain the Ozarks, totally inspires me. As large an area as modern Greece, the Ozarks continually fascinates me with its diversity. This is a big part of why I've stayed so long and decided to pull together this collection. This is why I spent days along the upper Roubidoux Creek long ago and think of this visit so often.

Over the decades, only a few books or studies have focused on Ozark people. Some wonderful histories and biographies have been written, such as the recently deceased Roy Reed's account of the controversial Orval Faubus, late governor of Arkansas and an experienced tie hacker. That was the big occupation here a century ago: turning oak trees into railroad ties with a crosscut saw and broad ax. Ozark oak took—and still takes—railroads West as essential support for the tracks. I have a few twisty tales to share about backwoods tie hacker families.

Each of the eight parts begins with a technical, how-to-do-it piece, then chapters of oral histories. Finally each ends with a memoir-like meditation. This collection shares many kinds of stories, all true, all gathered from people who have been eminently notable, esteemed survivors. A variety of oral history can be found on the Internet thanks to diverse archives and collectors. But these can be difficult to access and know what's reliable and useful. Some guidance in creating family and other recordings can be inspiring. These form the appendices.

* * *

This collection brings together profiles written during my years in the Ozarks as a reporter, an agriculture museum curator, a political campaigner and an oral historian. I also relate a few adventures as a freelance oral historian for 40 years and share insights on how to interview people. Listening is a skill all of us need. It can help in business, creative work and life in general.

Every person has at least one great story. Shortly before his passing, the late historian Vance Randolph, who wrote such diverse studies as *Pissing in the Snow and Other Stories* and *We Always Lie to Strangers*, observed his region had changed drastically in his lifetime. The old, independent hill crofters he knew from youth were fading out; modern folk driven by technology and wealth were taking over. But friends have told me that Vance recanted that view. He grew to see this region as continuing to attract independent, self-motivated people who question national obsessions with various false gods. Some follow the latest technology, most value tradition, a few true radicals thrive, all love this gnarly Ozark environment.

"I can help you out," this Cherokee woman said when I explained how, in my rush preparing for a drive to the upper Roubidoux, I had forgotten my cassette tape recorder. Tape was the state of the art back then. She said, "let's walk over to the tool shed." Her life's work was growing most of the family's food and medicine. Behind all the rusty hoes she found a dusty old boom box, which an uncle had used for recording and playing music.

"Let's see if this still works," she said, cleaning off the plastic case and plugging it in on her front porch. Luckily, I found some unused cassette tapes back in my truck. We popped one in and punched "play and record." Out rushed a few fat wood roaches. Nevertheless, the condenser mike on this venerable machine worked fine. We had a great morning of storytelling. This leads to my first piece of advice when writing or interviewing: never be shy in looking for a story.

—Mountain View, Missouri

Part I

My First Ozark River Oral Histories
Headwaters—Setting Forth in Oral History

Is oral history the most ancient form of literature? We all do oral history every day. It simply boils down to storytelling. To telling the truth. Listening and passing it on.

It's becoming easier for us to know our histories and where our people originated. When we know what's been important to the people dearest to us; it helps make clearer what your life is really all about.

I've been doing oral history projects for 40 years. I want to pass along some worthwhile skills and stories as well as highlights of trials and adventures. This first group of stories involves people living along some of the cleanest, clearest rivers in the world. Rivers have always fascinated me and most anyone who's experienced an Ozark stream even just whizzing by on old Route 66.

Each of the stories in this section has an introduction that explains how the information evolved. Creating oral history requires several steps, none too difficult, but all necessary to create a good outcome.

Oral history has received more attention since the 1940s because our world has become more complex. We don't have as many written records—letters, diaries, newspapers, etc.—to create the primary records of local and national events. So much happens via email, phone or in meetings where no one is taking notes. But, luckily, important events stay in our deep memory.

Even if there is an official record of some decision, exactly what it was and how it came about may not be fully described in any final report. Military historians have found that accounts from troops on the ground often differ from official records. With enough eyewitness reports, it's possible to reconstruct what really happened.

One of the most fascinating examples of the importance of oral history comes from an excellent book I reviewed for the *Oral History Review*. This case involves a Native American tribe living on the Olympic Peninsula west of Seattle. Failure to investigate local oral history cost the State of Washington more than $60 million and several years of bad blood.

How can failure to consult oral history derail a massive construction project? The issue of access to and support for tribal archives may make this study a classic. The simple explanation is that the state's archaeologist contacted only the tribal government, most of whom were a younger generation and unacquainted with the proposed construction site for a huge dry dock. The young leaders knew little of their tribe's oral history and were under pressure to create local economic development.

The surviving elders were not consulted. When construction began, ancient burials and bones began appearing in the backhoe buckets. As can be imagined, the issue quickly became emotionally heated:

> U.S. Senator Maria Cantwell decided to go to the dry dock site herself to see what was going on. She visited the Sunday after Thanksgiving, dressed in jeans and a sweater. She walked the beach line where tribal members were finding so many of their ancestors.
>
> "It was incredible from my perspective," said Cantwell, who, uninvolved in the project until that point, brought a fresh eye to the situation... "Who among us would go and dig up their relatives? I thought all the options had to be put on the table and explored. There is more there at that site than anyone imagined, and we have to explore all the options to deal with that. And this is just going to continue to be a more expensive proposition."[1]

Contributing to the conflict was the unresolved status of the First People in the region, the Klallam tribe of the Lower Elwa River, a river which flows into the Pacific at Port Angeles. Much of the tribe was wiped out by smallpox shortly after contact with American settlers in the 19th century. The remaining tribal members were gradually pushed aside by industrial development so that only about 750 members remained in 2000.

One of the world's largest sawmills had been built in 1913 on the site that was later selected for the proposed dry dock. Though in a month this plant could produce as much as 14 million board feet of lumber and timbers up to 150 ft., the mill was on pilings which protected rather than damaged a former village and large burial ground below it.

The gradual discovery in 2004 of the size of the nearly forgotten village and its graveyard stunned both the white and native communities. Part of the eventual settlement that doomed the transportation department's new construction project was a proposed museum for the tribe and economic development funds for the city. Other issues remain, as Lynda Mapes writes about in this fascinating book.

Part I—My First Ozark River Oral Histories

This is just one example of how discovering local oral history made a huge difference in a major metropolitan area such as Seattle.

Did you catch those statistics on the Big Mill? Can you imagine a board 150 feet long? They did some serious construction Out West!

Not too many years earlier than the building of the mill at Port Angeles, the Ozarks had the largest sawmill in the world. This was the mill at East Eminence on the Current River built shortly after the Civil War. By 1920 or so when Ozark forests were cut over, many timbermen went to the West Coast.

Oral history is not generally such a big deal. Usually it's family history mainly of interest to nearby relatives. Often oral history is used to attract tourist dollars or support local history museums. The oral histories I recall here mostly had the eventual goal of encouraging local pride and economic development.

1

King of the Ozark Rivers
Ralph "Treehouse" Brown

This guy inspired a generation who loved the rivers. Treehouse was known as one of the toughest, most ornery hillbillies in the Ozarks. I was honored to be at his funeral. Lately his daughter Rose has been running the operation.

I learned over the years that Treehouse had more brewing besides his cabin-based name, fame for shoot-outs and skills as a riverman. He came across as Paladin, "Have gun, will travel," but down deep he was a Santa Claus offering unexpected gifts to whomever took time to listen.

Maybe this is why I like doing oral history. It takes you down unexpected paths, as well as explains what's deeply important to a person. Treehouse had a love of Huzzah Creek, the nearby county seat of Steelville and the freedom to live as he chose. Several times I found him sleeping under a shade tree in mid-day heat with a log as a pillow. A nearby dog got most of the ticks, he explained. Air conditioning? Not necessary if you live near a creek.

This rolling countryside south of Rt. 66 in mid–Missouri features hilly pastures with a roughly equal amount of forest. This rocky Ozark land makes fine country for raising cattle, deer, raccoon and ruckus.

Ralph Brown was a part of my first sponsored oral history project. I had done a variety of interviewing and research earlier, but no one compared with Treehouse.

That is why I have to write this. What kind of man says this when talking about building his house by the river? "I don't know what they thought. I guess they thought I was crazy. I like to be crazy. If everybody thought I was the tops everything would be fine. It's much better for them to know that whatever I take a notion to do, I went ahead and did it. I got a lot of good neighbors. Most of them like me. But you never know who likes you and who don't till it comes to the showdown."

That's pure Treehouse, transcribed from the video I made in the late 1980s with a non-profit group after finishing my first oral history

Ralph "Treehouse" Brown was one of the first canoe outfitters in the Ozarks. He was famous for protecting his gravel bar and canoes. At one point, he lived in his self-built treehouse (illustration by Anna Bolt).

project. I got the bug to do more in-depth interviews. I had been a reporter, but I wanted to write more about folks than the typical newspaper story would allow in 700 words maximum.

Ralph wanted to share his point of view as well as his insights. Visiting his place offered unexpected pleasures. I also learned to be a little cautious. You never knew exactly what kind of project Ralph had going.

His funeral in summer, 1990, was that way too; it had surprises. With his family, neighbors and a few others who knew Ralph from his river floating business, the memorial service attracted a good crowd, maybe 100 people altogether. He lived along the Huzzah Creek for most of his 72 years. I sat next to a guy from St. Louis who told me before the memorial service began that he had become friends with Ralph during an altercation. He had landed his canoe on what Mr. Brown regarded as "his gravel bar." This spit of land along the creek bank constituted a constant source of conflict for Ralph.

"I had been floating solo all day, one of those beautiful spring days," the respectful young man recalled in a quiet tone. We talked briefly while waiting for the funeral to begin. This is the essence of his story:

"I was still high on a combination of beer and various illegal substances. I had to pull over because I knew it was unsafe that afternoon to try to run my canoe under that old wooden hog trough bridge at Scotia where Ralph had his business. There's a lot of water moving down that stream! I didn't want to get hung up under that old log bridge. So there I'm standing near the creek in the shadows late in the day planning where to haul my canoe. All of a sudden this big ol' burly guy comes up and tells me to get off his property. I didn't know who he was then. I still had to get down to Onondaga Cave where my car was."

"'Who says I have to move?' I say back to the big old boy."

"'Me, Ralph Brown. This is my place!' he says back at me."

"Okay, I'll just drag my boat down the gravel bar past the bridge, okay?"

"Nope, you're still trespassing. I'll whoop you good if you don't leave right now."

"I looked the old boy up and down. 'You think you're pretty tough don't you old man? Do you want to wrestle before I move my boat?'"

"I was still pretty high. Ralph looked me over, then tackled me. We begun to wrestle right there on the gravel bar. I wrestled in school, so I'm not afraid of much. Ralph was in for a good challenge. We ended up twisted together down on the gravel like two snakes. Eventually, after five minutes or so, it was a draw. We both gave up, pretty winded and shook hands."

"Ralph became a good friend. That's why I'm here today," the fellow concluded. Soon the memorial service began. About halfway through this guy stood up and told his story. Few others offered accounts quite like this.

The big surprise for most everyone was at a certain point during the service another young man stood up and introduced himself as Ralph's son from the Philippines. He lived 10,000 miles due west of the Ozarks. Ralph had been a U.S. Army medic during World War II and was based on the islands. Ralph had stayed in touch with the boy's mother and their son. He spoke lovingly about Ralph as a distant but concerned father.

I'm sure other stories were shared. There are no shortages as our video on YouTube, "Treehouse, An Ozark Story," suggests. It became available for free in 2018; we sold several thousand copies in previous decades. Part VI on my Freelance Projects has more details on producing oral history videos.

* * *

If you dig around on the net you may also be able to find the late *St. Louis Post-Dispatch* outdoor editor Tim Renken's May 19, 1985, article, "Brown is King of the Rivers," which has a few tall tales. It has a detailed account of the shootout at Harper's Ford and several stories about Ralph recovering plunder from overturned floaters and suddenly submerged motorcycles.

My favorite Ralph wisdoms involved his steady diet of raw potato sandwiches, buying new trucks and much else with hard cash, and vandals digging to find where he buried his cash. Ralph didn't trust banks. He used plastic lids on old canning jars so those with metal detectors would not locate his buried loot.

Floating on Ozark Streams

I first met Ralph after spending most of 1969 on active duty in Vietnam. My friend Pete Morrin—artist, museum director and then an Army reservist who had free time—suggested we go down to the Meramec. He'd heard stories about Ralph from his brother Kevin, who knew the Beletz brothers and a local canoeing club. They were all part of the canoe poling revival in the 1960s. They used to race upstream just using aluminum poles. Ralph and his brother Cliff were some of the toughest river polers ever.

Pete and I borrowed a canoe, hired Ralph to spot our car downstream and finally set off shortly before dark on a spring day. My strongest memory of that trip is Pete playing a flashlight's beams over a gravel bar in swift water as we cautiously looked for a camping spot in near dark. He chose the spot. We landed safely and undoubtedly celebrated with 905 beer, a local swill that ran about $2 a six-pack. It was a thrill to be out of Vietnam and in the Ozarks.

The Meramec River was an exotic place to me then. I had grown up in the St. Louis suburbs and rarely went west of Lindbergh Boulevard. I thought they still didn't have flush toilets in the Ozarks. The overnight float with Pete and meeting Ralph Brown may have inspired me to accept a job at the *Rolla Daily News* in 1972 shortly after I finished an MA in Political Science thanks to the G.I. Bill and St. Louis University. The Rolla newspaper covered the upper Meramec River region. Being able to write about a region as exotic as rural Missouri was a huge attraction. I also had an offer at the St. Joseph newspaper in western Missouri, but St. Joe didn't have anything quite like the Ozarks nearby.

Shoot Out on a Low Water Bridge

The *Rolla Daily News* offered young reporters an opportunity to develop a variety of stories. This book will reprint a few stories, which deserve a second life. My job back then basically involved coming up with at least one local story a day.

This challenge kept me hopping, but after a year I found myself getting more interested in feature stories, not so much in hard news. I particularly liked talking with older people. I realized that if I didn't write their stories, who else would?

Eventually I learned about oral history. It became part of the folk culture revival of the 1970s and '80s. Books such as *Foxfire*, produced by an Appalachian high school, and Alex Haley's *Roots* helped popularize researching family history and local culture. My first chance to do a thorough oral history project developed at a local government agency involved in regional planning, a job that followed my newspaper work. I was writing to assist local elected officials in six Ozark counties. We helped local governments win grants for roads, sewers, water quality, housing, etc.

All of these counties had rivers. These rivers were essential for farming, drinking water supply and recreation. Local people love their rivers and use them a lot. How do they actually use these streams? This was the basis of my first oral history project.

My boss at the Meramec Regional Planning Commission, Richard Cavender, encouraged me to write a proposal to the state humanities council. An Ozark native, Richard had strong feelings for the region. The humanities council and a local foundation supported my Ozark Rivers Oral History Project in the early 1980s.

To get the grant, I first had to write to local weekly newspapers and get a letter back stating they'd run these stories. Each agreed. Articles went to weeklies in Bourbon, Hermann, Owensville, Potosi, St. James, Steelville, Salem and Vienna. It was free local news to them. I've since learned that local weekly newspapers can be fascinating or as boring as a phonebook. They can tell a lot about rural areas. Even the local columns about who went to church or who was visiting who can be eye opening. Some local columnists just seem to have had huge families. Most of their news involved everyone with the same last name. But maybe these local news hounds paved the way for those reporting what they had for breakfast on Facebook these days. Everyone has news.

My First River Oral History

One of the first interviews for the project turned out to be a whopper. It's about one of the most infamous river men and hillbillies ever.

"Treehouse" Brown could be ornery. He shot first, and asked questions later. But if he liked you, Ralph would bend your ear for hours. Just as tough minded, his daughter Rose continues the business. Besides telling about an inspiring backwoodsman, this article helped lay the foundation to fund our oral history video that won local acclaim and national awards.

This is just as it appeared, my rambling run-on sentences and all, in the *Bourbon Beacon* (Crawford County) on April 28, 1982.

A Quiet Life Along the River— That's All Ralph Brown Wants

Ralph Brown is mellowing. A visitor to his canoe rental outfit at Scotia Bridge on Huzzah Creek may not notice the subtle signs of time's toll.

His gravel bar and hillside with its scattered pig pens, junked vehicles, canoes in various states of repair, and aged salvage looks much as it has since the owner began renting canoes in 1965.

Brown also continues to sport his longshoreman's cap, stubby beard and fierce smile. Still weighing over 200 pounds and able to carry a canoe with his one good arm, he says he is as ornery as ever.

"I am mean because I have to be mean," Brown explained his reputation. "They'll trample you to death if you let them. Ralph Brown never lets them."

What suggests Brown is beginning to enjoy his semi-retirement, and the sometimes subdued lifestyle of others who draw their Social Security payments, is a morning of talk during the recent winter with "one of the top river men of the territory," as he justifiably refers to himself.

With cold weather having slowed the river floating trade, Brown said much of his time is now spent taking care of chores that keeping 125 canoes in repair and in the water during the summer does not permit. His pigs take up a lot of time.

By his trailer, which is sited on a gentle rise in the heavily wooded valley, an old refrigerator without doors had its upper freezer compartment stuffed with various cuts of meat.

"At least half of this is still good," he says, picking up a kidney fondly. "I got it all salted down real good." He tossed it up once in the air then back on the pile of bloody hunks of hog.

Further down the hill he shows off another project: a half-completed outhouse built of fresh cut white oak logs, neatly notched to hold red cedar flooring.

"Somebody will probably come along and mess it up," he commented dejectedly. "You try to do things right and there's always someone who takes advantage of you."

But Brown can laugh about his difficulties. "Last week I thought I must have swallowed my false teeth after I'd spent an evening drinking with my buddy Junior Parker. You never saw a man so happy when they turned up."

Brown has not put in free long-distance telephone service from the St. Louis area as have other canoe liveries in the area. Social Security rules only permit him to earn $4,000 without penalties, so he says he does not need more business.

"A quiet life along the river," he said after showing off his place. "That's all that Ralph Brown wants."

What has made his reputation as an Ozark mountaineer, he said, has only been the necessity to defend himself and his property from theft, vandalism or trespass.

When asked, "Exactly how many people have you shot?" Brown responded without a pause.

"I've been shot at 10 times. I've shot back four times and I've only hit a person once."

That one incident involved an altercation with a rival canoe livery and a duel on a low-water bridge. Though the wound to his left arm has been slow in healing, he says he is still ready to defend his property, especially the quarter-mile of gravel bar along Huzzah Creek, from trespassers and anyone landing a canoe or parking a car without paying.

He bought the 12 acres along the Huzzah in 1948 mainly because he needed the gravel to fill a mud hole back on his nearby farm. Since the Huzzah property was the only land available to him in 1956 following a divorce, it was there that he built his famous tree house.

It is not really a tree house, just a three-room shack as he now calls it, built on logs about 15 feet above the creek. An oak grove shelters the structure from floods, which happen regularly, but haven't quite washed into the house or damaged the edifice.

"It is an eyesore," he said. "I expect they'll tell me tear it down because it is in sight of the creek, but I'm not about to. I don't believe in them telling me to do anything."

Brown's highly valued independence began at birth. Settling in the county from West Virginia five generations ago, the Browns farmed in a small valley a few miles west of Scotia Bridge, still a landmark on Huzzah Creek. An uncle had to use a pistol to persuade a doctor to attend his mother when he was born, Brown said.

The family of nine survived the Depression because of his father's skill in making molasses. All the children helped, he said, when the farm was paid off by cutting enough cedar and oak mine props to fill three railway cars.

"The Depression hit hard," Brown said, "My daddy, brothers and I produced up to a thousand gallons of sorghum molasses a year. That was our cash crop. We sold on street corners and door-to-door in Steelville. I stripped cane and run them through the mill and did everything to produce that molasses but cook it. We made the best that ever was in Crawford County, and I think I can do it yet."

Brown spent 41 months and 13 days in the South Pacific as an Army medic during World War II and a couple of years in a small arms plant in St. Louis during the Korean War.

"I didn't like the city, but I liked the money alright," he said about the work.

"My mainstay has been working in the timber cutting cordwood for charcoal and stove wood. But back in those days, I learned I could always make twice as much paddling a johnboat with a doctor or an attorney. They knew my brother Cliff and I were the best."

In 1963 Cliff and Ralph entered an Onondaga Cave to Meramec Caverns canoe race on a bet and ended up buying their first canoe. The next year they began renting two canoes and the following year Brown started serious business with a silent partner from St. Louis who helped him acquire a dozen aluminum canoes. The number of boats steadily grew to his peak year, 1975, when he averaged 125 canoes on the river most summer Saturdays and Sundays.

"It lifted me out of poverty," Brown said about the popularity of floating that has followed in recent years. Two daughters have helped him and one, Jeannie, at 16 was the youngest woman ever licensed by the state as a river guide.

Never one to mince his words, Brown said that other than problems with vandalism and the need for him to help maintain the county road by the wooden hog trough bridge, his only real worry is the new system of easements on lands purchased from the now deauthorized U.S. Army Corps of Engineers Meramec Park Lake.

"I know these easements are just supposed to protect the scenery." Brown said. "But thieves and trespassers will read the easements their way. The state better make it clear that us local people keep our rights.

"We've had to fight for them for years and I tell you, no one's going to take our property from us, period. If they try, they have to answer to Ralph H. Brown, and I mean it."

Editor's Note: Preparation of this article has been made possible by grants from the Missouri Committee for the Humanities, which is the state-based arm of the National Endowment for the Humanities, the Lucy Wortham James Memorial, of New York City and St James, and the Meramec Regional Planning Commission.

Results of Treehouse's Oral History

This article is typical of my early oral history and reporting. This is also a usual visit with Ralph. He was always busy. Everyone in the county knew him. Luckily, I learned more at his funeral and since.

Did you catch the part about Ralph's broken fridge in his trailer with the butchered hog parts piled up? It was by the front door, cold enough at winter for the hog parts and other food but still not very appetizing. Ralph gave me a big chunk, a green ham he called it. Luckily, not green with mold, just uncured. I brought it home, cooked it for Cath and one of our foster daughters. I didn't fully explain where it originated, but we enjoyed it. Many oral history informants have offered us similar goodies, all appreciated. Ralph surely enriched our vital DNA.

Doing an interview is a gift. It goes both ways. I think people appreciate being able to tell their truths and experiences.

2

Taking Care of His Creek

George Langenberg

This piece is also from my initial fieldwork, the Ozark Rivers Oral History Project. This interview may not grab you like Ralph Brown's adventures, shared in the last chapter, which was one of the approximately dozen profiles in the project. Focusing on how a German-American farmer takes care of his creek, the article helped create my career as an oral historian. The right people saw and liked the details on how to take care of a stream. I feel it's worth reprinting to give more insight into the kind of work I wanted to do.

While this mainly involves managing land, Mr. Langenberg's interview offers insights as fascinating as Ralph "Treehouse" Brown's wild tales. We're dealing with the northern Ozarks here, Gasconade County, settled largely by German Catholic families following the failed progressive revolutions in the old country of 1848. My wife Cathy's family is from this area, just west of Vienna on Little Tavern Creek. The rolling hills of this Missouri Rhineland region tend to have better soils than other parts of the Ozarks. Crops and families benefit.

In part because of this article, I joined several oral history projects the U.S. Geological Survey carried out in the 1980s and '90s from its Water Resource Division in Rolla. Anyone interested in fishing, agriculture or running rivers should enjoy Mr. Langenberg and his observations on the care and maintenance of streams.

This ran in the *Gasconade County Republican* from Owensville on April 21, 1982, and I have reduced it slightly.

George Langenberg maintained his farmland with skills he learned from his German ancestors, especially in the area of protecting against erosion (illustration by Anna Bolt).

If You Have a Stream, You've Got a Lot of Work

South of the town of Rosebud, Red Oak Creek makes a gentle bend by a field that seems as broad as any in Kansas.

George A. Langenberg, 87, who lives in town (about 5 miles to the north), knows the story of this field, all 189 acres of it. He has spent over 40 years working this land.

He has also studied Red Oak Creek. Knowing how and why and where the stream flows is part of the secret to keeping bottomland productive, Langenberg says.

Most times the Red Oak is such a small creek that it is not a problem. Fishermen rarely bother to even try it, Langenberg said.

But when a flood comes, the Red Oak becomes a torrent. Last year the floods were the worst ever. Neither George nor his son Arvil, who is now part owner and main operator of the place, were able to get any kind of crop planted.

"It was wet all the time," Langenberg said late last fall when he took time to talk about his field and the creek.

"It was frustrating not to be able to plant the crop. I like to turn the dirt," he said. "I like to see how good I can get it to come up. That's what interests me."

The condition of his farm buildings, rusty parts under an oak, an old tractor that still works, all have stories and recall challenges for Langenberg.

* * *

"It was July 10 or 11, 1947, I forget the exact day," he began when showing me the barn. "We had an awful rain up on Soap Creek and I'd been cultivating corn down there on the bottom. When it come up, I worked as long as I could, but I seen I was going to get caught. Oh, I knew it was going to get up big, and I'd left my fenders from the cultivator down on a stump there. I got down there and I see it's coming up good through that slough. Oh, it's a-going with one wheat shock after another floating down the middle of the Red Oak double time."

"Oh, then I got scared so I turned around and I couldn't get up this incline. The problem was my back-cultivator gang couldn't get up and it was slick there. The cultivator kept getting caught in these weeds. As foolish as I was, I went up to get a couple of log chains to put around each wheel. I shouldn't have done that," he said.

"The slough was already this deep and half-way up the magneto and over the axles. So I tried to back up but I seen I couldn't make it. I went off to the side of this forked sycamore and got up in it till it went down. All you could see of that tractor was the radiator cap and the steering wheel."

"If you had done something stupid, you could have been washed downstream," I said.

"I would have, if I tried to cross that slough," Langenberg said. "Big bundles of wheat were going down right past me. It shows a man's mind doesn't always think right."

* * *

Much of the Red Oak would have been permanently tamed by an impoundment, which had been proposed by the U.S. Army Corps of Engineers in the 1950s, he said, but the farmers didn't want it.

"We went and saw the state senator, Don Owens it was then, and told him it's no good for the farmers and he never was for it. But now, I don't know, there's not so many farmers. The Corps of Engineers might get what they want sometime in the future because the people don't understand these little creeks anymore."

After a quick visit to some Indian mounds, we drove to the bottom along the Red Oak. "If you have a stream, you've got a lot of work," he said. "Let me show you how I control the creek."

Two hundred yards down from the Highway T bridge, we left the truck next to a row of trees. They were sawed-off river maples that paralleled the road and formed a line perpendicular to the creek for several hundred feet out into the field.

"How'd the trees get that way?"

"I cut them off," Langenberg said. "You don't want big trees out here in the field. It'll shade out the crops a little, but worse, it'll catch all the logs and debris the flood brings down. I don't want that, I keep this line of short trees to slow down the current of the flood and let the big timber float on by. The high water's not bad. I don't mind the floods so much. See how I plow down here, against the slope. That makes it harder for that floodwater to take my soil. I get it from up above."

Once a nearby farmer complimented him for the good soil the bottom had, George said. "You ought to know how good it is," I says to him, and he just looks at me and smiles. He knows lots of it comes from his place.

"I've seen farms lose six inches or more off their fields in a flood. Or it'll change course and take an acre or ten if you're not careful. This bottom when I got it was all growed up with sycamore and sloughs. It was a jungle along the bottom, the best land. I had to start from the beginning, just like my father taught me. It was sure a lot of work."

* * *

We walked over to the edge of the field, which was maybe 10 feet above the surface of the creek and just about that far back from it. As we walked along the field's hard mud bank, George explained and showed the steps he takes to protect it and make the maximum amount of land available for the crops.

The basic principle to hold the bank is keeping the creek's flow even across its channel, George said. Any curve along the creek must be smooth and no gravel bars or root piles should be allowed to develop and deflect the current.

"If you let it hit one bank, then it'll hit it again down below," he explained. An obstruction-free channel causes less friction, so that any floodwater will be more likely to flow evenly by and not gouge out craters along the creek or take even bigger bites.

After a couple of minutes we came to a line of river maples along the bank whose outer-most branches had been sawed three-quarters through and left hanging.

"Along the bank you want to leave some trees," he said. "All those roots hold the soil. You can't plow right down to the edge anyway, so the trees help you. The branches when they hang out over the river are a problem though. They catch the trees and timber coming down with the flood and hold them, making a woodpile that's going to cause that flood to go over your ankle and take some ground with it. That's why I leave them hanging in the creek."

At some ledges across the creek, we stopped. "I had to get a cable and pull some of those rocks out of the creek. I put them in a hold on this side to keep the bank here. Now it flows good there, pretty good except just at the end of them, you see," he pointed across the creek. "There's a little gravel bar there. Just a few of those rocks falling off the little bluff did it. I'll have to go over and clean that up, get that gravel bar out of there because it could start something big."

The line of gravel along the bluff was barely six feet long, hardly even a foot into the channel and not big enough to support more than a few tiny weeds.

"It's really that big of a problem?"

"If you let it go, it is. See this," he pointed to a telephone pole that was wired to a pair of foot-thick maple stumps. "This is my newest project this fall."

The telephone pole had come from the electric co-op, which replaced a line crossing the farm. George had pointed it out earlier during our walk, saying he allowed them to do the work provided the crew cleaned up once the work was done.

"Well, by each of those holes, I found a handful of old copper staples. A cow would eat those and they'd kill her, but I guess those kids don't know that."

A whole two-foot thick burr oak tree had washed down in the last flood, hung up by some soft maples along the creek, and forced up against the bank, George explained the necessity for the 30-foot pole. It angled upstream and held the top of the oak into the shore and a pile of branches into the hole dug by flood. "Eventually that will all fill in with soil," George said.

* * *

As George spoke, a light German accent gave a slight musical cadence to his voice. His grandparents had emigrated from Germany and he was born January 1, 1895, the first of four boys, and was sent out by his family to help another farm family as his brothers grew able to do his chores. After serving with the Pioneer Engineers in France, he came back to settle in Rosebud, and married the former Laura Rosa Buehrer in 1923.

His service station became the first Chevrolet dealership in the area and a major truck repair garage along U.S. 50 when it was paved. The Depression wasn't bad for him, George said, but it meant long hours often late into the night repairing the big trucks and the hard times did "blow up" the bank in town, the doctor left, the hardware store closed up and one of the two mail routes eventually was lost.

* * *

"In 1937 I bought the first farm, 130 acres. My wife said okay, as long as we don't have to move out there. In 1942, I got the second one, 151 acres right next to it."

At the far end of the field, George asked if I was ready to go back. "Sure," I said. "Well, let me show you this first," he insisted. I followed him through a thicket.

"Look upstream." The creek shone blue against the deep shade near the forest, but upstream was a broad channel fit for swimming. Langenberg said it was half-polluted from the Owensville treatment plant and only a few inches deep.

"Now look down the other way." Several huge fallen trees crossed the creek but the gravel seemed so thick, what water remained seemed stagnant pools.

Walking back we stopped to look over at the far bank. "You see there's two sycamores there, but I just cut the one. That was enough. The creek was running too fast there. Putting that one tree in the creek was just enough.

"There's one other man down this creek who works his creek bottom like I do this. I've seen him walk along and study the creek, just watching it like it's an animal, something living. He learned the same as me, from his father. You've got to take time to see what the river's doing. I'll see where he's dropped one tree up along the bank. He could have cut others, but one's enough. He'll just take what he needs. You've got to study it, be interested in it. That's the secret to this whole thing."

* * *

The Farmer Who Loves his Creek

Did you notice the part where Mr. Langenberg points out several small mounds at the edge of his big bottomland field? I could tell they fascinated him, because he hadn't bothered them or dug into them, but the subject was tangential to the main focus of managing the creek.

Since completing the Ozark Rivers Oral History Project I became fascinated in the Native American heritage of the Ozarks. It's complex because most sites may involve different cultures over time. I feel it's generally best to not try any digging or artifact hunting because so much information can be lost in amateur efforts. Perhaps George felt this too. He cared for his farm in detail as some pamper their antique Chevy, Ford Mustang or hot-rod truck.

The main point George makes is that streams are alive and require deep study to understand. You can tell it's work George Langenberg enjoyed.

Maybe this doesn't grab you? To me it's fascinating in part because the management ideas for a stream came from his father and grandfather. Several hydrologists at the U.S. Geological Survey office in Rolla could see that I had taken care to let Mr. Langenberg tell his story.

One Result of a River Oral History

This one article resulted in my doing a group of oral history interviews for the U.S. Geological Survey along the Little Piney River to the west of Rolla. This small stream is known for its native trout population, challenging rapids for kayakers and the proud community of Newburg, which has the feel of an Appalachia coal town nestled into a deep valley. A short walk from town and the old Houston House hotel one of the best swimming holes in the Ozarks serves as the town's public swimming pool. I worked for Jim Barks, who was the head of the Water Resources Division, doing interviews along the Little Piney, then Robb Jacobson moved from Baltimore to direct a larger Ozark rivers project.

Robb and his wife Anne showed up at a summer solstice party Cathy and I had at our earth-sheltered house on the mighty Big Dry Fork Creek. We lived there about 25 years and created a lifetime of memories and friends, some of the best being this couple who shared interests in rivers, gardens, cooking, hiking, biking, art, wine and beer and other healthy pursuits. I worked with Robb, a PhD geomorphologist, about three years doing oral histories for his major project, which is the focus of Part III of this tome.

2. Taking Care of His Creek

I was doing other projects for the state arts council and giving talks for the state humanities program. Though I was challenged by these worthwhile opportunities, I wasn't making much money with part-time gigs. Luckily Cathy is a patient soul who had a good job as a systems analyst for the Missouri Department of Natural Resources. The only time I earned a decent salary doing freelance oral history work came from the U.S. Army when I worked on a major project at Ft. Leonard Wood. Oral history has other benefits, which is part of the reason I'm writing this now. I appreciate folks like Ralph Brown and George Langenberg who showed how land well used creates happiness equal to all the work required to keep up with the seasons.

3

Highlights of Ozark Rivers Oral History

Amazing People Downstream…

Farming and fishing make up the sweetest stories I heard on my first oral history project. To summarize this work, I wrote about some of these people and their stories. As I shift through this text I remember these people clearly. It's a little spooky, to feel these folks living within me after thirty-plus years. These tales still offer a variety of connections to present concerns and ongoing issues in the Ozarks. This is from a series in March 1983 that ran in another local newspaper. These observations form a background to the continuing issues of making a living in rural America.

Searching the Rivers of Memory

Roundy Craine, 95 years old, lives in a small house near downtown Rolla. Taking care of himself, he heats with wood, cooks most of his own meals and enjoys the breeze on his porch when the weather turns warm.

Roundy has a lot of stories to tell about the Ozarks, and especially about Ozark rivers. At the turn of the last century (the 1900s when he was a boy), he says he and his father could land a barrel of catfish in an hour on the Gasconade River just north of Rolla,

"The most beautiful fish I've ever seen," Roundy recalls. "You've never seen fat, white bellies like those cats had."

The Craines' fishing wasn't for sport. It was one of the few sources of cash for the family back then. The secret, Roundy says, was making a good trap.

"You take young willow and wrap it around a barrel. Then more willow goes up and down the sides to make a kind of huge basket. You take that barrel out of there, close the end of the trap and then put in a little door."

This basket-shaped trap, weighted down with rocks, was dropped into a deep hole and tied to the bank with grapevines. Handfuls of corn were thrown into the trap to attract fish, but it couldn't be ordinary shelled corn, Roundy says. It had to be fermented five or six days, until the kernels were good and sour.

"Before long, that bucket was just full of cats eating on that corn. Then you grabbed that vine and hauled up the trap before the fish could get out.

"I remember putting those fish into a tote, then going back to the other side of the river, where the wagon'd be waiting with a big barrel. Once we had it full, we went over the hill to Newburg, where the trains come in and took those cats right up to St. Louis, a hundred miles away."

Roundy Craine's stories cover other subjects too: guiding fishermen from the city; running a ferry that carried wagons across the river; traveling several miles by river in a winter storm to bring the midwife during his first son's birth.

Gathering stories like these has been part of my job at the Meramec Regional Planning Commission for more than a year. Our hope has been to add to the community's sense of itself by offering a portrait through local newspapers of the region that is focused on a primary natural resource, the rivers.

* * *

> Here's another story from these articles about a county administrative judge (now called "commissioner") who loved hunting and fishing. A region of rolling hills west of Ste. Genevieve, this part of the Ozarks was explored and settled by French fur trappers, miners and free spirits in the early 1700s. A few French-speakers still hold forth near the county seat of Potosi. Many parts of this county have distinct histories, which date back to early settlement, but most communities struggle with low income and unemployment.
>
> This is part of what I wrote about Bert Brinley in 1983. After this is a brief interview with his son, Cody, who was a boy when I visited their place long ago.

Bert Brinley's farm is on the upper Big River, downstream from the new Council Bluff Lake, a 440-acre impoundment of the U.S. Forest Service. Brinley, a former associate judge in Washington County, is a staunch conservative. His views on rivers and dams are interesting because they suggest a dilemma faced by many in the Ozarks today.

The Army Corps of Engineers' Pine Ford Dam was to have been built in Washington County, in the area where Brinley grew up, and some people thought that the dam and its 4,000-acre lake were just what the county needed. Though Washington County still has a strong rural character, it also has the highest unemployment rate of any of Missouri's 114 counties—26 percent in December 1982, much of it because of changes in the mining industry.

But Brinley is not sure that the Pine Ford Dam is what his county needs in the long run. He doubts whether the dam, which was recently recommended for deauthorization by the Corps of Engineers, would have had a significant economic impact on his county. And he and his wife, Evelyn, say that even the much smaller Council Bluffs Dam caused problems for Big River when the lake was filled two years ago.

"The river never really ran all summer, not until the middle of September, when they started letting water come through the spillway," he said. "And then it was rotten, stinky and smelly. We could just about smell it from the house. It was the water from the bottom of the lake, full of rotten leaves and stuff."

"I tell you, if a private individual had done that to the river, he'd be in jail. But a government agency can get away with it, and there's little the people can do about it."

Speaking as a farmer, Brinley says the river is a valuable asset that is gradually being ruined by increasing demands on its flow. And it also provides his favorite sport, gigging. He's often so successful that a winter night's effort can feed 50 or more neighbors at a gravel-bar fish fry.

* * *

> I haven't been by the Big River countryside in at least 20 years. I used to drive by Belgrade and the Big River going from Rolla to visit my parents at their cabin not far from Bert's place. It's outside of Belgrade, which looked like a sweet little community, a country place with most necessities and great neighbors. I decided I'd better try to call Bert while working to bring these stories together.
>
> I looked on the Internet and found out he passed away. He was born in June 1932 and died in November 2017. Luckily, I found his son, Cody, and daughter-in-law's phone number and called. I explained that I had written about Mr. Brinley years ago. They remembered the article and had it out as a part of family remembrances at Bert's wake.

"My dad served 14 years as a county commissioner," Cody said. "Now I've served 6 years on the commission. We're still a struggling county but we have a new company coming in that will hire 100 people eventually."

I asked about Council Bluffs Lake and the Big River. Is Cody as much an outdoorsman as his father was?

"I'm a workaholic," Cody said. "I've got a fencing and a tractor repair company and recently took out a lease on some of the pastures of the Edg-Clif Farm and Vineyard near Potosi to run my cattle. I don't have time to do any fishing in the lake or gigging on the river. My dad about wore me out with hunting. Don't have time for any of that."

"We took over dad's farm as he started getting weak and forgetful. It was a hard time for us, but we all got through it. Lila and I love being here now."

We only talked for a few minutes, but it made me want to get back there. Not only would I want to meet Cody and Lila and see their farm, but also the old French community near Potosi and into the Belleview Valley. This valley must have some of the best cropland and pastures in the Ozarks. Some of these old homes and farms are almost 200 years old. People struggle to keep their places working, but I remember there was a lot of pride. The nearby St. Francois Mountains have great trails and views into the valley and beyond.

Mostly I think about Bert Brinley and how he enjoyed his farm and his community. It's great to know he had a long time to appreciate it all.

* * *

These stories, fragments of much bigger events and lives, represent the end of an era. When I started at the Rolla Daily News in 1972, the first story I was assigned covered the last days of the two remaining one-room schools in Phelps County. The children from these two districts would have to take a bus to town. No more walking the rural roads or short cuts through the woods to the small, local schools. The neighbors had mixed feelings about the change.

Much of the same change was slowly evolving as I started working as a local news reporter, then became more interested in doing oral history. I learned how the agriculture in the Ozarks had been changing at a quickening pace from the 1930s onward. Farming was switching from a diversified family-based operation to specialized crops, usually calf production. Growing crops like corn or wheat went out; permanent pastures and mechanized hay production came in.

Luckily cow-calf producers, unlike chicken or hog farmers, have a variety of markets to sell their livestock.

One interview I did in my first rivers oral history project sums up changes in Ozark farms. This is from an interview in the *St. James Leader-Journal*, January 25, 1984, with "River Charlie" and Alma Smallwood on their farm.

A Farm Family Stays Till the End

Alma and River Charlie say they don't believe there are any full-time family farms left along the upper Meramec.

"They don't live off the farm like we used to, with the whole family working tooth and toenail," River Charlie says.

Alma joins in, "It used to be people around here got most of what they needed from their farm and garden. They bought very little in town. Every year I used to put up 200 quarts of fruits, and more of vegetables."

Although the big bottomland farms, with their rotations of corn, wheat, oats and rye—grown both for feed and cash—are gone, Charlie says the bottom land makes excellent pastures. "Floods won't hurt pasture grown up in thick grass."

Were the old days in any way better? "I like our new house up on the ridge better," Alma reflects. "We don't get snowed in so easily, but I don't see much difference between back then and now."

"All we've known is work. We've always worked. Charlie's out in his workshop now. I'm sure he would say the same thing."

* * *

Each family, each farm, has its own approach to choosing crops and the focus of its operation. This makes agriculture particularly fascinating for an oral historian. After working at the regional planning commission and finishing my first oral history project, I was fortunate to work several years at Maramec Spring Park outside of St. James helping establish the Ozark Agriculture Museum there.

My main job was designing the layout for display of a farming implement collection that had been given by the St. Onge family from rural St. Louis County. It included everything from small hand tools to a huge Keck-Gonnermann steam tractor weighing ten times

3. Highlights of Ozark Rivers Oral History

"River Charlie" Smallwood farmed along the upper Meramec River and made syrup by tapping sycamore trees along the river bottom (illustration by Anna Bolt).

more than any automobile. We had it operating once. That was enough.
 Those steam engines can blow up everything around them, but they are hugely beautiful when working. It was great work to keep this all in shape.

Memoir

At Trails End Camp

> What attracted me to want to write about people living along the Ozark rivers? This recollection may be typical of how people feel about a special place and time in their growing up.

Weekends can last a lifetime. Summers my dad took me to a run-down farm way out in the Ozark hills. Have I ever left this valley?

Will I ever forget Charlie Brown jumping overboard as we motored downstream?

"Here we are," Charlie bellowed, stood up, put one foot on a splintery gunwale, pushed his bulk up and out to belly flop into the river while we sped fast as a flying duck. Charlie was still in his bib overalls. He'd left his clodhoppers on the gravel where he kept his fleet of leaky watercraft.

My splash-soaked dad and I burst into laughter, the scene was so unexpected. Dad slowed the boat, turned around; I threw the anchor overboard so we could stay in the shade of a stately river bluff. We had on swimming suits and jumped in from either end of the old wooden johnboat to cool off with our guide and friend.

It was hot as hell. It's most always muggy and sultry June into September in the Ozarks.

Why do people live here? The eternal question of what makes any place attractive becomes especially problematic for the Ozarks. This was part way down my path into oral history work.

Deep at night, restless trying to fall back to sleep, I still walk along that sliver of a stream and its shadowy sloughs with silver minnows swimming through all the stories I love. This creek valley inspired dad and me to use an old seine net to catch lithe fish, which became our bait for catfish and goggle eye.

We would run the net across the rocky creek bottom, then round it up onto the gravel bar, trying to grab as many minnows as we could and tossing them into a bait bucket. Then we'd pop the net back over the stream to throw all the non-qualified benthic biota back into the creek. Carrying the pail down to the river landing, we'd have enough little guys to hook just below their dorsal fins and submerge by root wads where Charlie knew the big fish lurked.

At his camp/farm for much of the 1950s, Charlie had been a barrel maker, a big business in the Ozarks, and a factory worker. As bald as a cannonball with a belly even bigger, he just wore denim overalls, no shirt or drawers, and heavy boots without socks. Thick white fuzz covered his tanned shoulders and arms. He looked like a polar bear. In the early 1960s, Charlie was growing several big patches of tomatoes to sell at a nearby cannery. That was once a big Ozark business too. Charlie also perfected his own tomato wine, and canned fish with tomatoes and peppers to create "Ozark salmon" for winter dinners.

His wife took off parts of summers from working in a Kansas City hospital to be at the farm. Other than a few regular customers staying in the camp's two cabins and a tent house, Charlie's main companion was a big dog.

The one pup I remember most went everywhere with Charlie—in boats, truck and tractor. A large mixed breed, mainly a German shepherd, the dog was a good singer.

As much as a whole life built around days on the river, Charlie's ability to play music most stays with me. His dog also could carry a tune.

"I'm going to send a letter to New York to get you on television," my dad said, and Charlie would laugh that he didn't know how he would get 900 miles east. He had an old rattling pickup truck and no TV set in his valley near the Niangua River as far as I knew.

"You and your dog would be great on TV! Johnny Carson would love you!"

This must have been in the late 1950s, before the interstate highway changed the way we drove, before I became a teenager, before we invaded Vietnam, before everything got crazy.

Luckily this was not before tape recorders became available to the general public. Dad recorded Charlie playing music. Wish I knew exactly what happened to that tape.

Dad had a reel-to-reel machine, state of the art for the '50s. He loved high fidelity music and all the latest technology.

Saturday evenings, if I remember right, the Grand Ole Opry would come on a local radio station. Charlie and the half-breed German shepherd would be waiting.

Charlie's only instrument was a tin tomato can lid he had folded in half then cut somehow. The thing would vibrate in his lips as he hummed along with a song. He could do a few more trills, which added to an eerie warbling wave vibrating across the cabin somewhat like a bagpipe before the Scots charged into battle.

As soon as Charlie started playing along with the country music, his dog began a low howl that quickly expanded in volume and range. I remember them listening to the popular songs together to create a slightly harmonic racket. Dad just laughed.

I doubt if they ever sent a tape to New York. This must have been their main entertainment during the rough, grey season of winter into spring without a Mrs. nearby. Warm weather can last into December in this central part of the Ozarks.

* * *

My father began bringing me to Trails End Camp when I was about 10 years old. He had been going fishing there with a friend from work at his newspaper. I was surprised and honored to be invited to go on the three or four-hour drive from St. Louis down old Rt. 66, the Mother Road as it's now known, to the big town of Lebanon. We sometimes stopped there for a burger at the Cal-Mo Inn, then onto small highways north to Charlie's farm.

In addition to rivers and dogs, another thing about our visits to Trails End Camp involved learning to drink beer, usually a long-forgotten brew called "Falstaff."

"Run up to the cabin, open us a couple of cans of beer," I still remember my father asking. I didn't do it right. I just used the church key and put one hole in each top.

"That won't work," they laughed and explained the physics of the beer can. So I went back up the hill and put a triangular opening on the opposite side to let the air in. Whenever I open a beer, I still think of this lesson. As a teenager, I'd split a beer with dad and grew to appreciate how a small amount could dissipate the heat of the day and put one's daily problems into realistic perspective.

We spent a lot of time swimming and resting while fishing in the shade.

Life changed at Trail's End without school, friends or television nearby. The river seemed to breed millions of bright green fish called crappie, pronounced "crop-e," which knew how to unsnarl worms from our fishing hooks. They went to college to learn how to do this, dad said. Luckily, we had plenty of bait and time.

Our old casting rods taught us to be as patient as the crappie. We also would throw out lures like a Lazy Ike or a Jitterbug and the line would tangle up half the time. It could take an hour to take a bird's nest out of a casting reel.

There is never any rush on the Niangua. If you got thirsty, just dip your cupped hands into the river for a drink. Most nearby farmers made their own wooden johnboats and kept them pulled up on the banks. No locks on the chains. Just a spooky big ol' dried up catfish head nailed onto a tree trunk protected Charlie's two or three old boats. No huge and roaring outboard motors. Most had wooden oars and an old coffee can to dip out the river that gradually seeped onto the mossy wooden floors.

Charlie seemed perpetually happy, but he did complain about gully washers. A mile-long lane through the oak forest down toward the creek valley would wash out on steep parts during a heavy storm. Sometimes Charlie would have to meet us at the top of the ridge by the county road to pile us in the front seat and all our gear back in the truck bed.

* * *

On one of our last trips dad let me drive because I had a learner's permit. We argued about how fast I was going even though it was the limit. Despite being a major cross county highway, Route 66, back then, was mainly just two lanes. Dad had every right to be nervous about my driving. I was a distracted student, he knew. Parts of the highway near towns may have had four divided lanes, but I was raring to pass any cars anywhere going too slow. Dad perked up when I had to pass a slowpoke, but he coached me how to do it safely.

These long drives taught a lot of stuff, mainly about patience. Cars didn't have air conditioning back then so it was always noisy with the windows down. We could listen to the Cardinals and I sometimes practiced reading aloud.

Once or twice, we went with my Uncle Bert Russell and my cousin Gil, but I think they found it a little too rough. Uncle Bert had farmed in Pike County after serving in World War II so was no stranger to hard work in droughty times.

At least Pike County had decent soil. Known as the heart of the Little Dixie region in Missouri, Pike County seemed prosperous, I remember from family visits. Once dad said I should go with Uncle Bert to the barn to watch a calf being born.

But it was a breech birth. The veterinarian had to use a block and tackle to get out that bloody, stillborn calf.

At Trails End Camp, dad once asked me if I knew "the facts of life." Sure, I said, the boys talk about it all the time on the school bus. So my father and I didn't really discuss it. Later a book appeared in my room back home titled something like *The Facts of Life and Love for Teenagers*. I didn't discuss that with my parents either, but did read the juicy parts.

My mother never visited Charlie's place. No love of fishing.

Timon was a little like me, easily distracted at times, lots of interests. Luckily, we shared our mutual pleasure in fishing and hiking for many years. It helped when my parents briefly separated after Timon finally retired from the Pulitzer Publishing Co., where he had started out as a young reporter and worked his way up. But that difficult time was far before the weekends we spent at Trails End Camp.

I went to visit for a couple of days before being shipped off to Vietnam, but the river was flooding, which means it was no good for fishing. Charlie probably shared some of his tomato wine with me. I was old enough, 22, just graduated from college.

Nervous about the Army, I didn't know what lay ahead. My father, Uncle Bert and Charlie were all Navy veterans. They didn't dwell on those years, just some crewmates on their various ships and long months at sea. They were lucky to have survived the Pacific.

I would be lucky too. But I didn't know that. I didn't know if I would ever see Charlie Brown again, his wife or his tent house or cabins or even that creek valley along the Niangua River. Did I know water might never again be safe to drink right from the stream? I learned old folks living alone got to be tough and wise. Would anyone ever again hear a tomato can lid play a concerto with whippoorwills, a staticky radio and an old dog? I didn't know that Charlie's big bottom fields made the sweetest wine I would ever taste.

Part II

Working with the U.S. Forest Service
Techniques—Beginning in Oral History

"The oldest and strongest emotion of mankind is fear, and the oldest and strongest kind of fear is fear of the unknown."
—Howard Phillips Lovecraft[1]

Doing a family history conjures up diverse feelings, especially during a pandemic. The gift and fragility of each life becomes paramount when we think about recording stories from older people, or even youngsters. Interviews are often as traumatic as an unknown virus for both the interviewer and interviewee.

As I look back on my work investigating rural history, it's easy to forget the fear factor. Mostly, I remember the travel and tons of paperwork associated with grants.

Fear and the unknown tend to jump out at the very beginning of any project. One renowned oral historian has traced the importance of trepidation in our field, stating, "the interview has inspired fear in subjects and appealed to authorities as a powerful tool of disciplining."[2]

Despite knowing this, I was still quite surprised when my wife Cathy was afraid to interview her dear mother!

"I just don't know how to get started on this," Cathy said as we discussed the process of her recording an interview with Rita, then in her 80s but still as hale as the farm girl she had been along the Little Maries in the Missouri Rhineland of the northern Ozarks. "I don't know what to do and I don't want to mess this up!"

It surprised me because Rita was far from shy and her oldest daughter the same. But this would be something new for both, despite Cath's helping me out on various aspects of doing interviews and transcriptions over the years. It all worked out. Recently Cathy gave her four siblings CD copies of her interviews.

Family interviews can be tricky to say the least. Here is an overview of how to begin documenting your family, community, or other worthwhile groups. While snapping photos with your cell phone may be easier than asking a few questions, preserving someone's voice and stories can be more inspiring now and for years to come.

I also provide a list of books and a simple guide to interviewing in the Appendices.

✶ ✶ ✶

One great piece of advice on oral history came from Doug Wixson, the Okie historian who documented life on the High Plains (please see Part VIII). "Most people love to talk about themselves," Doug said. "Especially older people. The younger generation is often too busy to talk with them. All you need is a few good questions to prime the pump, and most people will orate all day."

Is it that simple? Sometimes. You can go to the Story Corps website, or family history sites, and find lists of non-threatening questions. One positive thing about the pandemic, many people may be thinking about their family histories.

Is it worth the trouble to interview family, friends, or others? It depends on your interests. How much do you care what's going on around you? Any topic has a history. If you find something fascinating, why not dig deeper to find the roots of your attraction? For example, a few years ago I did a project on people's feelings about trees, *Tree Dialogues*. It wasn't exactly an oral history, but people had stories about special trees, mainly from childhood. We produced a CD of stories and experimental music. I was slow in entering the digital age but learned through quirky projects that never paid much. Most of my endeavors have been environmental, but I also did one on a Navy destroyer in World War II.[3]

Beginning any kind of local documentation project is exciting. It's worth thinking about what most energizes you about the subject. Asking questions will help you understand what you most care about. Every project needs someone with the psychic determination to find out more. Every small business deserves a history; big corporations pay a lot to preserve records of their early years. Smaller firms need to preserve their histories too.

Valerie Yow, an elder of oral history and independent scholar, has created a thorough how-to manual listed in the Appendix. Here's her brief take on getting started:

> Imagining what topics the project will focus on and how you will do this is, of course, the first step in the research. Becoming conscious of assumptions, formulating questions, even defining tentative hypotheses, and critically examining all of these are necessary activities even at the beginning.[4]

Part II—Working with the U.S. Forest Service

Dr. Yow also offers helpful advice on how to structure the question-asking process, which is not always intuitive. When I began, I didn't know how to start an interview, but I followed her advice by instinct, in part from having been a reporter. Most people will begin with biographical questions, gradually move to specific questions, and return to the general thread of a person's life story as interviews and research proceed. It's pretty logical, often surprising and fun!

After grad school and a year as a reporter in the Ozarks, I decided I needed to broaden my experience. Luckily, I found a job in 1976 at the *Delaware Valley News*, in Frenchtown, New Jersey. In one feature story, I recounted neighbors' remembrances of James Agee working in town on his classic *Let Us Now Praise Famous Men*. They mostly recalled his pet goat, which accompanied Agee and his young wife on trips to and from Greenwich Village in the '40s. I also heard about a local farmer whose family had come over from England with William Penn in the late 1600s. This almost ancient history fascinated me, and as a Quaker, I was inspired by this peaceful heritage. His family had been conscientious objectors since the French and Indian War. I had to get one of those new cassette tape recorders to save this story! To get started I read Alex Haley's *Roots* and a couple of the *Foxfire* books, then went over to Bucks County to begin talking with Quaker farmers.

That started me on a sideline project that didn't turn out well because I was quickly overwhelmed with too many interviews. Now I am in the process of donating the tapes to a Quaker archive. At least I preserved the material and learned about the complexities of fieldwork in public history. I consider my work in oral history as actually beginning with the Ozark River Project described in Part I. After the river project, I had a chance to carry out oral history for the Mark Twain National Forest.

4

Palmer, Missouri

In the Valley of the Ghosts

This article comes from my Forest Service oral history in the eastern Ozarks south of Potosi. A mining region developed in the early 1700s, hills west of Ste. Genevieve led the French to cross the Mississippi from settlements in Illinois lowlands. These mines and their supposed great wealth helped create the infamous Mississippi Bubble in France that encouraged wild speculation as bizarre as Tulip Mania. The Bubble collapsed in 1720. Ancient mining remains still exist way out in the Mark Twain National Forest in Washington County, which some view as a hearth of Ozark history because of its early settlement.

My article appeared in the local newspaper of Potosi, one of the oldest towns in the Ozarks. It's written for the general audience of that old seat of Washington County, a place some 50 miles due south of St. Louis. The Forest Service owns most of the land around what remains of Palmer, the kind of barren place local kids were tearing up with their dune buggies and dirt bikes. But I had learned more lies hidden in the hollows. This helped me feel my oral history work had been useful.

This article is not oral history, just a summary of some aspects of interviews.[1] It's written mainly for people near the interview site. The goal was to show how local history can be protected when physical remains of a community gradually change and disappear.

Palmer in the Valley of the Ghosts

Twenty miles southwest of Potosi lays a valley of ghosts. The valley held the town of Palmer, Missouri, and dozens of small farms, mines, businesses and families.

4. Palmer, Missouri

These are friendly apparitions for the most part. Some even wrote letters to the editor of this newspaper several years ago urging the heritage of the area not be forgotten. This article seeks to help keep this legacy alive.

The town site and nearby mining areas are mostly within the Mark Twain National Forest. Until recent years the Forest Service had managed the area mainly for timber. Recreation has increased in importance, mining has steadily declined.

Following the 1950s, with less and less work available, people gradually moved away from Palmer. Mark Twain employees removed signs of their presence. Abandoned buildings tend to cause management problems.

This policy may be changing. Archaeologists and historians working for the agency wanted to learn more about the Palmer area. A variety of records as well as physical remains show the valley has seen a fascinating parade of human activity in just the last 200 years, let alone throughout the prehistoric past. Palmer may be the kind of place tourists as well as local residents would find interesting. It may be possible to teach some of the human struggles and triumphs of the past by interpreting a place like Palmer for future generations.

* * *

In the Spring of 1991 the Oral History of the Ozarks Project, a non-profit group I helped start, entered into a partnership agreement with the Mark Twain National Forest to do an oral history of Palmer.

Oral history is research based on questioning people in lengthy interviews during which memories have a chance to unfold. Joined with investigation of documentary records, oral history can add significantly to our understanding of recent history, the common history that is not always written down.

In the future the agency may use this research along with other resources and cooperate with local people and groups to do more interpretative projects in the Palmer area.

One summer is not a very long time to study a place as diverse as Palmer. But I was able to meet some friendly, knowledgeable people who were glad to talk about their memories of the valley.

I wish I could have spoken with more former and present residents of the area. There wasn't time to talk with everyone. The more I learned, the more interesting it became.

As I've lived in the Ozarks for about 20 years, working as a freelance writer much of that time, I've learned enough to know how little I know about the region. Each county, each community is unique. Over the years I've had a chance to visit a few similar ghost towns in the Ozarks. Not too far away was the community of Sligo, in northeastern Dent County, once a booming iron-producing town during World War I.

Much the same is true for Midco near Freemont in Carter County. It had a huge chemical plant associated with the munitions industry during World War I. Reportedly 5,000 people lived there then, but less than a tenth now remain and the plant is a ruin.

Maramec Spring and its old iron works are comparable to Palmer. Prehistoric and more recent artifacts including mining, timber and agriculture join with the beauty of the place to make this park in Phelps County a multilayered experience.

Unlike Maramec, however, most everything in Palmer has been removed or has fallen down or grown up. You have to be a detective to appreciate Palmer. The more you learn, the more you appreciate how life has always been a struggle for most people in this region.

The Mark Twain Forest has a few interesting resources on the area, such as a short history of the town written by Anne Cooper of Caledonia several years ago and a paper written on a Depression era self-help project in Palmer.

It may be as old as Potosi and communities further east in the Bellevue Valley, which date to the late 1770s. Once the town was known as Webster and located on the old White River Trace, which the Trail of Tears followed in the 1830s. My focus was on more recent history.

* * *

Dollye Cole Blunt was the first person I met who knows any of the history of Palmer. She was taking a walk early one June morning on a road to Palmer checking over her fencerows along pastures by Courtois Creek. She and her late husband, Howard Blunt, farmed and ran the store and post office for the community of Brazil due west of Palmer.

Brazil had 32 families during the Depression, when a lot of railroad ties were made and several moonshiners helped bring cash into the area. Now five families live in the Brazil area.

In those days everyone had it hard, but not many city people came to try to make a go of it in this part of Washington County, she recalled.

Her father, the Rev. Dollison Cole, was a circuit riding Methodist minister who served Palmer and other area churches, such as Belgrade, Council Bluff, Joseph Chapel, Marler Chapel, Sugar Grove and Sunlight. Born on a farm near the village of Courtois, Mrs. Blunt remembers Palmer as being the major community in the area, which included towns such as Enough, Goodwater, Quaker, Shirley and Viburnum.

Britz Halbert's store and hotel were the main attractions in Palmer but there was also a blacksmith shop, many homes for miners and buildings associated with mining companies. The Halbert store was taken down in the early 1970s.

"People felt bad when it was torn down because it had been there so long and had so many memories for them. It was probably the largest store in the area and had things others didn't." Her brother's business at nearby

4. Palmer, Missouri

Courtois was the last country general store in this area to go out of business, she speculated.

For Zelma Banta, a Potosi resident, the church at Palmer holds the strongest memories. Mrs. Banta celebrated her 94th birthday this August and has an excellent memory of her first teaching job, just after she graduated from the Potosi High School in 1915.

That fall she came to Palmer to teach. She was 17 years old and had 65 students in first through eighth grade.

"People said there was a rough element of people that lived out there. They were lacking in education, but they were good-hearted people, I would say. My father got this school for me, and I'm going to teach it," Mrs. Banta recalled of her determination to be a teacher.

"They said it was the best school they had in years. I knew how to control children. I taught them manners, courtesies, and they were all seemingly happy over my success."

Up until the 1940s, when a second schoolhouse was built at Palmer, the Palmer church served the community as both church and school. At the end of Z Highway in southwestern Washington County, the Palmer church is one of the larger wooden buildings in this part of the Ozarks.

Some people say it is close to 200 years old. It may be close to that. Both schools closed in the '50s, and the newer building exists only as a concrete foundation on the ridge above the old church.

Hazel White and Gladys Compton, two sisters now living in Potosi, grew up near Palmer and recall Mrs. Banta as being a teacher the whole community respected.

"Palmer was the kind of place where people did everything together. Nobody had anything, so we all just helped one another," Hazel White recalled. There were a number of black families who also farmed and mined, as did most other families there at that time, and though their children did not go to the Palmer school, they were included in other social activities and the church, the sisters said.

The girls and their parents moved to Frankclay so their father could get a job in one of the St. Joe mines and the girls could go to high school. They recalled leaving their farm was one of the saddest days of their growing up.

"I remember at the auction father had to sell our team of mules, Kit and Dine. We just cried and cried, because one of the miners bought our friends the mules."

"They were going underground in the mines and we knew it would then be a hard, short life for those animals," Ms. Compton said. "Those mules were friends for all the kids up and down Hazel Creek when we were little."

* * *

Palmer had a reputation as a rough town because it was a mining town where people could get rich quick, if they were lucky. Several people said in interviews that fortunes were found in a day and lost overnight in card games or bets. Flossie Welker, who lives north of Palmer on Highway 8 with her husband Steve, recalls her great uncle was one of those who discovered a valuable deposit of barite but lost in it a card game.

Barite, used for many purposes in oil, paint, medical and other industries, was, along with lead, the main product at Palmer. Almost 100 mines, or "diggings" as they are called locally, have been catalogued in the area.

Steve Welker, who says he is called "The Great White Hunter" for good reason, knows this territory as well as anyone, several people confirmed. Though he is closing in on his 80th year, Welker has not slowed down and still chases turkeys whenever they are legal game.

He grew up in Grassy Hollow, to the east of Palmer, went to the Seed Tick School and settled with the rest of his family in Palmer as a boy. Steve's brother Merlin and his wife Mildred are the last residents in the immediate Palmer area.

Much of Steve's life has been spent working in the tiff industry, the common name for barite mining. The diggings and washing plants, smelters and other facilities associated with the minerals have been owned by a variety of firms over the years, many of which employed Steve at one time or another.

The tailings ponds left by these operations are one of the most important resources from the mining days, he believes. These ponds have gradually grown up with vegetation along their banks and now provide good hunting and fishing environments.

"I'd like to see these lakes be improved if possible," Welker said. "This area has changed a lot over the years. Hazel Creek used to have more water in it and a lot more fish. I'd like to see the government do more to control poachers and those kinds of hunters who take sound shots when they think they hear game."

* * *

Bob Runner, a long-time Salem resident, also remembers Palmer from the early days. He recalls staying at the Palmer Hotel in the fall of '28 as part of a timber cruising crew from the S.L. Culler Lumber Co. of Salem. The firm had just purchased a 10,000-acre tract of virgin Ozark yellow pine south of Palmer from the J.W. Hughes estate.

"My job was to count trees. I had just been hired as an apprentice lumberman. I was 14 years old," Runner recalled.

"The hotel was large, but not very busy then. It was hard times. We had our meals there, and I remember the big china pitchers and basins in each room. There was no running water in the place."

The firm did not begin cutting this tract until a year later because in February 1929, the bottom dropped out of the lumber market.

"By June of that year we didn't have any orders at all for our milled lumber," Runner said. "Mr. Culler's crew took three years to cut the Hughes ground, then it was sold to the Forest Service to the best of my knowledge."

A lumber camp with some 20 buildings was put up near Palmer, he said. Fifty men worked on the job, one of the last large tracts of virgin pine to be cut in the Ozarks. The firm sold 12" × 20" posts 20 feet long, and longer for special orders, cut from this pine.

"The 10,000 acres wasn't all pine, but where it was pine, nothing else grew. The forest floor had no underbrush and was so open that the tiff miners could drive their teams and wagons through the pines to dig wherever they wanted," Runner recalled. "The Hughes family apparently didn't care to collect royalties on what was dug from their ground. There were holes everywhere."

These aspects of Palmer's history—the timber and mining—are important historic topics that would interest people visiting the area. Not quite so obvious is the mark of the Depression in the Palmer area.

* * *

Oliver Crocker grew up near Palmer and now works for the City of Potosi and travels on the back roads exploring his old haunts whenever he gets a chance. Crocker remembers the Depression well.

The Forest Service, in conjunction with other government agencies, worked to help people who were without resources, homes or the possibility of jobs. The then recently abandoned Berryman Civilian Conservation Corps camp was torn down and local men were hired as carpenters to build houses from the lumber for people in the Palmer area who had nowhere to go, according to Crocker and Steve Welker.

The government plan called for a community garden along Hazel Creek near the town cemetery. Steve Welker was a supervisor for part of that operation. A community canning shed and an artesian well were built nearby. Remains of these are still in the woods.

Both Steve and Oliver know many fascinating places in this area. Up in the woods on Forest Service land to the west of Hazel Creek is the foundation of the Mallow School, built in the '40s but closed in the '50s because of consolidation. Oliver was able to attend school there for only a few years because gasoline rationing during World War II made it necessary for him to drop out of school and help his father run the farm, getting in enough hay to fuel the draft animals.

Across the creek from the former Mallow School, Oliver pointed through the woods to the roof of an old sharecropper's cabin built on the ridge. "Sharecropping used to be common in this area," he said. "It was one way a young family could start saving a little money so they could eventually buy their own place. Or larger families or an individual could stay on if they were not able to buy their own ground. That doesn't happen much anymore."

Many more features of life in Palmer seem gone forever. They deserve further investigation.

For example, in the Forest Service's Hazel Creek campground, the remains of a large stone dam and what may have been a lead smelter merit examination and protection.

* * *

These are only a few of the stories I heard over the summer. My tapes have been summarized and a final report accepted.

The struggles of Palmer are not completely gone. A rock-walled town spring across from the old church still attracts visitors who must wonder how the stonework came to be here, in the middle of the forest.

The huge timber growing around this spring, in the cemetery and by the old wooden church gives a sense of what Indians and the first settlers saw. Maintaining the wild quality of Palmer is at least as important as the area's history, many people indicated in interviews over the summer.

This combination, of almost forgotten history, mining ruins and Ozark wilderness makes Palmer a perfect haven for ghosts.

What happens next will probably evolve slowly. That seems to be the nature of the place. At least some of Palmer's story is now preserved as oral history, as well as by ghosts.

—Article for *The Independent Journal*, Potosi, Missouri, 1991.

5

Grasshopper Hollow
Fieldwork in the Ozark's Largest Fen

> This is my summary of another oral history project for the Forest Service in 1992. Tom Burge, archaeologist, Kris England, forester, and Lynda Richards, biologist, must have liked my first project because they helped guide me to other Passport in Time projects. The agency wanted local contractors, without a lot of administrative paperwork. Portions of interviews which follow give an idea of local feelings about Grasshopper Hollow, one of the incredible, little-visited natural areas in the whole Ozarks. I tried to write summaries in as readable style as possible. Only the J.T. Nickel Preserve with its riparian pine and prairie near Tahlequah, Oklahoma, may be as unique.

Report on Oral History in Grasshopper Hollow

Introduction

If it is known at all, Grasshopper Hollow has achieved a modicum of fame as the largest fen complex in unglaciated North America. In my interviews this fall, I have learned few local people even know of the area, much less appreciate its scientific significance.

The prominence of the fens to those local people who do know the place comes through their importance for hunting resources, agricultural properties and history associated with timbering. This narrow valley of some 500 acres has been one of the most productive parts of the Ozarks in two senses: as a nursery for many forms of plants and wildlife, and as a place where many families lived during the height of the early 20th-century timber boom.

People liked the swampy gumbo soil because it didn't dry out in the depths of summer and ruin their gardens. The productivity of the hollow can provide a major theme for future interpretative programs, but it will also make management of the area more difficult: local people instinctively will want to hunt here as they did in the past and probably still do.

A cooperative agreement to manage the mixed ownership of Grasshopper Hollow has been developed by the Forest Service, the Missouri Dept. of Conservation, The Nature Conservancy and the Doe Run Co. This agreement currently prohibits hunting. Exactly how visitation is to be managed in the future is a major challenge for this area, and I believe some of the findings made through oral history will be useful to managers as plans develop.

The Setting

Grasshopper Hollow is located on the south side of the Bee Fork, a major tributary of the West Fork of the Black River in the eastern Missouri Ozarks. Five miles southeast of Bunker, Missouri, on Missouri Rt. 72, the hollow is most commonly approached from its head on the highway. In the last year or so Rick Martin, whose father was interviewed, sold a large farm at the lower end to Doe Run.

Except for small parcels on the edges of the buffer zone, which encompass the ridges surrounding the valley, most of the land is in public ownership. As the plat map indicates, the Forest Service owns most of the ridge land around the valley as well as the upper third of the hollow. The fens themselves, mainly owned by The Nature Conservancy, vary in character.

In an article in July 1989, *Natural History* describes the fens being the result of mineralized groundwater supporting various plants in various bedrock situations. The resulting fens can be deep muck or a spongy carpet of vegetation which undulate to the touch. Among fens, the prairie fen may be the most unusual, as Robert Mohlenbrock noted in his article: "Grasshopper Hollow's seventeen acre prairie fen is considered by local botanists to be the most pristine such fen in the world. Prairie fens usually arise along valley terraces with a slight slope. What distinguishes them is that tall prairie grasses and prairie wildflowers join the more typical fen vegetation."

Research Methodology

The current project was modest and preliminary and should be considered as more of a "windshield survey" than a true oral history project.

Only one of the informants has been interviewed in any depth. Nevertheless because Grasshopper Hollow is a relatively small area, I believe the fieldwork reported on below comprises enough of a survey to be useful in several ways.

The main thing I sought to do in these interviews was to fill out several themes that are significant in the history of the place. These themes may be useful in developing future interpretative strategies. Though this project began in June, prior familiarity with the place led me to suggest it as an ideal candidate for investigation through oral history.

For the first time visitor, the place seems remote and forgotten. The remains of a sawmill scar the upper hollow; the one gravel road off State Route 72 into the head of the hollow ends by the largest, most swampy fen and the ruins of an old stone house and various outbuildings. My interest was piqued at a dedication ceremony at the fens in September 1990, which marked the beginning of the cooperative management of Grasshopper Hollow. I subsequently camped in the area and became more interested in the human occupation of the land.

Summary of Significant Findings

In contrast to its present wild condition, Grasshopper supported many families at the turn of the century. These families worked in the sawmills and stave mills at Ohlman where the railroad ended. The railroad was built from the south, eventually ending at a roundhouse in what was to become the town of Bunker.

As many as 20 families lived from Highway 72 to the mouth of Grasshopper Hollow Creek. Each informant I interviewed had a different recollection of how many people lived in Grasshopper Hollow. These families chose to live in Grasshopper where land was fertile and made for good gardening; and the closeness allowed for working right at home.

They had squatters' rights; very few owned the land they lived on. Jimmy Clark, a blacksmith and tie-buyer according to Floyd Sutterfield, lived in Grasshopper in a house now torn down. He owned and built his house and carried out his trade there until the '20s.

Almost all signs of human occupation in the valley have been removed or weathered into the soil. Only the rail bed of the tramway along the ridge above Grasshopper Hollow remains a significant cultural feature. This rail bed could serve as a prominent attraction for visitors who wish to learn more about early 20th-century timber operations in this area. Indeed, Grasshopper Hollow provides one important site in this period of forest history as several informants said that the hollow had some of the best timber harvested by the Bunker-Culler operation.

Land in Grasshopper was rich with lime, another significant natural resource. It could almost be shoveled out, Mr. Sutterfield said. It was tested and found to be rich enough to spread on farms to enhance soil productivity. Farmers were paid during the Depression if they would lime their land. Small dugout spots remain up and down the valley: evidence of this activity and the federal effort to elevate financial distress and promote improved agricultural methods.

The whole Bee Fork valley was timbered; it may have been the last cut in Reynolds County because timber all had to come to Bunker. Gerald Angel, a prominent local historian in Ellington, said this part of the county was particularly hard to get to and hard to get timber out from. But the effort was worthwhile, especially for Grasshopper Hollow, according to Angel and others.

Grasshopper Hollow has long been known as a good hunting area; it may be hard to change this traditional use and keep people out. One informant, Amel Martin, reported treeing and killing 14 opossums in one night in the valley. A slow process of developing local understanding of the environmental significance of the hollow could gradually build support for protection of all natural resources in the valley. The town of Ohlman, at the head of Grasshopper Hollow, once had several hundred people and was bigger than Bunker. It was served by the railroad. In addition to freight and timber, the railroad also had a daily train—the Moose—which carried passengers. The old rail bed is a major feature that could be given historic interpretation in the future. There is some disagreement about the importance of Grasshopper as a fen; some local people feel that swampy areas around Crossville are larger and more productive. The charcoal kilns at nearby Reynolds may be worth interpreting. In the 1920s there were 50 to 75 people working at the operation. Today it is owned by Ellis Copeland and provides work for 5 or 6 people. Some original kilns are still there.

* * *

These comments are generally based on the more significant topics raised in the interviews, which have been summarized. The tapes and summaries have been turned over to Tom Burge, forest archaeologist.

Among those interviewed were:

Floyd Sutterfield, Ellington: thoroughly familiar with the history of the northern part of the county. Especially good on timber and the history of Bunker and Reynolds.

Gerald Angel, Ellington: knows many details about the county as a whole, less about the northern parts. Knows the railroad history. Believes that poaching and general disregard for values of rare plants may be a continuing problem.

Frieda and Elmer Vest, Bunker: long-time residents who farmed and worked in the timber. Elmer remembers walking 40 miles to a sawmill job and exemplifies the rugged lifestyle still valued in this area. He remembers selling ties to Jimmy Clark and several of the farms that used to be active in Grasshopper.

Ida and Charlie Black, Centerville: good stories about tie drives on the West Fork of the Black. Charlie was sheriff in the '30s and remembers the importance of pine above other species.

Hazel and Loeman Martin, Bunker: also farmers, remember the cutting of the pinery. Loeman remembered S.J. Bunker, the timber baron, as being well liked and very intelligent. He recalls many families in the area tried to farm in hollows with swampy places with mixed results.

Mary and William Burns, Bunker: they remember cutting hay for the Schultz family in Grasshopper.

Shirley and Don Hays, Bunker: recalled the Schultzes building the spring-fed pond in Grasshopper as a fish operation. They are close neighbors to the hollow and have mixed feelings about public ownership of the property. Articulate and friendly.

Other informants were interviewed informally and can be identified on field notes. Most local people were very friendly when I explained what I was researching. There is a great deal of local pride here in the ability to make a living in this rough country.

Discussion

These findings seem important for several reasons. The main one is that Grasshopper Hollow is not the wilderness it appears to be. It has been important to local people as a home place, hunting grounds and farm resource.

Apparently agricultural use of Grasshopper Hollow resources was most active during the timber boom of the early 20th century but continued in later years too. What makes this significant, I feel, is that it gives added dimension to the place. Not many people can appreciate rare plants as a valuable natural resource. Many more can relate to a unique, wild landscape.

That a particularly wild, swampy place once was home for many people adds that much more fascination to the place, that many more angles to interest the public in the importance of forest history, natural history and our common close relationship to the environment.

One topic I did not question informants on was any local use of Grasshopper Hollow for purposes other than hunting or agriculture. Informants raised no topics on other subjects, but a possible avenue for future questioning would be whether local people ever frequented the place for gathering wild plants or roots, and whether the diversity of plants was appreciated in any way.

Recommendations

What I am proposing is based on my interviews with local people and only secondarily on my own opinion. Because I only spent about 20 hours in actual formal interviewing, in addition to an approximate 40 hours doing related field work in locating informants, I am hesitant to claim my suggestion would have wide popular support among the community. But I believe these recommendations represent at least a consensus of the opinions of people I spoke with in Dent and Reynolds counties.

As far as my own bias goes, to get this on the table, I generally believe the less impact people can have on land the better. I tend to fit many of the stereotypic beliefs of the so-called environmentalist, though I am in no way opposed to hunting or other consumptive uses of the environment.

I do not have strong feelings on the future of Grasshopper Hollow but generally feel that the public should be allowed to visit the place in a manner which promotes understanding of its natural history and does not harm the resource. Publicity of the site should be limited, I feel, to protect the place.

My major recommendation based on the interviews is that local representatives from the community be invited to join the interagency task force, which is developing management plans for Grasshopper Hollow. I reach this conclusion based partly on what people told me during interviews, partly on evidence of an attempt to place a gate on the place.

One gate was put up at the Highway 72 entrance to the property earlier this year. USFS ecologist Lynda Richards and I noticed it ripped off its post when we visited the valley in October. This unfortunate loss could have been avoided with more understanding of local feelings about the hollow.

Earlier in the autumn I met briefly with Mark Copeland, son of Ellis Copeland, who runs a charcoal plant in the nearby town of Reynolds. He indicated in a conversation that hunting was very important to him and many others in the community and that Grasshopper Hollow is regarded as a good place to hunt.

* * *

It seems to me that the best way to win community support for a ban on hunting in the area is to try a more gradual approach, which will develop widespread understanding of why hunting is being ended in this area. Such an effort would concentrate on educational efforts in local schools and the press to build support for the area as a unique resource in this part of the Ozarks.

5. Grasshopper Hollow

On the remaining signs of human habitation, people had various feelings. As to the future disposition of the Widger sawmill, people felt that it was a more recent operation and had no great local historic significance. About the stone house, several speakers did say it does have more local importance. One person suggested it could be converted into a picnic shelter. Several people felt the man-made ponds in the hollow should be allowed to remain, but feelings were not strong nor extensively surveyed.

Several speakers said that the Bunker area has a unique forest history, being the last part of the Ozarks to be cut over in the harvest of the early 20th century. Grasshopper Hollow is one place that adds to this possible interpretative theme. Many other significant sites exist nearby.

My sense is local people would cause no problems and would continue to value the hollow as a unique natural area with a variety of qualities, one of which is rare plants. A few speakers seemed especially proud of the area. The right kind of educational program for Grasshopper Hollow will assure increasing appreciation for the property in the future.

6

Establishing a Farm and Hunting Fox

Amel Martin

What led Amel Martin to live and farm in the wilds of the Ozarks? Was it the chance to hunt possums all night? Or other pleasures of backwoods life?

My interview as part of the Grasshopper Hollow project with Mr. Martin offers a picture of such pleasures. Amel was one of the most enthusiastic, articulate storytellers I ever met. Maybe you can sense that in this portion of the transcript.

On the Bee Fork of the Black River and close by Grasshopper Hollow, Amel Martin's farm was a tidy little place off a small highway outside of Bunker, Missouri. This town has been called "The Arm Pit of the Ozarks" by a few locals because it's a rough, remote town in one of the poorer regions south of the Courtois Hills. At one time a medical waste incinerator was proposed for the area, but that never developed. During my trips there to talk with Amel, I got to know a general store in town that had decent coffee, biscuits and gravy, and fried pies. I haven't been back in years. In memory it's a community full of folks with strong biceps and independence.

* * *

Interview Portion with Mr. Martin, 1992, on Farming and Hunting Fox

    Q: But what did you do once you stopped working at the sawmill? Did you go back to farming full-time?
    AM: Uh-huh. After I got married, I went, you might say, altogether.
    Q: So, you were always able to do pretty good with farming?
    AM: Well, just get by and that's about all.
    Q: Well, you got a nice place here.

6. Establishing a Farm and Hunting Fox

AM: Yeah, I put everything in here.
Q: Really? Did you build this house, too?
AM: Built the house, all the buildings that's here.
Q: You did all the stonework, too?
AM: No.
Q: Who did the stonework?
AM: Old Mike Thompson. Of course, we put the rocks here. Me and another guy turned 30 sacks of cement one day, and I went fox hunting that night and stayed out all night.
Q: Jeez. What do you mean, turning 30 pounds of cement?
AM: Huh?
Q: What do you mean, you turned 30 pounds of cement?
AM: Well, you have to mix it with gravel and sand.
Q: You just did it in a trough with a shovel?
AM: No, well, we have a board—
Q: Yeah.
AM: —and you use a shovel to turn it, and you got to go and water it, mix it.
Q: You didn't have a cement mixer?
AM: No, we didn't have no cement mixer.
Q: You did it all by hand?
AM: (inaudible) turned it with a shovel. Mixed it up.
Q: Golly. And then you went fox hunting all night?
AM: And stayed out all night.

Later in this interview Amel talks more about hunting…

Q: You did some fox hunting?
AM: Oh yeah, I done both.
Q: Which did you like better, running the coon or the fox?
AM: I'd rather run fox.
Q: Why is that?
AM: Oh, I just get more kick out of the race.
Q: Were there many foxes around?
AM: Oh, God, there used to be plenty of them.
Q: Now, you don't see them much anymore, do you?
AM: They died out.
Q: What happened?
AM: They took the mange—and it killed them.
Q: So, there's no foxes around here anymore?
AM: I ain't seen a fox, a live fox, for six or eight years.
Q: That's really a shame, isn't it?
AM: Yes, it is. And I fussed about it, and I had some good foxhounds then, I liked to race. But after I found out they had the mange, the boys got to killing them, shooting them, chasing them around the persimmon tree, they—just kill a bunch of them. They had to have food. Well, I fussed about it, and seen they had the mange. We've got lots of coyote now.

Sidebar

Alford Forest Wins New Lease on Life

> This piece was written in mid–2020 about a forest further west, just north of Arkansas in Ozark County near Rockbridge, an old village now know for its trout population.

Not many self-taught foresters have pulled off a deal like David Haenke. Or have many Arkansawyers had the influence of Ella Alford. Together David and Ella did all they could over many years to assure the future of big chunks of Ozarks forests.

David developed his forestry chops through personal perseverance, living out in the jillikins near Bryant Creek and meeting his remarkable friend, Ella Alford.

Ella's father had purchased the Alford Forest in the mid–1940s as a retreat for his growing family. Young Ella fell in love with these hills and hollows. Eventually she was able to acquire her siblings' shares. Gradually Ella developed a way to preserve what she treasured in this land.

Her love of trees involved donating most of the 3,200-acre forest to the non-profit Ozark Land Trust (OLT), now based out of Columbia, Missouri, for enduring oversight, management and protection.

Alford Forest and the OLT have worked out a management plan to protect the forest, springs, streams and nearby Bryant Creek. You can read about it on their website. Ecological land management is clearly spelled out.

Further protection became possible in January 2020 when a project David has been working on for a decade finally came through. The California Air Resources Board Cap and Trade Program has bought for $600,000 the carbon credits resulting from ecological management of Alford Forest. The credits result from the high amount of carbon sequestration associated with ecological management of Alford Forest.

"It's a big deal because we believe these funds will provide a steady flow of income to assure the forest is managed and protected for the next

125 years," David explained. "The details of carbon credits are complex. Some people don't trust them. I think it's worth trying."[1]

* * *

A large tract to the east near Current River, the 4,000-acre forest at Shannondale, an historic mission project of the United Church of Christ, became the first carbon credit project in Missouri. Finalized in 2015, it's also the first carbon credits anywhere gained by a church.

Such experimental projects attract unique people. I know Haenke well enough to state this effort required all his reservoirs of patience, passion and acumen over years. Maybe he's a modern-day Thoreau. Ella Alford shared a similar expansive vision of what a forest deserves from owners and can offer the wider world.

I met Ella once or twice at the Ozark Area Community Congress (OACC), an annual gathering focused on protecting the regional environment. I met many inspiring folks at these bioregional sessions over the years. Unfortunately, the national Oral History Association conference, which I also attend, is usually held at the same time of year.

Part of David's secret is his gift for friendship and learning, especially from the late Clint Trammel, who for years managed the 153,000-acre Pioneer Forest near Current River, now administered as a non-profit corporation. David also increased his knowledge of tree quality and market value by running Alford Forest's sawmill and learning how to grade lumber. An art, business and science, knowing the value of wood products is one key to successful forest management.

"We had the benefit of oral and written history on the days of the Big Mill from Noble Barker, Sr., whose ancestors came into this area in 1830," Haenke wrote about how the forest management plan developed. Located in what's now Alford Forest, the mill ran from 1919 to 1929 logging virgin pine.

* * *

Individuals like Dave and Ella do not fit into any easy understanding of activism. Ella was a private person who benefited from her family's business experience in Texas and Arkansas during the boom and busts of the 20th century.

Saving Alford Forest was just one of her charitable projects. The more you learn about her and Alford Forest, the more hope might be possible for humanity.

"I know people in this area who received no-interest loans to save their farms," David commented when asked about what Ella has done to help the Ozarks. "No one really knows all the different things she helped. I think that's the way she wanted it."

Probably so. I know the land trust where Cathy and I lived for a few years before moving to Springfield benefited from Ella purchasing acreage so the start-up would not collapse. (An overview of the Greenwood Forest Land Trust is in Part VII.)

Ella's family and friends planned a memorial to share stories and songs after her death in May 2005. Her friend Susan Wiseheart helped coordinate recording of the event and still makes CD copies available. I'll pass on my copy to the State Historical Society of Missouri, which has archived much of my oral history work.

In many ways isn't a forest a living archive of people's use and respect, abuse of or dependence on the essence of life? Planting trees takes vision and big hearts.

Walk into a pine forest, you can hear all kind of singing when the wind blows. Some specialists say they're learning to listen to trees telling complex stories of helping one another.

It's fortunate some humans are listening to the Ozarks' piney woods and profiting in ways that will benefit all.

Memoir

Adirondack and Ozark Ancient Forests

  When I first settled into the Ozarks in 1973, I took our forests for granted. Trees, the Ozarks has beaucoup, esp. oak and pine, and many others. Pawpaw: gotta love 'em.
  I had an unusual problem with trees after I worked as a lumberjack one summer while in college.
  That was the summer of '63. It was my 19th summer. Bob Dylan had just released "Like a Rolling Stone," which played everywhere on AM radio. This was one of the best and worst jobs I ever had. To put it simply, my dad helped me get summer work with the International Paper Co. in the Adirondack Mountains of upstate New York. He was buying newsprint from IP for the *Post-Dispatch* and inquired for me. I was enthusiastic and appreciative of the help, but a bit nervous. I liked hiking the backwoods but had never used an ax.
  This was long ago, in the era of computer cards. Have you ever seen one? Cards, and magazine covers, needed high quality paper pulp, not the kind newspapers typically rely on. You know, the dark flecks and imperfections in lower quality paper? Higher quality paper doesn't have bits of bark.
  Our job, with a crew of about 10 gnarly dudes, was to go into the forest, cut and strip a band of bark 12 or so inches wide about chest high on hemlock and beech trees. This is called "girdling" a tree. We carried short-handled Hudson Bay axes to do this job and sharpened our blades every evening. Sometimes it was hard to strip the tree this way, especially on hemlock, a conifer with wrinkled bark. They wanted bigger trees, about two feet in diameter or more.
  Also, we had to carry a gallon bucket of a toxic chemical that, when painted onto the bare wood of the girdled strip, would kill the tree in two weeks. It would deaden the tree so leaves and bark would begin falling off shortly after we painted that nasty compound. Sort of made me sad, but in some ways, the job made me tough.
  It was something like "sodium arsenate," wicked stuff. If you got

any on your skin you were supposed to run and find a creek or spring to wash it off.

Of course we were spilling the stuff constantly. Our clothes were usually covered with it. Sometimes, the forest was relatively open, lots of sticker bushes, vines, and poison ivy.

Mosquitoes, black flies, and other stinging bugs were everywhere, so we had to wear long sleeves, heavy rubber gloves and head nets.

Usually every hour some flying creepy crawly got inside your head net. They went for the eyes and ears first. Or up your nose.

You couldn't swat them because of those heavy rubber gloves, the chemical-laden paintbrush and the bucket and ax in either hand.

It was summer. It got hot, and buggy, then buggier.

My fondest memory of that summer is staying at a run-down hotel somewhere in the mountains near Speculator, New York. Some serious drinking went on. I had severe airplane spins, dropped out of the bed I was sharing with another poor soul from our logging camp, and crawled down the hallway to the common bathroom to try to summon the energy to get my chin up to the toilet bowl and heave out everything churning in my belly. Only once since has that happened again: at a Buffalo Trace bourbon tasting and documentary video release at the annual oral history conference in Denver, 2011. My experience with Buffalo Trace left me feeling Buffalo Bill had slipped me a mickey, but I relearned a hard lesson.

We had great guys back in the logging camp, especially Harvey Elger, from the old timber town of Berlin, New Hampshire. We hitch-hiked from the Adirondacks to his hometown one weekend, almost 300 miles mostly through the wilds of Vermont. Coming back Sunday evening, about 1 a.m. we were still 20 miles away from our logging camp. At least there was moonlight, but no traffic at all.

"The bars usually close early on Sunday," Harvey said. "That means we're not gonna see any more cars till guys start work in the morning."

He was right. We walked the 20 miles and got to the job in time to start at 7 a.m. Amazing what a young person can do when there's no choice.

By mid–August I took early retirement, met my family then on vacation at Narragansett Bay and didn't want to see another tree, ever. I wanted to see forests covered with asphalt. Glad to be a college student, I loved parking lots, so neat and orderly.

* * *

I slowly outgrew my tree phobia by 1973 when I started as a general assignment reporter in the Ozarks. I wasn't a tree hugger, whatever that is. I wrote about how the Forest Service tried to manage all those trees to keep the public happy, the economy growing and forests protected for the future: multiple-use management was the Forest Service goal, not an easy balancing act.

Other than surrounding Ozark forests, an attraction for a reporter in Rolla, Missouri, was the variety of government research stations and a technological university. The U.S. Forest Service was one of the more active agencies. It manages some 1.5 million acres mainly in the southern half of the state.

People at this agency seemed hard-workers. Many had grown up on farms or timber towns. In some ways they reminded me of down-home career Army people I had worked with in Beckley, West Virginia.

In some sections of the Ozarks, the USFS wasn't all that popular because government management of land means regulations and bureaucrats to some. Lots of folks love to hunt and fish in national forests, but they don't want to be told what to do. Some bad actors would set arson fires just to damage the forests because they didn't like government in any form. But that stuff has slowed down as folks have accepted national forests can benefit us all. Besides, these forests weren't created in Missouri until the Great Depression of the 1930s. The Arkansas national forest, equally large but in more contiguous tracts, was created almost 50 years earlier by Teddy Roosevelt. Public relations with forests are different in the two states. Lots of landowners feel government-owned land means not knowing who your neighbors are, so the USFS folks in the Ozarks have always had to be super polite and used to being criticized from all sides.

* * *

The agency had several programs to hire contractors to survey aspects of compartments to be harvested. Archaeologists had to examine any prehistoric remains; biologists searched for rare plants and critters. As an oral historian I had several contracts to research communities that no longer existed in the backwoods.

One winter day I went out with a group of USFS archaeologists and cultural resource folks to look at an African American cemetery in the backwoods near Palmer, the early settlement on the verge of becoming a ghost town. Our jeep got stuck in a half-frozen mud hole. It took an hour to dig it out, then we got stuck again. We had to use sticks and rocks to move the vehicle out of the mire. They could have called the foresters back in the office to pull us out. But the cultural resources folks would have lost face, not good for your karma or the tavern after work.

Part of all my USFS projects was to summarize oral histories about communities that were just about gone. Few structures remained. The stories of their recent past resided in the memories of rare local residents.[1]

It was never clear to me how this material would be used in future management of National Forest sites. With no artifacts remaining in the landscape, current visitors may never know where people had once thrived but then left.

I learned there was more to places that appeared to be only trees; that was enough for me to feel the work had been worthwhile.

Part III

U.S. Geological Survey of Gravel and the River
Fieldwork—Researching Downstream and Up

Why do Ozark rivers have unending gravel bars? Are our streams filling up with sand and stone?

Old timers say they rarely see the deep fishing and swimming holes they knew as kids. Swimming holes were important back then. Other than caves or cellars, places to cool off were scarce. Rivers still attract attention in summer heat.

These questions led to my biggest oral history project, commissioned by a national park to help answer an important question: How have rivers changed over the last few hundred years? The quest for information boiled down to: What's the status and future of Ozark rivers? The report has become a classic, explaining how our rivers have changed. Oral history helped clarify these diverse transformations.

Early settlers planted corn, lots of corn. It created our culture, I learned as curator at the ag museum. Once the corn was laid by—it had its final plowing near the full moon in August—families would load up their wagons and go to a nearby river, or to a Chautauqua or camp meeting maybe. Cool river water and deep shade from big sycamores provided the best break from summer's heat and endless chores.

Usually by a big ol' rocky bluff, a hole can be 20 feet deep and a half-mile long. The hugest fish hang out in big holes. Kids jump off to cannonball their friends. But many local folks say whole river channels have become choked with gravel. Not so many big ol' holes!

My interviews involved some 40 older residents of the Current and Jacks Fork rivers which together make a national park, the Ozark National Scenic Riverways.

While doing these interviews I often stayed with Ted and Kay Berger, whose stories appear in this part, and who helped me locate people to interview.

* * *

The project was officially called "Historical Land-Use Changes and Potential Effects on Stream Disturbance in the Ozark Plateaus, Missouri." USGS Water Supply Paper #2484 is available online.

I was the co-investigator. Dr. Robb Jacobson ran the study and did all the data analysis. Shortly after we finished the project, I profiled Robb and his research in an article for the *Missouri Conservationist* magazine. The August 1996 article is still relevant and remains online. It gives a sense how a geomorphologist like Robb works. In one Appendix, I've included the list of questions, developed largely with Robb, for this project.

Because I liked rivers and rock climbing, I took an undergrad geomorphology course at Colorado College. That class proved surprisingly useful. I wish I had taken more geology to understand the antediluvian Ozarks.

* * *

As mentioned earlier, one of the most important aspects of doing oral history—or any kind of research where you talk with real people—is developing a personal interest in the topic central to your project. You don't have to love the focus, but you must find aspects which interest you in some way. Otherwise the whole thing may be a bore. This can be a problem. There's nothing worse than falling asleep when interviewing someone. I've done that. Very embarrassing. Also, your interest will help you not bore your readers when you write up your report, no matter how formal.

While oral history may seem relatively easy as research goes, details can make any project flop. Clarity is the main consideration—why the interview project has merit and how the information may be used and archived. Equally important is choosing the right narrators.

The closest I've come to learning oral history in any formal way was doing criticism for the *Oral History Review*. As the editor, Valerie Raleigh Yow took time to make sure important questions were explored in the 20–30 books reviewed in a typical journal issue. In 1994, the first edition of her classic manual *Recording Oral History* was published. It's now in a third edition. Other excellent overviews of the field abound. I began with Paul Thompson's *Voice of the Past*, now in its fourth edition. Each historian has a unique strength in writing about research methods.

In any project, a key part of an initial interview is developing rapport. Rapport takes more than a few minutes. "This means not following the interview guide slavishly but instead following the narrator's thought process," Valerie Yow writes.[1] Most older people I've interviewed take a while to understand why you want to talk with them about something from long ago.

In doing these interviews along Current River, for example, I had the advantage of explaining how I knew something about farming: helping set up the Agriculture Museum at Maramec Spring Park, a well-known Ozark institution, and working on a hay crew one summer. There's something inexpressibly educational about loading 50+-pound bales onto a wagon, then stacking them in a rickety old wooden barn when too exhausted by heat and work to talk or think.

That experience helped build a background to do these interviews. Still, it takes a while to establish the ease of good rapport. I'd tell students—it's what used to be called "good vibes" (luckily kids still know the Beach Boys' most famous song). However, I was also somewhat intimidated by Robb's project. Basically, I'm a suburban guy in awe of folks who keep their hay baling equipment going, know how to doctor their cattle, juggle finances, and keep a farm from going broke.

Besides choosing the right people to interview—those who had memories of 40 or more years of life along rivers—the next most important thing was to do at least two interviews with someone ideally within a day or two of the first meeting. I think many researchers do not appreciate the importance of a second interview. In some ways it defines oral history. A single interview is the norm when we are looking for information from someone.

An oral history interview draws on mutual rapport to present your interviewee with an opportunity to explore his or her experience in depth. That's rare in our society. You pay your interviewees an awesome compliment by taking the time to hear and record their stories.

More than just honoring a person, additional time spent unlocks a storehouse of memories your narrator may not have explored in years. This can be a great pleasure as well as an opportunity for you to show respect and learn something new. Surprisingly, researchers have found speakers who claim to remember things from their youth 80 or more years in the past probably have fairly accurate recall. This is because certain details from the past have powerful resonances for each of us.

However, it's rare that an initial meeting will evoke these deep memories, but I have seen many informants come up with amazing details during a second interview. This happens because the interviewee will (ideally) have a night to sleep after your initial interview. In sleep, the subconscious mind goes to work, silently recalling aspects of the past he or she has not consciously thought about until meeting with you.

* * *

"For better or worse, our recollections are largely at the mercy of our elaborations; only those aspects of experience that are targets of elaborate encoding processes have a high likelihood of being remembered subsequently," writes Daniel L. Schacter in a fascinating study.[2] Much research has been devoted to the neuroscience of memory in recent years. Schacter's book may be slightly dated, but it shows how certain kinds of experience create reliable, persistent recollections. It's a highly readable collection, a compliment from a guy like me with mild ADHD.

Just setting up the initial interview in an appropriate place can be an important first step. The right setting can evoke memories. Going with an interviewee to a scene of significant memories can be particularly useful, as can recording feelings about photographs.

My goal in an initial interview involves chronologically exploring a person's biography and main steppingstones of life and career. A second and follow up interviews offer opportunities to explore the focus of the project and most of the important questions related to it.

Keep track of the key things said after the recorder is turned off. Something unexpected usually pops up. Keep a notebook handy. Remember what needs a follow-up when you have a chance to record again.

7

Gardening for a Life of Abundance

Ted and Kay Berger

> My friends Kay and Ted Berger have been long-time inspirations. They produce incredible fruit and veggies on their farm, which lacks air-conditioning, TV, Internet and flush toilets. Their two grown children live in cities with great jobs and use all these seeming lifestyle necessities.
> The Bergers' farm lies in a half-mile wide valley on the South Prong of the upper Jacks Fork River. I stayed in their garden shed or house many times while working on the Historical Land-Use Changes and Potential Effects Project in the 1990s.
> That's why I put the Bergers in this section; they're true river rats who know how to appreciate the upper Jacks Fork. They've been great friends to Cath, me and many others, and helped me find people who know their river. This begins with Ted talking…

* * *

"We were at a party where wild hogs were roasted. The conservation agents had been called to put traps in the forest which our ol' buddy David Haenke has been managing for many years. These wild hogs have become real ornery pests in the Ozarks lately. Trapped about eight young ones, 40 pounds apiece. Cooked up four hams as part of David's 70th birthday party."

"They tasted really great," Ted continued. "Nice and tender. It reminds me of when we had a problem with a neighbor's hogs. It was while we were still getting settled into the Ozarks in the late '70s…"

"Mary North had them. I forget how many. Some would supposedly get loose and end up at our place rooting up our gardens and wherever they chose to go. She didn't care where they went and was even a little proud they were smart enough to go eat off the neighbors' places. They were all huge, but usually we could scare them away before they caused too much of a problem."

"I was working for another neighbor as the off-bearer at his sawmill and was rushing off to work one morning. This big ol' boar hog looked up at me while rooting in the garden. I just wanted to shoo him off good, maybe with a little buckshot in his rear end. So, I grabbed the 12 gauge and went out to the garden."

"He looked up at me when I hollered to 'get on home!' Instead of running away, that critter charged me! I had no choice but to shoot it between the eyes, and hurry off to the sawmill for work, though I did stop by to tell Mary quickly what had happened. Put in a good day, then that afternoon our friend James came by. He was working for Mary North."

"'You better get off to Mexico,' James said. 'Mary's got the sheriff to issue a warrant for your arrest.'"

Kay jumped in, "That's what I remember, you came by school just as I was getting off from teaching in the afternoon. You didn't know where to go and what the sheriff could do."

"Finally I did end up in court," Ted said. "Small claims court. She sued me for loss of that big boar. So, I sued her for damages to our place."

"Mary even brought in the big pig's head. She's kept his head in the freezer to show what a huge critter he had been. The lady judge was mightily impressed, she ruled against me, but then found for me too. Mary got the bigger judgment. All because she brought in that half-frozen boar's head."

* * *

That was long ago. Cath has been stressed because we're going on a long trip. This afternoon she's become unusually happy.

"You should see what Ted brought by," she says, hurrying me into the kitchen. It's a bushel basket of veggies: organic green peppers, a variety of huge heirloom tomatoes, okrey, string beans, corn smiling in its shucks, onions and garlics. The only thing lacking is sweet potatoes, but it's August. They'll be harvested in another month: Ted's Reds, famous in our corner of the Ozarks. This gift of veggies powered us all the way to Steamboat Springs, Colorado, where we visited Ted's sister who accepted half the bounty.

Ted has been growing organic veggies commercially for four decades on a rocky few acres along the upper Jacks Fork. Weekly, he hauls garlic, sweet basil, jalapeños, and more 60+ miles into Springfield from his farm north of Willow Springs. Last autumn, he joined the sustainability revolution with two shimmering plastic hoop houses—one 20 by 48 feet, the other 60 feet long. Friends helped him finish the job with stout plastic covering, then he hand-dug dozens of growing beds over the winter. His carefully planned structures have changed his family's lives. Now he can grow veggies all year.

"This is why I hang out at the river when it gets hot like this," he said

7. Gardening for a Life of Abundance

in July. "I'd go bonkers if I worked all the time I could. I've learned to kick back when we can."

* * *

Most Thursday afternoons during July and August a bunch of us would go to some nearby river and hang out in the shade, swim, fish and drink beer.

One week Ted had marinated veggies Kay had chopped up so small he felt they might fall through the grill. We built a driftwood fire. When it was down to a big bed of coals, Ted hauled a sandstone slab from the riverbed, flopped it on the glowing embers and in 20 minutes the rock made the finest grill possible for some sausages and bluegill along with all their produce.

A big guy, originally from rural Ohio, Ted has been living in the deep Ozarks since the couple came here in the early 1970s. Working outside on his farm almost every day has made him strong, but that takes a toll. He visits our Quaker dermatologist buddy Van Stoecker in Rolla annually or more to get his skin cancers checked out. Both he and Kay don't run along their nearby county roads for fun and exercise as much as they used to. Knees can act up occasionally.

Ted bikes now when he can. A few years ago we went to a potluck before an Ozark Mountain Daredevils and Big Smith concert, two of the better local bands. Ted wanted to ride his bike back to the farm instead. Good exercise: 20 miles to Willow Springs, then another 10 to home. It was a summer evening but he made it by dark on a busy U.S. highway then the twisty local one. He wore a reflective vest. Everything planned, that's Ted's way.

* * *

This planning inspires his winter adventuring. More than anyone I know, Ted loves to explore the Ozarks. He has little desire to visit other regions or states; his neighboring hills and hollows offer enough excitement. Only one person might equal him—his buddy Mac Gum, who used to be principal at the middle school where Kay was a sixth-grade math teacher for several decades.

Mac and Ted resemble the famous Smith brothers; do you remember them from their sweet cough drops? Trade and Mark, was that their names? I most remember them with their big beards on little cardboard boxes that held the tasty medicine. That's what Mac and Ted have, giant fluffy grey beards, summer and winter. Good for catching beer foam.

* * *

Winter is traveling time in the Ozarks, no ticks or snakes. Henry Rowe Schoolcraft set the pace for winter exploration here 200 years ago. Ol'

Henry rambled south from Potosi into Arkansas Territory to study mining in hopes of landing a plum federal job. Spent much of his time hungry and lost.

Ted's rarely lost. He loves studying maps and planning routes and keeps records of where he's been, where he wants to go, and who's been on these expeditions that usually last just a day. He has to stay close to his dairy goats; it's hard to get off from farming. Not many people hike the way Ted and Mac do: off trail, up and down the ridges, following the creeks to find a spring, cave or high bluff.

We've seen marvelous places. One of the better hikes was into the Roger Pryor Backcountry in the Pioneer Forest. A timber operation purchased in 1951 by the St. Louis conservationist and forester Leo Drey, Pioneer has been managed as a not-for-profit foundation since 2004. Leo and his employee Roger made a productive partnership. They collaborated to protect many pockets of Ozark wilderness during their 20+ years of work, which ended when Roger succumbed in 1998. A rotund, happy guy like Shakespeare's Falstaff, he was full of life, folksongs, and anger at those who despoil. Did his disappointments at our collective lack of passion for the land hasten his death at age 53?

Just as Roger was a boisterous, outspoken advocate for the wilds, Ted's the opposite—a soft-spoken radical who will occasionally write letters for various causes but prefers to hike, make jokes about the holier-than-thou's, or brew beer rather than pontificate. Twenty years ago he spent many winters writing short pieces about his Ozark experiences, but he found efforts to get published hardly worth the endeavor of polishing his prose.

Besides, winter's best for hiking. Big Creek on the middle reaches of Current River, and at the heart of the Pryor Backcountry, once harbored a lively community of timber workers, farmers and families, a general store, churches and schools. Now no one lives along this great small-mouth bass stream, one of many "Big Creeks" in our region.

* * *

Hiking the ridges can take it out of you. Ted and Mac run up them. Most of the rest of us huff and puff. Ted's routes often avoid trails, so human signs are rare where he likes to go. Still we're often surprised to find old cabin sites back in the hollows. It's not uncommon to find masses of jonquils nodding in early spring sun where no one has lived in decades. Ozark wilderness carries signs of people trying to make it here, even if it is just a rusty trash dump or a pile of cherty flakes from Osage knappers along a high creek bank. It makes me sad to see once productive fields on creek bottoms now grown up in greenbrier and cedar. Little farms never made much money here, though they did pretty well raising happy families.

Climbing up and down these ridges reveals why folks settled here originally. It's incredibly beautiful and fertile in the creek bottoms. The hillsides

7. Gardening for a Life of Abundance

grow huge timber—pine, oak, and hickory—which must have been the big attraction for many. It was all free for the taking. Because of the karst topography, springs and streams tend to run year-round. In winter, which sun can warm into the 40s, we spend a lot of time taking boots on and off to cross streams. The freezing water stings but makes us laugh and feel alive too.

* * *

Ted played mandolin for a while, but now concentrates on crops, his goats, coming up with solar or labor-saving devices and keeping up with family and friends. Years ago we knew his sister Lee who helped out at Plumbottom Farm, before she moved to Colorado. A registered nurse, Lee and her husband Dwayne hosted Cath and me when we went west to escape August heat and brought the aforementioned Bergers' surfeit of veggies. Both brother and sister and their families have adopted the popular "paleo diet," which features eating no grains or beans, to focus instead on healthy meats, veggies, and fruit. Ted and Mac usually have ample supplies of venison and wild turkey, which makes such a diet easier.

Kay's not quite as enthusiastic about paleo fare, but Ted does his share of cooking so she doesn't complain. It's sort of a joke to Kay, like Ted's running up and down the ridges. Kay goes her own pace and catches up quick enough. Conveniences like an outhouse, an artesian well, and wood for heat and cooking meet most needs. When you live in a quiet valley in paradise, you only have to watch for ornery neighbors, like armadillo from Texas migrating north due to climate change.

* * *

"Our father was a big influence on us as we were growing up," Lee explained as we went hiking in the Colorado mountains one day. "Dad had a subscription to *Prevention* magazine and was an organic gardener in the 1940s and '50s." That's part of the reason Ted got so interested in farming.

Ted explained later: "When I was in college during the '60s the comedian Dick Gregory was invited to speak on campus. I was very impressed."

That surprised me; I'd forgotten what an activist Mr. Gregory had been. I heard him at least once in St. Louis where he grew up and found some of his funniest material. I was living near Delmar Boulevard at the time, a major street, which Dick said is the longest in the world. "It goes all the way from Africa to Israel." The beaten-up inner city gradually gives way to wealthy suburbs in the west.

"Dick Gregory was on a hunger strike at the time," Ted recalled. "He was just drinking juice to protest the Vietnam War, and was thin as a bean pole, just skin and bones. It got me to thinking."

"I wondered, how lean I could be till I was disqualified from the draft."

Most of my friends were thinking similarly about this time. Who has compiled strategies for avoiding Vietnam?

"They changed the draft when I was in college. The military assigned numbers to all the guys who had registered. Each year only so many men were needed," Ted said. His lottery number never came up. But he lost a lot of weight and became more interested in diet, health, and agriculture. Kay and Ted met in college, worked in youth services, and eventually found an ideal farm to live their dream in the Ozarks.

As back-to-the-landers, they've been successful at staying true to the ideals of their youth from Thoreau to organic agriculture. Kay usually carries a cell phone when out and about, but they're the only folks I know who lack the tech toys that most now consider necessities.

The trade-off has more than paid off for the Bergers. Lately they've been harvesting strawberries in December and have greens all winter long. Though Ted started farming with oxen he trained himself, he now uses Italian BCS tillers, which he makes last for a decade or longer. His homemade beer is as good as anyone's, but he confessed that since he's a paleo-person and all those carbos aren't too healthy, they might have to start growing wine grapes.

8

Gravelbars and a Thief at the Corn Crib
Rev. Cecil King

> The Reverend King has written a history of his community, Yancy Mills, one of the early Ozark settlements initiated by Scots-Irish mostly emigrating from the upland South and Appalachia rather than from St. Louis and the north. A new edition of this history was edited by Rolla writer Garrett Gabel in 2011. Three years later Cecil died at 92. This summarizes our interviews.

* * *

The Reverend King lived along one of the prettiest streams in the Ozarks, the Little Piney, which meanders 20 miles from headwater springs northwest toward the Gasconade. One of the largest rivers without a dam in the Midwest, the Gasconade may have been named by French fur trappers in the early 1700s.

Many of these trappers were Protestants who left the old country when King Louis clamped down on religious freedom. The old region of Gascony along the Atlantic coast harbored freethinkers. The Aux Arcs offered opportunities which attracted entrepreneurial spirits.

A deep thinker, the Reverend King had a tidy yellow clapboard house with white trim along U.S. 63 where it crosses the Little Piney. He and his wife kept a garden in raised beds near the house, visible as I sped by, often heading south to Arkansas. That highway slices through the heart of the Ozarks from the state capital at Jefferson City south to Mammoth Springs at the state line then into cotton fields and Memphis.

The Kings' home was a beacon for me. I remember our visits because they were the first on this multi-year project. As I roared downhill toward the Little Piney, I knew I was out of the Rolla area and heading towards the wilds of Texas County, the largest jurisdiction in the Ozarks. Many friends lived out here scattered in homesteads, but I always needed a map to find them once I got nearby. This county attracted lots of back-to-the-landers because property was more reasonably priced along upland ridges away from the big streams.

Across from the Kings' lies the mill pond that gave this community its name, Yancy, after an early Virginia settlement. The site accommodated several mills over the years, but just the pond remains. I interviewed Cecil in May, 1991.

Before interviewing began, we talked informally about Cecil's current interest—research on Yancy Mills and its spring, a community established in 1823. He collected photos of one early mill, a five-story structure built in 1848, as well as a large commercial distillery active at the turn of the century. In the photo it's possible to make out some drill holes in a warehouse, according to Cecil, made by a local resident intent on tapping into one of the huge vats. The last commercial business at Yancy closed in 1940.

After we finished the interview, Cecil had one other story about a neighbor from years past. This fellow noticed someone had moved a board from his wooden corn crib. Right away he figured some two-legged thief had been swiping dried ears of corn.

A coon couldn't have pulled off that board. It had to be a person, a bad guy. The farmer set a small leg-hold trap with solid metal jaws hidden in the top of the corncobs.

The next morning he came outside to do his usual chores. Who should he see but a neighbor from nearby with his arm wedged tightly into the corn crib? The man was grimacing with pain.

After freeing this guy from the trap, the farmer invited the man in to treat his bloody hand and to have some breakfast.

"If I ever see you near that corncrib again, I'll have to kill you just like I'd do any other varmint," Cecil told the humiliated robber as he sent him on his way.

Cecil also emphasized timber in this region was in better shape when he was young in the 1930s and '40s than it is now. The forests were more extensive because no heavy equipment to move logs existed then.

"When I was a boy, they didn't have the means to get out into the timber like they do now," Cecil said. "You used a horse or mule and dragged them [logs] out. You had no way to haul them a distance. Your mill would have to be close by. I remember steam engine mills. I guess you could say they were portable because you could move them, but it wasn't easy to move them."

This and other interviews confirmed the hypothesis Robb Jacobson had developed for this investigation—a variety of landscape disturbances through these watersheds have affected stream quality.

The common feeling among many residents of the Ozarks has been that timber cutting in the boom years of the early 1900s had been the major cause of erosion, which created extensive gravel bars and sediments to fill streambeds. This USGS report shows that blaming the timber industry for extensive erosion is simplistic.

Jacobson used analysis of oral history and available land use data, including aerial photography over decades, and radiocarbon dating of wood debris in sediments, to determine stream instability was more complex than just runoff from timber cutting. He studied factors such as hog populations in the Ozarks. Most counties in this watershed and along the Current River had many more hogs on open range than they had people. These hogs often spent months hanging out along the streams wallowing in mud. They tore up the riverbanks according to historic reports and verified by the oral history. Also row and grain crops were more common a century ago. Erosion may have come from farming and road building more than from timber cutting. But this can differ in each watershed or community.

Now most bottomland areas in the Ozarks are covered in pastures, not grain, for grazing cattle. Stream instability from a century ago is gradually subsiding. Spring burning of the woods is not so common after the 1960s, and that has affected runoff too. But will changed weather patterns—more frequent strong rainstorms with long periods of drought due to climate change—affect these rivers? Only time and more studies will show.

Longer excerpts from the Reverend King are available online in USGS Water-Supply Paper 2484. Twenty pages of the 84-page report are devoted to analysis of oral interviews. Because farmers do not typically keep records of how they change their operations over time, oral history proved to be one way to see land use changes during recent decades.

Robb's analysis of the interviews shows his persistence in sorting through a great variety of comments. In general, our rivers will tend to get shallower and wider, his findings show. This is what the late Reverend King, a devoted fisherman, had suspected.

9

"We are losing this river…"
Jack Toll

The interview summarized below typifies work for the USGS "Historical Land-Use Changes" Project. This is the type of report Robb Jacobson, the principal investigator, felt he could use more readily than a transcript, the usual oral history product.

Back then the transcript was king. Lots of effort went into making verbatim reports of interviews including every "umm," "cough" and "laugh." I even erased cassette tapes so they could be reused, in part because I was such a tightwad. The recordings were secondary then.

Summaries were somewhat easier to create than a transcript, but no one saw them as a primary document. The transcript was considered the primary document and the main goal of carrying out oral history. Now the digital recording file is considered the primary document because it can be used in ways that were too difficult or expensive in the days of analog tape. Recordings can still be transcribed, but digital files can be used in radio, video voice-overs, podcasts, and other media.

At the end of each paragraph a tape counter shows how many inches of tape passed the magnetic recording head. Digital recording is still much the same, but it's a time code similar to video recording. Robb sorted through these interview summaries to find sections which referred to topics included in his schedule of questions. I did two interviews per interviewee: one to develop rapport and introduce the project, then a longer follow-up interview to go over the schedule of questions and see if the informant might have additional information or photos. This exciting part of oral history makes multiple interviews necessary.

* * *

This second interview with Jack is significant because he clearly states overall stream quality has decreased during his 60+ years of living in the area. He's clear what the problem is—the thousands of acres of forest bulldozed by owners with little regard for the land they are thrashing. Out-of-state operators have created a huge "landscrape" of cleared steep slopes in the upper Jacks Fork that erode during heavy downpours.

Is this a problem elsewhere in the Ozarks? Probably, but forest health and cover does not garner much attention. State and federal agencies such as the USGS monitor long-term issues such as river quality. Luckily the National Park Service, which funded Jacobson's project in collaboration with the state Department of Conservation and the USGS, sponsors scientific research on resources in its jurisdiction. Whether taxpayers and voters will support such work in the future is an open question. Interview was completed May 28, 1992, for the U.S. Geological Survey.

At His Home North of Mountain View, Missouri, on the Jacks Fork

Introduction

Nancy Echols, who owns a health food store in Mountain View, suggested Mr. Toll as a source. Several other informants also suggested he knew the river well. This more than proved to be true.

Jack is retired from the U.S. Fish and Wildlife Service, but bought land on the upper Jacks Fork in 1960, and thus has been able to revisit boyhood haunts for many years. He is one of the most articulate, knowledgeable informants interviewed. He walks and fishes the main channel and both prongs of the Jacks Fork, so knows the stream thoroughly.

Summary of the Interviews

Jack was born in 1927. When he was five his father lost a Depression era job and left the East Coast to return to family roots two miles north of Arroll. The farm had a spring that flowed into a tributary near Grassey Hollow. He remembers a particular fishing hole where Grassey comes into Jacks Fork about three holes above Chimney Rock. It was called Grassey Hollow Hole. The family would go there several times every summer, but now this hole is extremely shallow. He remembers it as being much, much larger.

Is there a possibility that a comparable hole has developed in other reaches up or downstream? All of the river from the VFW camp and two miles up each prong are steadily filling up, no new comparable holes are being created, he said. Some new, smaller holes do get created, but the overall trend is shallower holes in the last 25 years. (200)

Usually gravel appears to be the main sediment washing in, but last year mud was washed in from the Highway 17 bridge and on up the North Prong. Never seen such sediment before. Only saw it on the North Prong for about a mile. It was like a muddy pond, but it has since flushed out. His children own a mile on the river, and they report the same findings about the channel. (240)

Asked to speculate about the source of the gravel in recent years, Jack mentioned the possibility of increased road grading and gradual deposition of gravel, but the real problem is not additional gravel but additional heavy flooding caused by extensive clearing in the upper watershed of the stream. Jack mentioned the clearing on H Highway west toward Cabool that is on extremely steep slopes. Such clearing has been going on for years, especially on the South Prong. The flood levels seem to be higher in recent years as well, adding to the problem. (290)

Responding to the prepared survey questions, Jack said the forest when he was a boy was filled with big, over-mature "wolf trees" (big old solitary tree) and young stuff that would be harvested when it got big enough to make a tie. Not much big pine. His father's farm was cutover via crosscut saw for boards when he was a boy, but just mature, moderate-sized trees. There was pine along the river itself. (320)

His grandfather and father had a freight business and Jack recalls seeing pictures of huge pine in the area, but the cutting in the upper river tended to be done by individuals on small patches rather than by big firms. Jack tells some about his family history and his luck in coming to the Ozarks. Anyone who had timber would cut a certain amount on a regular basis because that was one of the few sure cash resources, other than livestock, during the Depression. He estimated that 20–40 percent was cleared. There was more timber then than now. (420)

Many fields were growing back into forest. Now the timber is little islands among the fields, then it was the reverse. Burning the forest was common, but his father didn't believe in the practice and protected his woods. It was always spring burning. Burning and the free range went together; so when the vote closed the range, there was no incentive to burn. The range was closed in the '40s. The burning must have had a big effect: no leaf litter on the ground. He remembers free range in Wayne County. There hogs were "very erosive" on the forest. (520) Sorghum was the one row crop he remembers, especially in new ground when trying to establish pasture on cleared land.

Side 2

Jack doesn't recall any conservation programs being active in the area other than one sponsored by the state called Conservation Knights, which was geared to wildlife issues for young people.

When asked about flooding, Jack said it was a common problem he remembers because his school bus was often delayed. As a boy, he stayed away from the river during high water. Recently he has noted floods have had particularly hard effects on timber downstream from the remaining deep holes in the river. Granny Hole on the North Prong lost its slough this year due to flooding; Hattie Hole was also lost. Gravel appears to be moving more as a result of flooding, closely tied to loss of holes. (610)

"I haven't talked with anyone who thinks the river's getting any better," Jack summarized. "Everyone thinks the holes are disappearing." About gravel hauling over the years, Jack said he believes such digging of material has had no effect on the overall buildup of sediment in the stream. Only mud and other fine sediment could have adverse effects, but he knows only one gravel mining operation on the South Prong in the watershed. Thirty years ago a man named Miller had mining operations along the stream, but Jack doubts whether the operation was of significant size to have much effect.

Bank erosion appears to be more common now, he said. Several places along the South Prong have had their banks clear-cut in recent years, which has had immediate environmental effects. No stream straightening has occurred other than on the South Prong where a gravel operation had equipment in the stream for a mile making extensive modifications (730).

On fishing, no species shifts have occurred to his knowledge other than the regulation of smallmouth bass, which has made larger bass more likely to be found. He doubts whether the total numbers of fish have decreased in recent years because, to his knowledge, fishing is still good in the Jacks Fork. (780)

Logging was not very extensive in his neighborhood as a boy; fire was more likely to cause environmental effects in his opinion. Only selective cutting took place in the basin in the '30s and '40s. Whether any of the major tributaries were affected by other land use practices during that period he could not say. He did not travel near Peter's Branch, Leatherwood or Piney Creeks. (830)

"We are losing this river," Jack said at the end of the formal questioning. In particular he mentioned how huge algae blooms have become common in the river and near the prongs beginning in mid-summer. Cow manure and fertilizer may be the main cause. Springs have also decreased in size, he said.

"The problem's upstream, way upstream," he said. The loss of forest cover is the main problem; only ceasing to clear steep land could slow down the problem. One particular cattle operation near the intersection of U and HH in Texas County has cleared several hundred acres in the last year, removing almost all trees and all vegetation on even the steepest slopes. Such clearing of thousands of acres, more than riparian clearing, is what is destroying the river in his opinion.

About other problems, Jack recalled extensive clearing in a few places along the river and some farming operations which allow cattle unlimited access to the river. But these are minor problems in comparison with the clearing, he believes. (950)

—This summary of a 60-minute interview was completed by Alex Primm on June 23, 1992.

Memoir

Almost a Great Job for an Oral Historian

Most of my oral history projects were funded by grants from government agencies. Earlier I worked five years at an organization involved with natural and cultural resources in the northern Ozarks.

The job fascinated me in part because an operating foundation is a hybrid between a private business and a government agency. The James Foundation occasionally makes grants but meets diverse needs using funds generated generations ago. It's managed by the New York Community Trust in Manhattan.

A constant balancing act, my job was at the pleasure of a true Ozark character. Luckily, I had survived a year in Vietnam which served as great training for the unpredictable non-profit universe.

Learning to navigate despite uncertainty must be one of the challenges more workers will face as regular 9-to-5 jobs become scarcer. I can't claim to have survived the museum world with any great finesse. Those years were a cautionary tale that I look back on as a monument to my indecision.

* * *

This fascinating opportunity at Maramec Springs Park popped up unexpectedly. I was offered a museum job in 1983 at one of the most beautiful, historic corners of the Ozarks in part because I had worked one summer on a farm hay crew. My meditation on this experience, *Hay Journal*, was published by The Press at Colorado College in a limited, hand-bound edition of 150 copies. Perhaps I gave a copy to my boss at the time, Richard Cavender of the Meramec Regional Planning Commission.

Richard and I shared a love for the Ozarks during long drives on agency work. A master of managing federal grants for local governments and economic development, Richard suggested I talk with his father-in-law, Ford Hughes, director of the James Foundation. That was the important first step. This is how things work: if the right person can put in a good word, it always helps, especially in a place like the Ozarks.

It helped that I was a veteran, had a master's degree and had always been intrigued by agriculture. My parents had friends who farmed, my Uncle Bert had given it a try and my godfather David R. Francis, grandson of a governor who became an ambassador, ran pigs for many years. I was also familiar with museums, having won a scholarship to a summer art school in Skowhegan, Maine. I was lucky to have a decent background to be the founding curator of a new agriculture museum in the heart of the Ozarks. Woo pig sooie, as they say in Arkansas!

This was a great time in my life. Cathy and I had worked together to build a solar house and decided to become foster parents when we learned that we would not be able to have children of our own. Luckily, we enjoyed helping several great kids while being part of this well managed state program. I was able to do some teaching at rural schools for the Arkansas and Missouri arts councils. Things were going great.

The James Foundation office was in St. James, an historic town on the mainline of the Frisco railroad and Route 66 roughly 90 miles southwest of St. Louis. Its major facility is five miles east of town where the state's sixth largest spring bubbles up. It's spelled "Maramec" as it was on the oldest maps of the region, but the nearby river goes by "Meramec." Our house was on a back road between Rolla, home of the state's tech university, and St. James, home also of Johnnie's Bar (and Museum) on Old Rt. 66.

The countryside of the northern counties shares a sunken relief with much of the Ozarks. Our hills may not be very high, but our valleys sure are deep.

Fishing is one of the main attractions at Maramec Spring Park. Hundreds of anglers can be on the mile-long spring branch on an average day. The state conservation agency manages the fishery. When I worked there, the foundation offered historic ruins, a campground, restaurant, pavilions, museums, driving and hiking trails, some 1,000 acres, and employed roughly 20 seasonal workers on a $1 million+ budget.

Enjoying picturesque sites at the park makes a great day for reunions and picnics. I toiled many weekends at the Ozark Agricultural Museum selling souvenirs and sprucing up the museum. This was a small part of my job, which mainly involved designing the exhibits, finding farming donations and restoring the old equipment.

Not a lot of time for oral history, but I did manage to do a few local interviews. I don't know what happened with them. This is a reoccurring problem in oral history: interviews get lost or end up in archives unused.

Maramec Springs Park had a life of its own because work was seasonal. Life revolved around the major activities: trout fishing, camping and picnics. Visitation slowed with autumn into winter. That's when new exhibits at the ag museum could be developed.

Within a few weeks on the job I learned that the local director of the

James Foundation could be a wild card. Ford Hughes ran the operation as a personal fiefdom. The biggest challenge of my job involved anticipating what Ford wanted done.

A proud Arkansawyer, Ford ran the foundation with personal style. He loved farming as he knew it in Arkansas. Ford had taught vocational agriculture at the local high school. I quickly learned to get along with him in part because I learned he'd been an Army company first sergeant. While I was a reluctant draftee sent to Vietnam, I absorbed bureaucratic cultural peculiarities while overseas. Sergeants don't want to be challenged. They need things to go smoothly so they don't get hassled by the brass. As long as it looks good, Sarge is happy and can drink all the beer he wants at the NCO club.

Ford could change his mind on a dime and reportedly designed the huge barn that became the ag museum on the back of a paper picnic plate. Ford hired good people; park staff did most of the museum/barn construction.

I still remember one visit I had with a donor to the museum, the late Walter Snelson, retired insurance man, farmer and local historian. While in his early 90s, Mr. Snelson was still driving and piloted his big old car to the front of the museum. He hopped out and strode to the main door with the agility of the bushwhacker Quantrill raiding Kansas. He had something in a sack.

"Where's that little farm forge I gave you recently?"

"Let's go into the museum where we have the blacksmith shop," I told Mr. Snelson I knew he would want to know what happened to a small blacksmith rig he had donated recently. Donated or loaned, it was not clear. I heard second-hand from another employee that Ford had traded Walter's farm forge to another employee for a bigger forge to go in the blacksmith shop display. We visited the blacksmith exhibit and Walter must have sensed something was amiss. Most of Walter's previously donated tools were still in place, but he wanted to know the fate of everything he had donated and especially that little forge.

"Are you sure that's the forge I donated? It looks different," Mr. Snelson commented. I really didn't know for sure if this was his donation. We didn't have a firm acquisitions or registration of donations policy in place. I told him I would check with Mr. Hughes on the phone.

"That would be great because I have another donation for you, a water keg. Every farm used to have a water keg handy during threshing season."

On the phone, Ford said to take the new donation and show Mr. Snelson other new donations to keep the man happy. There were so many objects that we ended up spending an hour going through the storage room. Walter was happy, he even recited one of his poems from memory about threshing wheat during harvest.

I still recall one of the most unusual donations from Mr. Snelson or another local retired farmer: a hand-made canvas turkey breeding jacket. This was a heavy piece of material with loops for the wings of a hen turkey attached to a cover to protect her back so an amorous Tom could not spur her during mating.

To get the museum started, Ford had accepted a large tool collection from the St. Onge family in St. Louis County. I learned how to display plows as if they were turning dirt and to hang farm tools as flying sculptures. It was a one-man operation but other staff at the foundation provided great suggestions and support. Unfortunately, there was no budget for much change or growth.

It's not nice to disparage those no longer with us. Ford was such a charismatic presence while living that these comments should be seen as homage not criticism. He's almost disappeared on the net, which is not surprising as he died in 1999. But I did find he was inducted into the Missouri Park and Recreation Association online hall of fame along with some 30 other more well-known Ozark conservationists including Pat and Ted Jones, Leo Drey, and Ed Stegner. I knew many folks in the digital temple of worthies and appreciate how hard it is to tease out who has served the public interest with the greatest persistence. The Ozarks has inspiring, rich environmental history; Maramec Springs deserves attention as a hearth of early development.

Ford mainly had to keep his boss and a board in Manhattan happy. Lucy Wortham James, a major heiress of the Dunn and Bradstreet fortune, established a multi-million dollar trust to help create Maramec Spring Park among other goals in the 1940s. I interviewed people who knew her, a progressive woman of her day who had dumped her diplomat husband to live on her own terms. Some of her special interests were creating a prize Jersey dairy herd, establishing the region's first electric service for her farm community and various cultural and women's charities in New England where she lived most of the time. Because she had grown up in St. James, the old iron works received special attention while she lived and from her trust following death in 1938.

I tried to avoid local politics surrounding the foundation's efforts in St. James, which included a library, in-town park, cemetery and eventually the town golf course. I could see little possibility of working my way up to take over Ford's job, though the thought crossed my mind.

I was lucky to stay on part-time for several years after the museum had been completed. But it was a disappointment: the ag museum had a limited future. Luckily this holding action allowed me to develop independent oral history opportunities.

* * *

What lacks in the Ford Hughes legacy at Maramec Spring Park may be sensed if one can imagine the remarkable site it could become. Now it's basically a local park with limited historic interpretation and gaps in information about everything from mining in the area to the abundance of Native American sites, including a major route on the Trail of Tears, that came to the iron works.

One of the real gems of the park is an historic home where Phoebe Apperson married George Hearst, which serves as a park supervisor's home. Only parts of the Hearst family's Ozark story can be easily located on the net.

An attractive Ozark farm girl, young Phoebe was the schoolteacher for the miners' children in the 1850s. She met the dashing mining engineer after he returned to Missouri to see his family. George had struck silver in California and Nevada. Lots of it. The couple married in 1862, honeymooned in Panama, and established their home in San Francisco. George found more valuable minerals, became richer and richer, fathered one son and became a U.S. Senator. You maybe have been to visit the son's famous home south of Big Sur—San Simeon. The Hearst Castle began in the Zarks.

And how about George's great granddaughter, Patty? You may recall her story from the wild politics of California. Patty Hearst joined the Symbionese Liberation Army shortly after she had been kidnapped and held for ransom in 1975. That played the national news and became an even bigger story in Rolla, where I was a part-time features reporter.

Someone called the editor to say he had seen Patty at the Greyhound Bus station in town. Maybe Patty was coming back to her great grandparents' roots? That's what the editor sent me to find out.

I interviewed a few colorful characters at the depot. No one claimed to have seen Ms. Hearst or anyone wearing an S.L.A. t-shirt or even any brunettes from California riding cross-country buses recently.

* * *

Previous to Ford Hughes's tenure, a local engineer, Robert L. Elgin, did much of the initial work to establish the park.[1] It had been a pre-industrial ruin. Bob became an industrial archaeologist whose work in several fields has been archived at the Missouri State Historical Society. With his wife Carolyn, Elgin had a group of friends—Bob and Margaret Wilson, Marylou and Art Corn, Pete Kirgan and several others—mostly World War II vets who were informal advisors or formal advisory board members to The James Foundation programs in St. James. They all enjoyed an occasional bourbon, tended to do a variety of traditional crafts, had great parties and often supported Ford's efforts to maintain their town's lucky inheritance.

Ford was The Man. He loved organizing things like the big hoopla for the March 1st annual opening of trout season. Leo Cardetti from town often cooked at this event. He operated several local restaurants, made sure good wine was available and volunteered with the county historical society. Once I had to spend the night at the ag museum with Ford's favorite toilet paper salesman. Luckily we didn't have too much wine, so we were able to cook breakfast and welcome the thousands of visiting trout fishermen at one of the town's biggest festivals.

Ford could talk almost anyone into doing anything. Perhaps that's what it takes to run a major recreational enterprise. Working at the ag museum taught me persistent pragmatism, or, as they say in Arkansas, "Root hog or die."

* * *

One person at the park especially inspired many—Raymond Haffer, a blacksmith who had grown up near the upper Meramec River just 20 or so miles away. Ray helped with building exhibits while repairing old farm equipment and sharing stories about the old days. The part of Crawford County where he grew up, Cherry Valley near Huzzah Creek, holds a variety of small farms (mainly cattle operations), state and national forests, and struggling communities usually centered around local churches.

After serving in World War II, Ray worked with his brother-in-law hacking railroad ties in the forest during the late 1940s and early 1950s. A good man could hack the four sides of a log to create a tie in about an hour. Back then Ray would get about a buck for a tie. Every Friday a tie buyer would come to the woods where they had been working to count, mark, and buy their ties. Ray liked the freedom; the two men could work at their own pace. He was among the last of the true tie hackers and kept strong until the end.

Of course, Ray talked about much more than this. He had the patience to repair or build about anything; both his sons, Bob and Rick, are the same way. For a long time, he lived in town with his wife Mary in a double-wide trailer he'd modified and expanded over the years. Ray was able to take out most of the mobile home's interior to put up new walls, floors, siding and a wrap-around porch. An unusual way to build a house, but Ray made it comfy with a big wood stove.

In many ways, Ray was the opposite of Ford, but the boss depended on the old blacksmith to keep equipment going both at the park and at his home. Everyone who worked at the park and most everyone who lived in St. James depended on Ray to fix their stuff, find them a decent working truck cheap, or know where to find deer or fish. If Ray didn't know it or have it stored behind some shed, he'd help you find it.

When he finally retired, Ray could be found working near his shop by the house fixing vehicles or farm equipment for neighbors. He even helped Jim DiPardo, another park veteran, set up mining equipment at his sandstone quarry outside of town. Often Ray would buy old automotive or electronic equipment, burn it with leftover shipping pallets, punky stove wood, or old tires, then harvest copper and other material for scrap to bring in a few bucks.

Ray didn't like sitting around. This kind of salvage work may not have been the healthiest activity for an old guy, but probably no worse than drinking bourbon or watching television. A staunch Baptist, Ray Haffer was the man who kept things mellow wherever he was. Laughing whether things went right or wrong, Ray had seen it all and could do it all. The world would not have run right without Ray Haffer's 86 years in the Ozarks.

I never did a recorded interview with Ray. But you can see him show how to hack a railroad tie on the Oral History of the Ozarks' *Treehouse* video, which lately has become available on YouTube. Ford gave Tom Shipley and me license to shoot part of the award-winning video at Maramec Spring Park. That setting, its forest, historic spring, nearby river and Ray Haffer added a lot to our production.

Part IV

Marching with the Military Again
Enlistment—Public Service
Interviewing in the Ozarks

Fort Lost in the Woods lies near the heart of the Ozarks. I was lucky to experience it as a civilian, not as a draftee for basic training.

Many friends endured marches to the rifle range, gas mask drills, and low crawls below barbed wire and machine gun fire overhead as they came under the control of a dreaded Drill Sergeant. My basic training occurred at Ft. Bliss, Texas, a fittingly named post for my close-order drill in the desert, October–November 1967. We even had buses to take us to the grenade throwing pits and related instruction.

Is this kind of training good for young men? For young women?

Questions and memories invaded my mind while working part-time at Ft. Leonard Wood from 1999 to 2003 as an oral historian.

This four-year project evoked mixed feelings because the Iraq War raged while I worked with Dr. Richard Edging, an archaeologist who managed a variety of research projects at the sprawling base. We documented this historic region centered on the remains of Bloodland, a conveniently named town that became part of the base on the eve of World War II.

Occasionally I saw busloads of American G.I.s heading from Ft. Wood to some far-off deployment. Did I have flashbacks of my own deployment to Vietnam? Probably. But I went overseas as a lone soldier on a Boeing 707 with orders to an Army unit outside what used to be known as Saigon. My heart went out to these active-duty G.I.s, but my apprehension for their mission was subsumed by desire to document a resilient Ozark community. I was glad to be working on a project that seemed worthwhile even as I had concerns for being part of the military again.

My oral history at Ft. Wood researched life in the area that became a military base in early 1941 with six months of preparation. Politicians knew America would likely be at war in Europe and Asia. They wanted another inland training facility. Ft. Leonard Wood became a huge construction site overnight. Six towns and hundreds of farms were sold within a few months to create the post.

Ft. Wood, mainly a training center, now covers almost 100 square miles. Federal regulations stipulate archaeological and historic research be reviewed before any new construction begins. My work was part of a new pre–World War II history of the region. Administrators at the funding agency felt the phrase "made it in the timber" from one of my oral history interviews was too suggestive. It described how residents made most cash income from selling logs. Thus, the shortened title, *Made in the Timber*.[1] Steven D. Smith cooperated with Dr. Edging to write this history with thorough professionalism and used the whole phrase as the book's epigraph. Unfortunately, it's a rare volume now, but valuable local history if you can find one.

The main thing I learned on this project involved tempering my preconceptions. I came to understand this region was still "Ozarky" despite the 80-year history of the military base. I also developed a new appreciation for the diversity of the military. It's a huge operation but offers a variety of economic development opportunities despite the usual military propensity for wasting resources. Being at Ft. Wood made me feel we should consider public service options for young people other than the military.

A few stories inspired me from these years in the field. A stop along the infamous Trail of Tears, nearby Waynesville has a citizens group that restored a pre–Civil War hotel among other projects. Dedicated professionals and volunteers have made Pulaski County and Ft. Wood models for historic preservation and environmental conservation.

10

Hogs and Midwives

Interviews with Ft. Wood's Early Settlers

> From the score of people interviewed on this project, a few capture the challenges and euphoria of life in the Ozark backwoods before the new Route 66 and nearby Ft. Wood were completed. Virgil Mozelle Shelton farmed near the famous community of Devil's Elbow downstream from the military base on the Big Piney. (Named for a sharp turn, this river bend features a huge boulder mid-stream that regularly busted up timber rafts floated down by local crews.)

Settlers ran hogs to provide meat. Fish were also plentiful before Ft. Wood was built, but deer were almost extirpated from the Ozarks by the 1940s. Mr. Shelton worked part-time as a fishing guide and was a first-class storyteller. His interview explains how the community gathered up their free-range hogs in autumn.

"You've heard of a cattle roundup. How about a hog roundup? Usually the hogs would gather up where the later crop of acorns came in, a big north hillside. There would be more acorns there. Sometimes we'd build a pen up there. Other times, we'd just start taking corn up there. We'd dump a bushel of corn where the hogs would come to eat.

"I attended two of these hog roundups. My granddad had a big old Airedale dog, big old rascal, and they'd point him at a certain hog and tell him to get it. He'd invariably catch him by the left ear. He wouldn't bark. He'd just grab the hog by the left ear and hang on. Well, that hog would drag him 30, 40 feet. He'd brace his feet, then in the stock pen the pig would just go around and around and around, but that dog would hang on. Finally, he'd sit down, open his mouth and the pig would just fall.

"Well, each farmer who had hogs there would bring a wagon with a covered top and a swinging end gate. The hogs had the ear marks. If the hog was one with pigs, an old sow, her herd of little pigs would stay with her. Oh yes, you'd hear it squalling. Of course, the old sow with the ear marking, we knowed where that pig belonged. There'd be a man on each side and in front. We'd get her by the front feet and the ear on each side. We'd pick up, and into the wagon she'd go."

Homer Hildebrand, who lived and farmed further upstream near the Piney, also had stories about the importance of hogs and watching out for wild porkers when hunting: "An old sow'd eat you up if you're out in the woods where their little pigs was," he said in our interview. Homer had been suggested as a knowledgeable long-time resident by friend Paul DeSmedt and his late wife Jane who lived in St. Louis and often visited family in the area. The Hildebrands had lived in the southern part of Pulaski County for several generations and generously shared their local knowledge. Homer remembered, "My mother was a midwife to no telling how many people who couldn't get a doctor. She had no training, not that I know, but off she went everywhere and did that. A verse in the Bible, I don't know where it is and no one's ever said, and she never told. Someone'd have an animal hurt, something wrong with it, be a'bleeding to death and she could take that Bible with that verse and stop that blood. Now, a lot of people said you can't do it, but she did anyhow. Well, she was a veterinarian as well as a midwife."

South of Ft. Wood, Paddy Creek provides a protected 7,000-acre wilderness area. How many know this U.S. Forest Service site takes its name from James Ohio Pattie, the first Anglo-American to see the Grand Canyon, in 1825? The Pattie family had an early sawmill along the Big Piney. They gave it up to travel west. Father and son had many challenges as they headed further west to California, a narrative too complex to share here but an inspiring adventure worth following from its beginning in the deep Ozarks of yore.

* * *

Sharing this fascination with local history, Napoleon Bonaparte Ramsey grew up on a farm further upstream from the Sheltons on the Big Piney. His family's place became Ft. Leonard Wood's beautiful golf course. When I had a chance to interview him, the retired chemical engineer was living in Virginia. He occasionally returned to the Waynesville area to visit friends and family.

Boney had strong memories of seeing tie rafts floating by the family farm. Rafting railroad ties downstream to buyers began after the Civil War. The Big Piney provided one of the major sources for ties, which were usually cut during winter, allowed to dry in the warm season then rafted to markets with autumn rain that raised river levels. But rafting ties could be done at any time, as Mr., Ramsey explained, in this slightly edited transcript from October 18, 1997:

"They were rafted down this river, down to Jerome [on the Gasconade] where the railroad is. I saw one tie raft, the last one. That was in 1926, could have been as late as '27, but no later.

"I was with my Dad. I was about 5 years old. We walked down to the river from this farm, the little farm we lived on. There was a raft tied up. My dad knew those fellows ... there were about 5 or 6. As we approached them, Dad said to me, 'Now, they'll offer you some food, don't you take it because they don't have very much.'

"When we got down there, I'm glad he warned me not to take anything that was offered. And they offered me some things. But the thing that smelled the best was cornbread. They put it on a board and spread it out till it was about ½ inch thick. They put a prop, a rock under it and let the radiant from that fire cook their cornbread. Did that smell good! Nice brown cornbread...

"Yes, they told my dad, this is the last one. He said, 'I'd like for my son to ride on this raft.' They said, 'Be down here by 7:30 in the morning and you can ride it as far as you want to.' Yes, we did ride. We got on there and we rode that raft down past Stone Mill Spring which in distance would be about 4 miles from the Rolling Heath School. Then I rode it about 4 miles.

"I could hear them signaling. They had a signal, the man in the front of the raft—there was a couple in the middle area—then there's a man at the back with the break pole which was stuck down between a couple of ties. This was dug in the bottom of the river with certain yells they would make. They would know to let up on the break or to apply a break.

"If the back end of the raft tried to overtake the frontend, it pushed it over against the bank. They wanted to keep that raft, you know, in the middle of the stream.

"It was a beautiful day and it was warm—I guess it was in June. We would walk along on the raft. It would sink down. The water would come up on the top of the tie.

"My dad said that when he was young he used to have a fly rod and he would get on one of those rafts and he would fly-cast for fish. And if he found a good hole, he could just walk back on the raft and keep casting in the same place.

"But that was the last raft, there won't be anymore. I would say it would be about, oh golly, it was less than a quarter of a mile long. Going around the bends in the river, the lead rafter at the front of the raft which was guiding it with poles in the water, he couldn't see the fellow—this was before two-way radio communication—his yell would tell the fellow in the back and also the 2 men in the center of the raft to break or not break. They knew what was happening and they wanted to keep it away from the shore also.

"There's a tie slide right down here, not far, about oh, less than a half mile. I think it's called the Ramsey tie slide. What they did there, they made ties up on the flat level and with horses, they'd take them over to the top of the hill there where that tie slide was. The tie slide was made out of wood. And it was all sort of greased with hog lard. They would put those ties up on that slide. It was, as I remember, maybe about 2 feet wide and it had a high board on each side maybe 8, 10 inches, something like that because

10. Hogs and Midwives

only one tie at a time went down. And they didn't want any lockups on that. That must have had about a 60 degree—it was off a bluff—not quite straight down.

"Well, of course, there were fellows out there swimming around to get those ties and they would nail them in the raft. They would use 3 saplings; I'd say 2 inches in diameter. And the bigger sapling was right in the middle and they'd have a space, maybe they'd have about 10 or 12 feet of ties. Now those ties weren't right together. They were about 6 or 8 inches—3 or 4 inches apart as I remember. That was for the guiding and turning the bends in the river.

"I thought riding that raft was fun. I was sorry that it was the last one—the first one and the last one I'd ever ride on. They said after that the sawmills would be doing it. And by then, they were getting trucks that could haul it to the railroad.

"I'd have liked to stayed on it all day. My Father rode with me. Then we walked back home. It was very enjoyable for me and it was quite an experience that I'd never forget because it was the only time. All the old rafters are dead."

This tale of the last Big Piney raft memorializes a trade and time in Ozark history gone forever. Thousands of men, and a few women I've been told—at least one stout gal near Freeburg in Osage County—hacked ties. They turned oak and other timber into railroad ties. Probably hundreds of millions over a century or so. They used crosscut saws to drop trees, chopping axes to score the four sides every 12 or so inches, then broad axes to clean them smooth.

A good tie hacker could make ten to twelve in a day. Now it's done in sawmills with big trucks to haul in the logs and haul out the sawn ties.

No more rafting timber. A hearty crew on the Current River recreated tie rafts in September 2009 and 2016 for the traditional Labor Day celebration in Doniphan, Missouri. It was an honor for all involved to help build these rafts. A sawmill produced some 200 ties in the spring that were dried over the summer then hammered into three or four blocks with sapling poles to hold them together. Coupling poles joined these blocks together as hinges. The rafts were flexible in floating downstream on the twisty river.

A few old timers, like Bill Debo from Devil's Elbow, have dug up and made use of ties that sunk when they became waterlogged along the Big Piney. But these "deadheads" are gradually disappearing and being covered with gravel as the river meanders over time.

* * *

You can find the one major monument built for America's tie hackers in Wyoming near the Continental Divide in the upper Wind River Mountains just east of the Grand Teton National Park. The 14-foot-high limestone relief sculpture depicts a tough young guy with a broad ax, fellow workers and horses in the background. The Rocky Mountains supplied a lot of tie timber, but building rail across the Great Plains was a job for Ozark oak.

Arkansas actually has a monument to the railroad tie industry, but it's not a statue. The state's largest park, Hobbs State Park-Conservation Area, at over 12,000 acres, was donated in part by the family of the late Roscoe Hobbs, a railroad and timber entrepreneur from Rogers. The Friends of Hobbs Park has a history on how the park developed in the late 1970s with local support and advice from The Nature Conservancy, which began its Arkansas office at this time. My parents were friends with Mr. Hobbs' daughter, Warrene Schlapp, married to a St. Louisan but always proud of her Rogers roots. Named for the nearby War Eagle Mill, Warrene and her father shared an interest in conservation. Just east of Rogers, the Hobbs tract was managed by selective cutting. Now it's the only state park in Arkansas that allows managed hunting. Luckily the Ozarks has a tradition of successful entrepreneurs and others being recognized for their conservation efforts on honor rolls such as the Arkansas Outdoor Hall of Fame and other sites you can find at some public agencies and websites.

Of course, many Ozarkers will not be included in any hall of fame. Many individuals who have done something worthwhile for conservation and their communities will never be memorialized. Maybe you can add to the future for conservation?

11

The Lady with the Bull Dick Cane on TV

Aileen Hatch

Aileen Hatch introduced an essential aspect of oral history as the foreword of this collection, "A Wagonload of Fire." Some events and stories seem unforgettable. This story is one. It captures an essential aspect of the Ozarks, at least for me.

This event, the loss of a wagonload of furs, creates what psychologists have called a "flashbulb memory," a shocking or novel event freezing a moment forever with associated personal details. For many Americans, where they were when they learned of traumatic events such as the assassination of President Kennedy or the 9/11 attacks act as flashbulb memories. In addition to being such a powerful image, the burning wagon represents the subsistence way of life that has been a tradition in the region. The relaxed nature-based lifestyle of the Ozarks was celebrated by the folk historian L.L. Broadfoot in his 1942 masterpiece *Pioneers of the Ozarks*, by novelist Donald Harington in his Stay More novels set in Arkansas, by popular theme parks and by the persistence of the hillbilly in regional culture.

Mrs. Hatch loved the Ozarks. *Aileen: Ozark Pioneering Spirit*,[1] her self-published autobiography, written with the help of her cousin Iris Culver Meadows, says it all. She was a go-getter all her life. Growing up as the youngest of five children in rural Texas County, Aileen was born in 1912 and became a tomboy almost as soon as she could crawl. Her three brothers, in birth order, Oberon, Orland and Orban, and older sister Aula made for lively home times and at the family lumber company. Aileen's actual first name was Iola.

Graduating from Southwest Missouri State College, Springfield, in 1936 with majors in math, science and physical education, she was on the track, soccer, hockey, basketball, volleyball and softball teams and president of the Women's Athletic Association. Aileen married the superintendent of the Licking Schools, Joel Hatch, in 1937 and had

Part IV—Marching with the Military Again

two sons. Her youngest son, Dr. Dan Hatch, a retired science teacher in Licking, has reviewed this for accuracy. Aileen died in 2002.

The transcript had been the heart of oral history. The spoken information was the nugget researchers wanted, it was thought. That has gone out the door with cassette tapes. The primary document has become the actual recording whether voice or video. Of course, transcripts still are made, but specialists realize the human voice with its intonations, pauses, emphasis, and unexpected stops and starts, tells much about the speaker beyond the literal meaning of his or her words.

This transcript shows that the pressure of getting guests onto his nightly show caused David Letterman to be blindsided by his Ozark storyteller.

A friend of the family told David Letterman's staff about her and the rest is history. This document shows how popular entertainment depends on novelty and how oral history differs from other forms of interviewing. See if you can picture this scene taking place at 11:30 p.m. March 2, 1995, in Manhattan, New York, via CBS to living rooms across the country:

DAVID LETTERMAN: Okay. Our next guest has a fascinating story. This woman is a four-time Senior Olympic Champion and what, what ... how did you ahh...?

AILEEN HATCH: In Archery.

LETTERMAN: In Archery!

HATCH: Yeah.

LETTERMAN: That's good. Four-time Olympic Champion.

HATCH: Yeah.

LETTERMAN: She's also a nail driving expert and co-author of this compelling book about her life in the wild called *Ozark Pioneering Spirit*. Please welcome, Aileen Hatch. Here she is. Hi Aileen! Good to see you! Take your ... just back a little bit there. Couldn't see your face.

HATCH: Okay.

LETTERMAN: Welcome to the show. Welcome to New York City. I understand ... have you not been in New York City before?

HATCH: Never.

LETTERMAN: Share with us if you can your impressions of the city.

HATCH: Oh it's great.

LETTERMAN: Yeah?

HATCH: You really gave us the red carpet treatment today.

LETTERMAN: Well, there's been some sort of mistake. Where ... are you having fun?

AILEEN HATCH: Yes.

LETTERMAN: How long will you be in town?

HATCH: Ahh until tomorrow night.

11. The Lady with the Bull Dick Cane on TV

LETTERMAN: And you're gonna be able to do a little sightseeing and so forth.
HATCH: Yes.
LETTERMAN: Now where exactly do you live in Missouri?
HATCH: Ahh do you know where Fort Leonard Wood is?
LETTERMAN: Hmm...
HATCH: You don't know where Fort Leonard Wood is.
LETTERMAN: Is it, is it near St. Louis?
HATCH: Well, 150 miles...
LETTERMAN: Well, sure. Then I know where it is. I know exactly where it is. You live in a small area there?
HATCH: Yes. I live out in the hills.
LETTERMAN: Uh-huh. And have lived there pretty much all your life?
HATCH: All my life.
LETTERMAN: And I understand also, in addition to being your first trip to New York City, this was ... is this true? Your first trip on an airplane?
HATCH: Oh yes.
LETTERMAN: Wow.
HATCH: You're the only one that could have gotten me up there.
LETTERMAN: Well that's very sweet of you. I appreciate it. What, what was that experience like? Was it exhilarating for you? Was it anything like you had imagined or...
HATCH: Well I was scared to death.
LETTERMAN: Yeah? Did you have trouble opening those airline peanuts?
HATCH: No! Yeah! I didn't open my spray...
LETTERMAN: Yeah. Now, is it true that you were gonna be here yesterday but yesterday was the opening day of trout season and you don't miss the opening day of trout season.
HATCH: Oh no.
LETTERMAN: Now what is so special about the first day of trout season?
HATCH: Well, I've done that now for—this is my 56th consecutive opening day.
LETTERMAN: Wow. Are you a fly fisherman?
HATCH: Yeah. Well, I was a fly fisherman 'til I got older and then it got so crowded that I had to go to ahh, you know, use the spinning rod.
LETTERMAN: Uh-huh.
HATCH: 'Cause you can use that in smaller area.
LETTERMAN: Right. You know what else is good. It's dynamite.
HATCH: Yeah! Yeah! Yes. Now that would get 'em. We can have a fish fry with that.
LETTERMAN: But what about opening day is so special to you?

HATCH: Ahh ahh right at first, you have to get your fish quick 'cause that's when all the dumb ones bite.

LETTERMAN: Ha! Ha! Ha!

HATCH: If you wait awhile, there's like five or six hundred people fishing. And each one uhmm hooks a fish and then it gets old, educates them and they won't bite anymore.

LETTERMAN: "Don't go over there ... you're gonna get hooked..."

HATCH: That's right.

LETTERMAN: We're gonna go ... do we have time to do this? Do we have time to.... Do you want to drive some nails?

HATCH: Yeah! Let's drive some nails.

LETTERMAN: You've actually won competitions for driving nails, is that right?

HATCH: Yes

LETTERMAN: I didn't realize you could compete doing this but let's go over and we'll learn everything we need to know about this. Come on.

HATCH: Yeah and as we go over, I wanna give you a little gift.

LETTERMAN: Oh man, I love gifts.

HATCH: Okay, I thought you would. I wanna give you my walking stick.

LETTERMAN: Alright. Now, here we go.

HATCH: Ahh, but first though I got to have you guess what it's made of.

LETTERMAN: What the walking stick is made of?

HATCH: Yes.

LETTERMAN: Ahh looks like teak.

HATCH: Well, no. Shall I tell you?

LETTERMAN: Well, I guess I have to, now. Or you could just say it's just teak, sure.

HATCH: They wanna know?

LETTERMAN: Uh-huh.

HATCH: It's a big 'ol Angus bulls...

LETTERMAN: There you go.

HATCH: I gave this to you.

LETTERMAN: I know. You know, you could still be trout fishing. Ah, it's great fun meeting you. I'm glad you could come to New York City and I hope you're having a great time and ahh see the city and enjoy yourself. Travel safely back to Missouri. Nice to meet you Aileen.

HATCH: You bet.

LETTERMAN: We have to do a commercial. We'll be right back here with Dave Stewart, ladies and gentlemen.

HATCH: Thanks very much.

LETTERMAN: We've run out of time here.

[COMMERCIAL BREAK]

11. The Lady with the Bull Dick Cane on TV

Part of the humor is not included here because it's visual. Aileen told David the cane was made from a Black Angus bull's penis. He immediately dropped it as if it were a red-hot potato.

"It was like the walking stick was poison," Aileen's son Dan said when I had a chance to visit him and his wife Cookie at the family business in Licking, Missouri. Their daughter and son-in-law accompanied Aileen on the trip.

"Aileen had studied the show for a good while before going to New York," Dan explained. "She wanted to play a little joke on David because she knew it would get a laugh all around. She hinted to the staff how she was going to zing the host, but he didn't know about the gift ahead of time. She just whooped it right on him! Right away he dropped it! A friend had given her the cane, one of those treasured items she rarely used and wanted to pass onto the right person."

The bull dick cane exists as a rare folkart item somewhat in a league with a toothpick made from a raccoon penis. One such handcrafted item is enough to create a lifetime of laughs.

* * *

Some of this segment has been cut here to show Mrs. Hatch's fun-loving inspiration. Also, this section demonstrates a particular kind of interview, the unexpected celebrity. How many guests to the Letterman show had never flown on an airplane or been to the Big Apple? Aileen plays along with the opening routine by offering an easy rapport with the host. Each plays their role until Aileen springs her gag. A transcript only suggests how the joke on David went across with the audience much less the host.

That Aileen Hatch would be jetted from Texas County is not that surprising in some ways. The March 1994 cover of *Missouri Conservationist* magazine had featured her in a full cammo suit hidden by a big oak, arrow notched on a wicked-looking compound bow. At 82 Aileen sort of looked like a kindly grandma, but the setting suggested otherwise. With additional Paul Childress photography, the accompanying profile by Lori Simms gives a thorough biography of a true conservationist.

When visiting Dan Hatch recently I had to ask about an incident I'd heard from Texas County friends long ago. Aileen had been involved in an incident with canoeists on the Roubidoux Creek on her farm.

"Yes, that did get some attention at the time, but luckily no one was bodily harmed," Dan said. "Aileen regarded the creek as her property and didn't like trespassers. She almost always would give permission to floaters or fishermen who asked to be on the stream.

"But these two guys in a canoe just came floating down not paying any attention to signs or a fence. An argument ensued. When the guys got down to her home, she rammed their canoe with her four-wheeler. Messed it up pretty good, but she got her message across."

More details could explain this incident. But is it relevant? To some slight extent, yes. The Ozarks have incidents involving outdoor enthusiasts who do not respect or don't know about private property rights. One Meramec River floater was killed a few years ago by an irate landowner, who is now in prison. It's tragic people just don't retreat and try to be respectful when tempers flare.

Another reason Aileen Hatch was the perfect guest on *Late Night with David Letterman* may be that the two personalities were made for each other. A recent thorough biography[2] by *New York Times* critic Jason Zinoman offers a great overview of a comic genius and cultural icon bigger than his television presence:

He was increasingly mentioned as the talk-show avatar of post-modernism, a movement marked by self-awareness and challenges to dominant narratives that were then shifting.

Dave began his career on radio and television as a wisecracking weatherman and disc jockey. His love of improvisation made his show over decades new and unexpected. The biography gives fascinating details on how the host worked with a staff of writers to keep things fresh.

Even the first exchanges in the Hatch-Letterman transcript shows they shared mutual respect but were feeling each out live on air, almost like debaters or prize-fighters. Something more than Aileen making wisecracks about driving nails and fishing was in the offing. It was that zinger of an elegant walking cane that became too hot for the host to handle.

12

Missouri Moonshining Days
George Lane, Waynesville, MO

> Mr. Lane was the grand old man of Pulaski County politics when I interviewed him long ago. Having served many terms as county clerk, he knew all the old-time residents of his county. Despite being home to one of the largest military bases in the country, Pulaski County has many families who have been living in the region for generations.
>
> The Forest Service owns tracts along the Big Piney River north of Ft. Leonard Wood, which hold the remains of a private resort.

* * *

"It was good money, making moonshine, and it wasn't considered criminal. It was just a way of making a living. There were several people who were known as good whiskey makers. They had a reputation in St. Louis. It eventually ended up in St. Louis. If it were selling for $1 a pint, you'd get $2 for Pulaski County's. Well, they had a reputation for making good whiskey.

"Every family had someone in it that could bootleg. It was essential. Just part of the family plan, you know. While the rest of them were plowing, they was minding the still. Even Baptists would trade to get sugar for whiskey making.

"Making whiskey gets ahold of you. It's an easy way to live. By God, it was White Lightning too. Strong. It wasn't bad tasting, but by God, it'd hit you before you knew it.

"I was always hanging around the courthouse. The sheriff had an old sawed-off shotgun—I guess it was either a 16 or 20 gage. I don't know who owned it. It always was in the sheriff's office.

"I was a big boy and always in there. Every time they'd bring anyone in I'd be there. One day, I guess I was about 14 or 15 years old, I was walking across the courtyard. It was on a Sunday. The sheriff come over the hill, him and his son. They were pretty big operators. They were trying to rid the county of bootleggers and everybody in the county was against them. I don't know how they ever got elected.

"I was going across the courtyard and the sheriff said, 'George, come and go with us. We're going to raid a still, the Scott boys.' And I said, 'Hell, I can't do that. I'm about halfway kin to them. They're my friends.'

"Well, the sheriff's son was a smart-aleck, so he said, 'I deputize you.' I didn't know what they meant. I said, 'Hell, you can't deputize me.'

"He said, 'Hell I can't. I deputize you. Come with us. We're going to raid the Scott boys.'

"I said, 'Hell, I was raised with the Scott boys. They're my friends.'

"'You're deputized now, you have to go!'

"He went in the courthouse and come out with that old shotgun. I was afraid to shoot it but I took the damn thing. We went out there and stopped at a little old cabin. Mr. Scott had his still down there below it.

"So the sheriff said, 'Now if we go down there, they know us. They'll run.' He said, 'You go down and get Scott and bring him up here and we'll arrest him.'

"I went on down there. Scott came running and he said, 'What the hell you doing, George? What you doing with that damn gun?'

"And I said, 'Hell, the sheriff's up there and they want me to bring you in. You start running. I'll shoot and you run.'

"'Hell,' he said, and started running. I went down there by that still and lifted that old gun up and let off a blast. Damn near killed me, it went over his head. By God, I never saw a guy run like he did, knocking over trees and everything else. Of course, I went back up there and said I saw him but he run and I shot at him. They asked me if I hit him and I said I don't think so cuz he picked up speed.

"Well, I never thought much more about it. About 20 years later, first time I run for office, Scott moved to Richland and had a garage over there. A hell of a fine man, a good man. And by gosh, I dropped in, campaigning.

"I had forgot shooting at him. I'm there just having a big time and he said, 'George, I'm going to vote for you. By God, I ought not to, you son of a bitch, you shot at me.'

"I said, 'Scott, if I'd a shot at you, I mighta hit you. I just shot over your head.'

"He said, 'The leaves just sprinkled all around me when you shot.' But he was fine. When I took the shot I was only 13 or 14. He did vote for me several times after that."

—Interviewed in Waynesville, Missouri, Pulaski County Courthouse, May 1998.

Sidebar

Ambrosia on the Piney

> No kind of expert on this, I've heard many stories about gigging, but only been a few times. It's enough seeing a river running with black channels of fast water, maybe beaver or hellbenders deep in darkness swimming away, and our boat wrapped in night.

* * *

God help any fish above the old Ft. Wood dam on the Big Piney last night of gigging season. Or early winter anywhere throughout the Ozarks, on a river or creek big enough to hold a johnboat and a man or two up front. On a platform ready with 15-foot spears and lights to brighten a watery circle, look deep into the river a gig's reach.

Suckers are the usual game. Most giggers won't pass up drum, red horse, carp, buffalo or hog mollies either.

Best is right there along the river, rolled in corn meal and thrown in deep hot grease with onions, hushpuppies and taters. Out comes light-golden puffs or slabs steaming in your greasy, dirty hands. You pull off chunks or just take bites. The slight crunch of cornmeal melts to the lightest, purest communion with flesh maybe possible beyond love.

This is reason enough for adults, mostly men, to spend a thousand dollars or lots more for a boat, necessary equipment and long cold nights slowly patrolling streams for fish. Still, there's reason beyond a chance to eat the catch bringing giggers out in the Ozarks.

* * *

In January it's not a particularly friendly place. Gigging with a dozen or so others in three or four boats on the Piney the last of the season causes some slight apprehension because of the frigid edge to night. On the water a steady hum of the motor and generator for lights attached to the bow below the gigging platform soon becomes a monotonous normalcy. We begin passing whiskey, schnapps and brandy among the three of us sitting amidships.

Marvin Mace was the mayor of Edgar Springs who knew all the best fishing holes on the Big Piney River. He routinely organized the greatest fish fries in the Missouri Ozarks—few women were privileged to attend (illustration by Anna Bolt).

"Sometimes they get so drunk they fall in the river even when they're just standing on the bank," I've heard said. That's when it's all over and you're feeling good.

When the first one's hit, we all hoot and holler as the gigger jerks the pole behind him and knocks the sucker off the trident into the bottom of the boat. The poor sucker flopping soon stops but silence holds till lateness of night shows we'll find no big mess to feed everyone waiting.

The wind finally does us in. Ice bad too. We start up one slough going around an island where fish lay thick because of good feeding in roots. The further up the narrow passage, the thicker the ice.

Marvin Mace, lifetime fisherman and mayor of Edgar Springs, stands up front holding onto the simple railing to catch giggers from falling.

"We're into it now, let's keep her going," he hollers back to us. "Rock the boat. Keep her rolling!"

We start shifting our weight side-to-side, holding on tight till water about sloshed over the gunnels. The boat's lurch breaks the ice and keeps us from riding up on it as the 10-horsepower motor powers us up a dark channel. For ten minutes we crash through, getting 500 yards on up. Despite all our rocking, finally we can break ice no more. It only gets thicker. We beach on top of it.

Marvin catches his breath, and turning back to us, "We can't do no more good up here, let's head back," he says. Slowly we push out with gigs to motor towards Happy Hollow Beach. But ice no boat has tried to break stops us again. The wind comes up too, rippling the river, making it impossible to see down.

"We've had fish so big it took three of us each with a gig to lift him into the boat," Marvin says. "And we've been out all night and never got a thing. That's rare. There's a lot of what they call them rough fish, that's what we're after."

* * *

The wind ends gigging for other boats too. Everyone's few fish go into the same pot. "Usually it's just some of my sons," Marvin says, "Me and the Jenkins boys. But on the last night of season like this, a lot of the guys from Edgar Springs and around, Gerald Harris, Walt Jones, Delbert Harris, everyone's down here. I'm related to just about everyone here in some way or other."

On the bank the fire grows waist-high, so the slightest gust blows swarms of sparks over the 50 or so guys standing around the fire to keep warm, talk and drink. Two propane cookers keep busy for a half hour frying fish, then chunks of onion, taters and hushpuppies. Soon enough everyone's eating, laughing, drinking or passing on a bowl full of something hot and fishy. No one eats slow in freezing wind.

After the final sucker's cooked and boats are loaded onto trailers, the few remaining blazing logs are thrown into the river and coals scattered. Potato peelings, and the silver-glinting fish scales, bright as stars in lights from the trucks, remain final signs of the giggers on the hard frozen gravel bar.

Rolla, Missouri, February 1982.

13

The Cadillac Mayor of Crocker, Missouri

Norma Lea Mihalevich

Folks move around a lot in the Ozarks. Part of it must be the soil, or shall we say, the lack thereof. Some areas have more; they're richer. West Plains was so wealthy they stayed with the Union during the Civil War.

Crocker didn't even exist then. It's a railroad town along the old Frisco line built when the tracks were extended west from Rolla to the Great Pacific Ocean after that bloody conflict.

You might wonder what keeps small towns such as Crocker, Missouri, going these days. There are no factories, yet lots of houses nearby and plenty of small farms dot the hills. Many Ozark towns had shoe factories, various kinds of mills or at least a tomato cannery.

It helps that Ft. Leonard Wood lies miles due south. Fort Lost-in-the-Woods has become much bigger in the last few decades. It still has Basic Training and several new schools such as Chemical Warfare and MP training. Thousands of military retirees nearby take advantage of necessary Army services such as those good deals at the PX.

Still, that doesn't explain why Crocker hasn't gradually faded away as have so many Ozark towns.

I had a chance to find out one of Crocker's secrets to success: a long-serving mayor who loved the place and devoted her life to its people.

* * *

I met Norma Lea Anderson Mihalevich some 20 years ago when I was doing oral history on the Ft. Leonard Wood area. The focus of the project was to record information on this region, as it existed when the base was created in a few months shortly before America's entry into World War II.

13. The Cadillac Mayor of Crocker, Missouri

Ft. Wood was built so fast that they had to raft pine logs down the Big Piney River to be sawed into lumber right where the barracks were being constructed.

Mrs. Mihalevich remembered all that. She had other memories. She loved growing up in rural Pulaski County near the region that became Ft. Leonard Wood.

Will another generation experience as much change as Mrs. Mihalevich has seen? Her childhood could almost be a medieval epic.

I remember her memorial service in June 2010. So many people crammed in a small church, then all enjoyed a feast that paid homage to the region's German heritage. Her daughter, our friend Jenny Smith, gave a touching eulogy where she related stories about her mom's 24 years as the community's mayor:

One day a city patron came into the mayor's office and handed her mom a $10 dollar bill and said, "Mayor, here is ten dollars to fix that pothole in front of my house." In response she returned the $10 and apologized to the man and said, "I'm really sorry but we don't have any $10 potholes in Crocker."

Cathy and I used to visit a nearby German community, Brinktown in Maries County, where her mom, Rita Bauer, grew up before going to work in St. Louis. Norma Lea was able to stay in the area partly because she met the right match, a local doctor with family roots in the Ozarks. Her children have been as active in their communities as their mom was in hers: an incredible, living tribute to their mother.

Much of this involvement may have been due in part to her parents who were both schoolteachers. So was Norma Lea. This section of her interview, from August 1996, is part of the Ft. Wood cultural resources survey.

* * *

"I love children, and there was something about teaching that was inspirational. If you can't receive a lot of reward just from teaching, then you shouldn't be in the business. The only thing I didn't like about teaching was it became so routine. You had fifteen or eighteen children in all eight grades, which means seven or eight subjects for each child. You had to stay on your toes all day long, there was no relaxing anytime. Then to do the same thing every day was very difficult for me.

"When I first started at Rolling Heath School I was nineteen, fresh out of high school. I studied more than any child I had in the room to keep ahead of them. I stayed with my sister and brother-in-law on his family farm, the old Ramsey place right where the golf course is now at Ft. Wood. Some of the children came by boat, but I drove a school bus. It was a second-hand '36 Chevy car with two doors. We could use that because it didn't have four doors. They thought the driver could more or less protect the two doors, then the children in the back couldn't get out except going out the front seat.

"It was wild country all around the school. They didn't have a church anywhere nearby, so they would have a revival at the school sometimes. It was thick with woods. You could find the road, but you could hardly ever see a house, even from the road. They didn't kill out forests then like they do now. It was wilderness looking."

Memoir

Dancing with the Spirit of Vietnam, May 2014

While doing oral history at Ft. Leonard Wood I occasionally recalled my time in the Army. Vietnam during the war haunts most vets, but it isn't all bloody nightmares.

Being able to return to old battlegrounds with a small group of veterans helped me. This trip put my military experience into a larger context. It freed me from bad memories and guilt.

After returning I felt compelled to write about the visit with the Veterans Vietnam Restoration Project. The group started in 1988 sending small groups of volunteers to help build schools or other facilities in the former war zone and continued until 2014. This was the last group from VVRP. Its goal was to help restore both Vietnam and American veterans.

I had to write about these three weeks as a personal journal entry, a chance to ceremonialize rather than reach final conclusions. I reflected on how members of our group have been able to change themselves through working with fellow vets and returning to sites of significant memories. Perhaps seeing how places once known have changed helps us to change. Seeing how others have faced their doubts and concerns has helped me too.

Though all these guys were new acquaintances for me, we had shared powerful experiences common during active duty. Mostly we all wanted to change, to grow in new ways. We were there for each other to share what we were learning while being back in Vietnam.

It seemed almost as intense as being on active duty all over again. I want to relive this trip to share what that conflict did to some of us and how we've survived. I don't want to relive my past, only share this inspiration. This time we were in Vietnam by choice and that helped free me from the worst of the past.

* * *

For a small group of veterans, Memorial Day has lasted a full month this year, 2014. We began our observance in Vietnam where we volunteered to build schools.

We were part of a group traveling to Vietnam's verdant Central Highlands, which many of us remembered from long ago. These three weeks in former enemy territory offered memorable adventures, mainly in and around the old capital city of Hue nearly destroyed in the infamous Tet Offensive of 1968.

Our trip united twenty-five veterans, five partners, and one daughter to help build two modern kindergartens. I was the only Missouri guy. Wayne Purinton, a retired farmer from western Kansas, is last president of the board of Veterans Vietnam Restoration Project, which sponsored the trip. Several California and Colorado guys, freethinkers and healthy adventurers, dominated our contingent which represented all regions but Dixie.

Also, on the trip I had a chance to get to know Tony Shaw who grew up in suburban St. Louis, went to Mizzou and graduated in 1968 as an R.O.T.C. Second Lieutenant. Soon he found himself a 25th Infantry Division platoon leader running around the jungle in armored personnel carriers. "At that time I felt the war against Communism made sense," Tony says. "I've changed a lot since."

Our trip was Tony's third back to Vietnam as part of a VVRP volunteer team. A board member since 2007, he now lives in Prescott, Arizona, where he practices law. (He retired in 2019.)

On one of our first days together, Tony, all the vets, partners, my wife Cathy and I went to two different cemeteries to pay respect to those buried within, Viet Cong and North Vietnamese soldiers killed in action. This wasn't required, but we all participated, at least physically.

Our leaders purchased bundles of incense sticks and alone with our thoughts, we walked from memorial stone to memorial stone, placing tiny smoking slivers into small, sand-filled vases. Our first site was actually a gym-sized memorial hall with some 3,000 names engraved on tablets. The other was a rural cemetery beginning to sprout mossy weeds spreading from encroaching jungle.

Both of these graveyard visits subdued us, reminding us of our own mortality and luck. Then we went to schools to haul building materials for a few hours.

Luckily toward the end of the trip, we cut loose from this work. At a barbecue with lots of beer-inspired singing, we line danced around a bonfire with aging local Viet Cong vets who hosted us, most of whom spoke as little English as we spoke Vietnamese. The common language of music, beer and vittles brought us together with new hopes to celebrate life, fate and spring under the full moon.

"This was a great trip for me. I wish every veteran had a chance to do something like this," Tony said about his third civilian experience back to Indochina.

"I first volunteered in '07, then brought my oldest son with me in '11. This year we had the biggest group ever to go with VVRP. We all got along, and I think the Vietnamese really understood why we came over again," Tony said. "One of my most amazing experiences was after volunteering and going by motorcycle to some of the old battlefields I knew as a platoon leader west of Saigon.

"I visited a woman who runs a restaurant in Tay Ninh City near where my 25th Division had its base. She's a highly decorated Viet Cong veteran and I had met her on two previous trips, so she remembered me this spring. She was probably one of those VCs who popped out of their tunnel system to fire rocket-propelled grenades at my tank.

"Now those tunnels are part of a museum, and she has one of the best restaurants in town. I hadn't eaten anything since six that morning. When I came in for lunch, she remembered me right away and gave me a big hug. She wouldn't let me pay for anything and kept giving me lots of food and beer."

Tony recalls his former enemy saying in effect, "You're a good guy, you come to help us." They lacked a common language but still communicated.

"Back home in Arizona I go to schools, service clubs and vets' groups showing slides and giving talks about what we've done in VVRP," Tony said. "Some vets have health issues; some just don't get it. They think we're crazy to want to go back. Some think we're traitors. They're stuck in the past."

Tony said he encountered no hostility from any Vietnamese towards Americans on his trips. National and local governments at first were reluctant to allow American veterans to begin the volunteer program 29 years ago. Each year VVRP has sent one or two small vet teams to volunteer on construction projects at schools, clinics and other facilities. One of the main purposes is to help vets deal with personal anger or guilt at serving in what many see as a questionable war and the resulting post-traumatic stress disorder.

"This year, we had a great range of veterans, but the trip was bittersweet because it was the last one. VVRP is sun-setting. The Vietnam vets are getting too old to do this kind of thing. We aren't finding many who want to go. The VVRP has been unique. No other organization has sent so many vets, maybe 200 altogether, and we did it without government aid."

Shaw's family has been involved in real estate and public service for decades. Tony is named for his grandfather, the sixth mayor of Clayton, a St. Louis suburb, who helped found Shaw Park there during the Great Depression. A well-known defense attorney, his father served as a B-17 navigator whose bicycle foray from a German P.O.W. camp inspired Steve McQueen's *The Great Escape* film.

"Dad was proud of my service in Vietnam," Tony said. "We never had any falling out over the war, but I came to see it as an illegal and immoral conflict. You can't force democracy on people. My family in St. Louis has been very supportive of what I've been doing to heal the wounds from Vietnam."

* * *

Wayne Purinton, president of the VVRP board and a retired farmer in western Kansas, has had somewhat similar experiences. Some guys in his hometown still won't talk with him because of his volunteering overseas.

"It's sort of sad," Wayne said. "They're still fighting the war, still angry. My best friend then was killed in a rice paddy. I lost part of my soul in that firefight. I came back to Vietnam to try to do something positive, as I did when volunteering for the draft in 1966. We've helped build several schools. My life has come full circle mainly because I have been able to return to Vietnam."

After 25 years of farming, Wayne wrote a unique book about his Vietnam experiences published by Langdon Street Press in 2011. Based on letters home he had forgotten writing and rediscovered in 2000, the story follows official records, staff journals and officer's logs from his unit he located while researching in the National Archives and Records Administration in College Park, Maryland. A variety of other documentation make his book both personal and inspiring.

Wayne is that kind of veteran, someone changed forever by his military experience. For more from Purinton, search for his Memorial Day columns in his local newspaper, the *Western Kansas World* (archive, "Vietnam"; attribute @authorPurinton).

While both Wayne, Tony and most on the final VVRP trip had volunteered before, this was my first time to Indochina since 1968–69. I had been a glorified Remington Ranger, a clerk-typist-editor on Army duty outside Saigon. My war centered on a sprawling base known as Long Binh Junction, infamous for its brig, steam bath with attractive attendants and nearby Chinese restaurant all designed by some concessioner to keep us rear echelon troopers in line and mellow on something other than pot smuggled onto the base.

Occasionally I had a chance to report on our unit's missions elsewhere in Vietnam; the more I saw, the more curious I grew.

Later I used the G.I. Bill to study Mandarin, because one of my officers said we'd soon be at war with China. That spooked me. More endless wars? What did my future hold? So China gradually has become an obsession for me. This spring was my first chance to explore a peaceful Vietnam north of the former Demilitarized Zone after five trips to China.

* * *

The first week we were in Vietnam, we worked lugging sand, brick and other building materials at schools under construction in the mountains west of Hue, an old imperial capital. The second week involved mostly visiting rural schools VVRP had helped build in previous years.

These highland forests impressed me with their wild fertility, not unlike Ozark bottomland grown up in cane as the explorer Henry Rowe Schoolcraft experienced 200 years ago. Designed for kindergarten-aged kids, all so young and cute, the schools VVRP built seemed like living temples in the jungle.

Even this bit of volunteering in retrospect seems worthwhile because at the least I learned to appreciate how hard Vietnamese work. When I was in Vietnam fifty years ago, I shared the common misperception Vietnamese were lazy and ignorant, mainly wanting to steal stuff from us wealthy Gringos rather than work. Cultural miscommunication is common, to put it mildly, in war.

Before working at Ft. Wood, I had a chance to do an oral history of a U.S. Navy destroyer from World War II. As I prepared for these interviews I read a classic study, *War Without Mercy: Race & Power in the Pacific War*[1] and could not help but reflect on my own experiences. During World War II itself, anti–Japanese sentiment in the Anglo-American camp became entangled with larger fears concerning Asians in general (the Yellow Peril) and "colored" peoples as a whole.

When I was in Vietnam, it was common for us to call the locals "gooks" or "gookamese." When arriving in-country I had nothing against local civilians, but I quickly saw how different they were from folks of whatever color back in Missouri. I occasionally ate local food. Now Vietnamese food has become popular and refugees from the war have been welcomed and accepted in most U.S. communities. Even the Ozarks has a large Vietnamese community in Springfield and Carthage.

In addition to racial rifts, differences persist nationally among veterans about the basic conduct of our war. Some feel more firepower against communist troops in the north was required. Others feel the conflict was lost because our allies in the South lacked leadership. Our group didn't have these differences. We generally felt it all was a huge mistake and moved on. Why hadn't our government done more to reconcile differences with Vietnam after the war? We did this in Europe and Japan, why not Vietnam? Is constant preparation for war a necessity for American capitalism to thrive, as some argue? We discussed all this, but mainly we agreed that seeing Vietnam now at peace was essential. More veterans need to see what 50 years of relative peace have made possible here.

If more understanding with Vietnam has gradually become possible, why not with China? We don't have to agree on diverse social and political issues, but why not cooperate on bigger issues like world health and climate change? We discussed all this and drank a lot of their fresh beer in the process.

* * *

The humid heat we all remembered from back in the day shimmered across the highlands, reducing most volunteers to a slow drag by 11 a.m. while hauling building materials up scaffolding. The local building crews worked past high noon, then took lunch then a long nap under tin roofed lean-tos which served as their kitchen and bedroom until each of the schools was completed. Once the day cooled down, the crews would start up again and work till dark, six or seven days a week until the school was completed.

The longer I was in Vietnam, the more I realized it was a totally different country than what I imagined a communist state to be. While intellectual and political freedoms apparently remain controlled, religions of all kinds seem to flourish. From what I saw, the main religion is making money. Robert Templer's investigative study *Shadows and Wind: A View of Modern Vietnam*, 1998, shows how it helps to have connections with the party in power.

Hue has been rebuilt. Parts of the imperial palace remain in rubble, but small-scale capitalism surrounds the citadel with rebuilt homes all featuring small gardens. Luckily our trip coincided with an international arts festival. I met two young women from Russia who had heard one of the best rock bands from our town, Springfield, Someone Still Loves You Boris Yeltsin, playing in Moscow. Cathy and I also visited the moss-encrusted Tu Hieu temple on the outskirts of Hue where the peace activist Thich Nhat Hanh first became a Buddhist monk and spent his final days.

The quiet perseverance of a few apparently totally destitute people I noticed in Hue leaves almost as strong an impression as does the hopeful appearance of the new schools we visited. I think most visitors would agree local and national government has done much to help average citizens. The Ozarks might be more needy in some ways. It would be interesting to compare health and economic statistics.

We didn't see any grass-roofed hooches, which were common back in the day. Most rural housing seemed solid cinder block or brick with metal roofs.

Touring the VVRP-built schools, I noticed one ancient mamasan as thin as a skeleton walking around a highway construction site trying to sell cans of Red Bull she carried in a plastic bag. She could hardly walk, her pathetic progress was slow, her skinny legs bowed and rickety, but she kept trying to find someone to buy her goodies.

She was a survivor, just like us veterans who visited Vietnam this spring. We all were huge and indeed chubby compared with the locals. We felt blessed with incredible luck and grace to be here, still alive, still able to maneuver ourselves, seeing places we knew personally or by reputation from long ago, now peaceful. Gardens filled nooks and crannies in towns. Renewal and renovation appeared constant. Everyone seemed to have a motorcycle or scooter, even little kids, though most rode an astounding array of new and old bikes.

Some of our group contributed to a fund to buy bikes to help kids. Isn't this what brought us here in the first place? Like Thich Nhat Hanh, we have danced around the whole circle.

PART V

Journalism into History
Deadline—Every Day a New Story

As political contention and technology continue to develop, journalism has become increasingly problematic. I've always thought reading a number of different sources offers the surest objectivity about this crazy world.

When I worked for the *Rolla Daily News,* my job was to come up with a story every day. Just something local. Anything. I loved the challenge.

I learned to bang out stories fairly quickly, especially with a rough mental outline of where it was going. Working on deadline teaches a lot. These pieces deserve a second life, as these individuals all inspired me and others in the Ozarks. The longer I worked on newspapers, the more compelled I grew to learn how older people make their life decisions. Oral history had more appeal than covering city council meetings. Yet I still believe, as my editor Bob Yates used to say, local council meetings can be more dramatic than anything on television.

My transition to digital recording took several years in the '90s. I had used a cassette recorder occasionally while interviewing people for articles. Early on I adopted a personal policy of reading back over the phone or showing quotations via Internet to anyone featured in a piece. A former reporter, my dad drilled into me Joseph Pulitzer's motto, "Accuracy, accuracy, accuracy." Also essential in oral history.

One source for best practices in interviewing can be found at the Oral History Association's webpage. Also look for the Institute of Museum and Library Services' sponsored guide to a collection of articles on "Oral History in the Digital Age" as tech affects contemporary practice at http://ohda.matrix.msu.edu.

14

Two Special Parents for Special Children
The Earl Adamses

> This is one of the first pieces I wrote for the *Rolla Daily News* in 1973. Other than growing up in a newspaper family, the only training I had in journalism was a basic course after being drafted at the Defense Information School at Ft. Harrison, which was an active base during the Vietnam War. These military instructors also emphasized accuracy as the necessary basis of news reporting and public relations. They warned that leaving details out can be a form of censorship.

* * *

When I saw the child, my first reaction was to look away. She was just a little girl huddled up on a couch, but her skin had a dark, grayish tinge and her head was slightly misshapen.

I asked Mrs. Adams how long she and her husband had been foster parents for handicapped children.

"I don't like to call them handicapped," said Mrs. Adams. "I call them 'special' children."

"Life deals enough hard blows to kids without these children having to carry around a name like that," she said.

As we talked, Mrs. Adams's foster daughter went to sleep on her "sister's" lap.

Mr. and Mrs. Earl Adams, of St. James, estimate they have served as foster parents for about "oh, my goodness, I don't know how many children," Adams said. After some discussion, she and her husband agreed the number was about 85 children in the last several years.

They've forgotten how they became foster parents. Mr. and Mrs. Adams finally concluded the first foster child came into their home while they were living in Iowa. A probation officer she knew asked if they would take in a homeless child, Mrs. Adams said.

"I've loved every one of them," Mrs. Adams said. "That's their special need. They need lots of love."

Most of the children the Adams have opened their home to here were referred by the Rolla Regional Diagnostic Clinic. Some were referred by the county Welfare department.

All of the children have been with the Adams just temporarily due to shorter difficulties within the child's family. Once problems in a foster child's family are solved or a permanent home is found, the child leaves the temporary home.

"As long as you know the child's for the better having been with you, you can't regret their leaving," Mrs. Adams said.

No Motivation for Play

"You have to do this in the interest of the child. No foster parent makes that much money. We haven't had a raise in the funds we receive for each child's care in five years. The motivation is to do something for some child. It's not a salary you get, but a service you perform."

As Mrs. Adams talked, a boy whom the Adamses had picked up earlier in the afternoon at the Cerebral Palsy School climbed into Mr. Adams' lap. Though he was actually six years old, Mrs. Adams said his development was diagnosed to be equivalent to a child of one and a half years. Mr. Adams played with the child while his wife talked.

They have four children now and Mrs. Adams said at times they've had 10 in their home. They have no children of their own.

"I really enjoy it," she said. "I don't want to do anything else. I wish we had started it when we were younger.

"I think most people are afraid to take on a foster child because they think they'll be tied down. We go wherever we want and bring the kids."

Mr. Adams said he works four nights a week as a night watchman so he is able to spend much of the day with the children.

As we talked, the youngest child woke up. She slid off the couch and took short, halting steps toward me. She stood at my knee for a minute and then, without saying anything, climbed into my lap.

She Sees Some Hope

"Some kids become practically normal. One child was with us for two or three years and then went back to her parents and a normal school. That little girl," she said about the child on my lap, "didn't move when we first got her. She would just lie still all day."

The little girl had found a pad of paper in my pocket and was flipping through the sheets of paper.

14. Two Special Parents for Special Children

She looked carefully at both sides of the paper before turning to the next sheet of the notebook. After slowly turning the notebook over and upside-down several times in her hands, she opened the cover and began to tug on one piece of paper.

"No, no," Mrs. Adams said. "That's a no-no."

The child looked at her, let go of the piece of paper and began to flip through the book again.

"We do go through toys pretty quickly here," Mrs. Adams said. "The Jaycees sponsor a Santa Claus who comes to our home and the Methodist Church has a Christmas party where we also get some toys. And Mrs. Mercier has parties with the help of Rolla service groups at the school."

Jane Mercier is director of Rolla's Cerebral Palsy School. The school has 12 children who attend special morning classes. Last week, for the first time, classes were held five days a week.

Help in Many Ways

Mrs. Mercier said the Adamses not only help by taking care of children, but also assist in fund raising and taking children to and from the school.

The little girl was tugging on the paper again. She was curious about everything and soon was scribbling all over my notes and being as captivating as any child.

"That's what it takes," Mrs. Adams said. "The more determined they are when they play, the faster they learn and get better."

"I once had a minister tell me he thought the children I had were repulsive. Later he thanked me for helping him see the beauty in them."

—*Rolla Daily News*, 1972. This family inspired me in part to suggest Cathy and I become foster parents when we were not able to have children. We enjoyed the process almost as much as the Adamses did, though not taking in nearly as many children.

15

Bass Fishing Tournament
Basil Bacon

> This article challenged me. I hadn't been fishing in years, much less on a huge inland lake. It was also a chance to stay at the Playboy Club Resort.

When Bacon Fishes, He Means Business

Basil Bacon, who had been a regular along Pine Street until 1976 when he sold his furniture store, was waiting patiently in a 16-foot bass boat.

The cold wind didn't bother him because he was wearing a heavy insulated jumpsuit and was fortified with black coffee.

Shortly after 7:30 a.m. he and 21 other fishermen gunned their engines and headed in search of smallmouth bass. Catching enough of them would be worth $4,500 or more to the winner of the Bass Caster's Association grand national tournament, the event that brought Bacon here.

He makes his living fishing. "It pays for my habit," he said. He estimated that he is one of about a dozen persons in the nation who support themselves through tournament bass fishing.

His earnings from BCA this year have amounted to about $10,000 so far, Bacon estimated. He is also paid to represent the Ranger Boat Co. of Flippin, Arkansas.

With stakes so high, the contest here offered something different than the usual fishing trip.

The day before the tournament, however, the pressure on the fishermen was not quite as great and Bacon said he would have a little time to talk as he fished in preparation for the two-day tournament. Under BCA regulations, this was the only time that contestants could fish on Lake Geneva this year.

15. Bass Fishing Tournament

Tuesday was the day to practice, to see where the fish were and what they were most interested in eating. Bass fishermen call this "finding the pattern."

"If I can just get onto the pattern," Bacon said late that afternoon, "I'll clean house. I think I've got the right bait here to do it."

At 6 a.m. Bacon was ready for fishing. Several hats, about a dozen fishing rods, a half dozen boxes of tackle and other equipment were lined dress-right-dress in the rear of his van as he pulled away from the Playboy Resort where the bass fishing organization was putting up the contestants.

"This isn't early," he said. "I've started doing a fair amount of guiding over at Lake of the Ozarks. That means getting up around 4 a.m. so I can meet my customer for the early morning fishing."

Was Getting Rusty

"I got into it because I found I was getting rusty between tournaments, losing my touch," he said. "It's interesting and pays $100 a day. Last week I had a three-star general who looked like he was 35 years old. He jogged or rode a bicycle every morning. He was 51. You should have seen him when he pulled in a three-pound bass, biggest fish he ever caught, he said."

Bacon was pulling one of the 22 completely rigged and identical bass boats that BCA had acquired for use and promotional purposes at the contest. Parking his van, which he had driven up from Rolla the day before, with the boat in downtown Lake Geneva was no problem, however. The streets of the off-season resort town were nearly empty.

Inside an all-night café it was just as quiet though the counter was filled with working men silently contemplating cups of coffee and an occasional newspaper.

The fisherman ordered, then lit a cigarette, not his first that morning. Two more contestants—wearing bright red jumpsuits and talking in heavy Southern drawls—came in after parking their van and bass boat in front of the place.

Heads Turn

Heads began turning at the counter. The Southerners sensed it and laughed about some joke as we sat down.

"I didn't know you guys were in town yet," the waitress said as she brought the menus over. The fishermen studied them silently and the whole front part of the restaurant quickly filled with bass fishermen.

Actually almost all the contestants—Midwesterners and Southerners in the vicinity of U.S. Army Corps of Engineers reservoirs—had full-time employment. They had been selected for this tournament on the basis of their performance in similar contests, but with $150 entry fees, earlier in the year.

One of the fishermen glanced at the day's headline. "Pole Elected Pope," he read aloud. "I hope he has a good sense of humor," he said and showed the newspaper to his friend. "You know, Polish jokes," he said. The friend smiled briefly.

Bacon ate quickly but took time for a second cup of coffee while he had a thermos bottle filled. He kept looking out the front window for Jimmy Nolan, another representative of Ranger Boats.

Someone at the café mentioned that Nolan had last been seen at 1 a.m. in front of the Bunny Hutch disco at the resort with a carrot tied to the end of his fishing line. He was reportedly casting the bait into the club to catch one of the waitresses.

Driving back to the resort, Bacon passed Nolan who waved and smiled sheepishly in the early morning light.

On the Water

At 7:30 a.m. Bacon had his boat in the water and was speeding across the lake to a group of docks a map he held indicated as a good place to start fishing. He had till 3:30 p.m. to learn as much about the lake and its fish as he could.

Suddenly a plastic bag that had been covering a life vest blew out of the boat. Bacon went back for it, saying that he didn't want to mess up the lake, then continued on at nearly 50 m.p.h.

Once at the docks Bacon began fishing with a bright frog-colored lure that had a propeller. That night one of the reporters commented that he had recently seen Missouri Governor Joseph Teasdale using similar bait.

"The governor was throwing this lunker lure out there and reeling it in as fast as he could," the reporter said. "I told him the lure was designed to be reeled in slow, but the governor said he was too busy being governor and didn't have time to reel it slowly. He just kept reeling away as fast as he could."

Bacon took his time. He said he was not comfortable using the boat provided because it did not allow him to stand on the very front and cast. His own 18-foot boat, equipped with a 150 h.p. engine, has a hand-controlled electric trolling motor.

Held on the front of the bass boat on a stand that allows it to be quickly raised out of the water, the trolling motor allows the fisherman to guide his craft as he fishes. It and other new equipment has changed the art of fishing and has helped make bass fishing a semi-professional sport. The main engine (only 115 h.p. on the contest boats) is used for reaching potential fishing spots quickly.

15. Bass Fishing Tournament

On man-made lakes a 50-mile run to a good fishing hole is not unusual, Bacon said. He has also said he has encountered waves up to 12-feet in height and has weathered them in his bass boat.

After 20 minutes Bacon had his first strike of the day, but he did not get particularly excited. "Could have been a perch," he said. Bacon struggled with the foot-controlled trolling motor then gave up on fishing at the docks after a half-hour of trying various surface lures.

Looking at his map he found another spot, a rocky point that went into the middle of the lake, he wanted to try and was there in a few minutes. He cast along the submerged rocks with a 4-inch, black rubber snake-like lure but had no luck.

At 3 p.m. he stopped fishing again. He had been casting steadily for nearly a half-hour and had come up with nothing. "At least I know now they're not biting at 30 feet," he said. "The pattern has to be something else."

—Lake Geneva, Wisconsin

* * *

> This is the first of a two-part article, from October 1973, on Mr. Bacon at this fishing tournament. I spent a day watching him fish while I took notes and tried to keep warm in Wisconsin autumn winds. I remember being so cold I started smoking cigarettes again briefly.
>
> The second part deals with the tournament itself, during which he caught only one fish but came in fourth place. If you want to see that piece, please check out my website. Basil Bacon is commemorated in the Bass Fishing Hall of Fame at Johnny Morris' Wonders of Wildlife National Museum & Aquarium in Springfield, Missouri.

16

Area Inventor Looking for Business Partner

Louis Moore

> The next profile represents a juggling act. It attempts to present a portrait that is accurate as well as entertaining; respectful but aware of bizarre potentials. Mr. Moore was a Canadian attracted to the free spirit of the Ozarks.

* * *

Louis Moore of rural Edgar Springs—you can spot his place by the concrete dome, the only one in the area, he proudly points out—is looking for a business partner.

This partner needs to have a few specific skills. The main one is administrative ability. It also wouldn't hurt if the partner could raise several hundred thousand dollars—plus.

Moore is an inventor who believes he can develop an automotive engine that can power an average car with a 40-miles-per-gallon efficiency while producing half the air pollution of the standard internal combustion powered vehicle.

Moore will provide the mechanical know-how for the development.

Data and a record of correspondence associated with the proposed engine, called by Moore "The Monobanger," reveal the inventor is not the kind of person easily dissuaded from his task.

"He's different alright," said Dr. Charles Remington, who teaches design of internal combustion engines at UMR. "He's been coming in here, sort of drifting in periodically, over 10 years or so.

"He's quite disgruntled over his inability to get a federal grant to develop the engine, but I've never had a chance to review his work so I can't comment on it," Remington said.

16. Area Inventor Looking for Business Partner

Louis Moore was known as an inventor who would not give up creating futuristic machines in the backwoods (illustration by Anna Bolt).

An Odd Bird Indeed

Moore readily agrees he's different. When asked if 3 p.m. would be convenient for an interview at his home, Moore said, "That will be 2 p.m. my time. I don't see any reason to switch over to Daylight Savings Time just because everyone else does. I do things by reason, not by what the crowd does," he said.

The inventor has lived on his farm here since 1965. He has supported himself mainly by producing plastic doll heads with a molding process he invented. The products are sold to metropolitan manufacturers, he said.

"I like the rocks and the bluffs around here," Moore said, explaining his move to Missouri from Arizona. "And Edgar Springs is not too crowded. It's always easy to find a place to park.

"The only disadvantages are the copperheads, the mosquitoes, taxes and the hay fever," he said.

Born in Days Land, Alberta, in 1921, Moore finished his formal education at age 13 to begin "odd-jobbing around, working on farms mainly, until I joined the Royal Canadian Mechanical and Electrical Engineers during World War II."

One project, realized as a working air compressor, is Moore's MOEEO engine, which he explained is an oscillating engine "in which all parts run at their natural frequency like a pendulum clock. The kinetic energy transfers to potential energy at the end of the piston's stroke in each cycle."

"I was just going to call it my oscillating engine experiment," Moore said. "But my friends said it was an experimental ornament, so I've come to call it MOEEO, for my oscillating engine experimental ornament."

Monobanger Prototype

A prototype of his main project, the Monobanger engine, has not been built he said. It is a reciprocating engine, like most internal combustion motors, and is planned to power another of Moore's projects, the Economobile.

"The Monobanger has two pistons which would be forced apart at the same time," Moore said. "This would turn two shafts in opposite directions which would then turn two fly wheels that are in synchronization. That's where the power would come from to the single output shaft."

According to a letter from George P. Lewett, chief of the office of energy related inventions in Washington, D.C., "Evaluation is to be performed as a service to the Energy Research and Development Administration which, in the case of a positive evaluation, may fund development of the invention." Several forms were included in Lewett's letter for the Edgar Springs inventor to fill out about the Monobanger.

In April 1976, Moore heard from Lewett's office: The Bureau of Standards had to stop its investigation because Moore's design lacked technical detail.

"A detailed disclosure of an invention that is not yet invented is an impossibility," Moore responded in part.

Through continued correspondence with Lewett—and President Carter's staff, Missouri 8th District Representative Richard Ichord, Jr., and Senator Thomas Eagleton—Moore was able to secure an additional review of the proposal.

That also resulted in bad news for the Economobile. The second review claimed to find disadvantages in the unorthodox design of the crankshaft,

16. Area Inventor Looking for Business Partner

connecting rods and pivot assemblies which reportedly would create problems in lubrication, bearing wear and engine vibration—all points that Moore disagreed with in further correspondence.

Searching for Cash

In January last year, Moore noticed an item in *Time* magazine that quoted California Governor Jerry Brown describing his state's energy program.

"Americans seem to be getting less inventive," Brown said. "I'm going to try to stimulate things the best I can through energy innovation."

Moore zipped off a letter to the governor. "As yet all the politicians that I have contacted are 'All Blow and No Go.' Here is your opportunity to see what you can do," Moore wrote.

Unfortunately, the response was not from the governor, but from the staff counsel for contract services of the California Energy Resources Conservation and Development Commission.

The advice was that Moore should apply for a United States letters patent.

And that's about where the project stands now. Moore contends the Monobanger is a workable, unique and potentially valuable engine and challenges anyone to find a fault in his theory.

—*Rolla Daily News,* 1978. Louis died in January 2013. I learned later his inventions never received funding.

Sidebar

Fine Art from White Oak Forests

> This was a short visit that reminded me how much this basic Ozark industry has contributed to the world's sense of quality.

* * *

My friend Carolyn Brooks has developed an unusual career: bourbon historian. Yes, the liquor, not the French royal dynasty.

Developing gradually, her career has been lots of fun for her family and friends as well.

A few years ago Carolyn and her husband Peter Morrin were cruising the Ozarks. "Would you like to visit one of the largest bourbon barrel makers in the world?" I asked.

From working in local news, I knew the town of Cuba had a number of successful local businesses. We were driving from St. Louis along Old Route 66 where McGinnis Wood Products occupies several big factory buildings on the east side of town. They are big supporters of community activities in the area.

Also big timber buyers. Stacks of White Oak logs three-stories high lie near their factory buildings. Leroy and Ovia Marie McGinnis, both in their 80s, share a tidy office just big enough for two desks, lots of file cabinets plus many historic photos and awards filling their walls.

"Sure, we can take a few minutes to visit with your friends from Kentucky," Mr. McGinnis says. "They'll enjoy seeing where their bourbon will spend several years!"

Carolyn became a bourbon historian from managing an historic home in Louisville, then writing nominations of properties to be on the National Register of Historic Places. Several distilleries called her to do historic architectural research.

"History and heritage are very important in the bourbon industry," she explains. "There's lots of fake stuff out there, so I have to be careful!"

We ended up spending more than an hour talking with the McGinnises

Sidebar: Fine Art from White Oak Forests

and seeing the factory and barrel wood storage areas. Their business has grown steadily since it began in 1968, now employing 200 people and sending products all over the world.

What's special about Ozark oak?

"We had a Scottish research firm here recently," Ovia Marie says. "They compared our Missouri wood with French oak. Ours was just as good for making Scotch whiskey.

"Our White Oak is so good," she explains. "You can taste it. You can tell if the wood comes from different places. Our oak has excellent taste for wine too. We air dry White Oak for three years once it's cut into staves. For bourbon, we air dry staves for a year then dry it further in a heated kiln. That seals any pores."

Leroy takes us to see the men working to make barrels. We could see building barrels takes a craftsman's eye. Each of some 40 staves to make a barrel is chosen by hand, then joined by metal hoops. Once formed the barrels are tested for leaks and toasted by controlled flames for particular tastes. Lots of noise and sweet smoke.

It looks like hard work. We were impressed with the skill and hospitality inspired by White Oak which makes the Ozarks essential for this respected snake bite medicine. And wine.

17

Local Prophet Carves Wide Swath

Rev. Joseph Jeffers

One of the great studies of American regional lore must be the amusing, unprecedented *Let Us Build Us a City: Eleven Lost Towns*[1] by the late Ozarker Donald Harington. The nearly 500-page tome begins with a map of special towns in Arkansas, all communities that never quite became cities. Yet all these places used the word "city" in their names.

An art history professor as well as an artist who spent his last years in Fayetteville, Professor Harington wrote several expansive novels based on the lonely Ozark outposts. Most have a magical, almost surreal quality somewhat in the spirit of fellow Arkansawyer, Donald Roller Wilson, a painter who often imparts human characteristics to a cast of critters. I wonder if either of these artists knew about the "Jonesboro Church Wars"? Is there something in Arkansas that produces such genii?

I didn't know anything about the church war until recently. That's when I had a chance to spend some time with the online *Encyclopedia of Arkansas*. This ever-growing resource offers much to amaze any visitor, so I am suggesting you hop over there to read about this long-ago conflict in Jonesboro.

This encyclopedia entry should be read because it offers unexpected background for the profile that follows, a man I interviewed long ago. Luckily I tried to be fair and accurate with the Reverend Jeffers. He appreciated this article after it ran.

Local Prophet Warns World of Dangers

What's in a name? For Dr. Joseph Jeffers, of St. James, a name has been his driving force, his reason to live and his livelihood for nearly 40 years.

That name is "Yahweh." As director of Kingdom Voice Publications, which is also based in St. James, Dr. Jeffers is spreading the word about Yahweh.

Pamphlets, magazines, radio programs, telephone calls, lectures, interviews on television programs—just about any means possible are used by the prophet to spread information about his religious and political beliefs.

The term "prophet" is one Dr. Jeffers might momentarily shy away from, but in a recent interview, he did describe his main line of work as "making prophecies." He also said he is "the only preacher who is the voice of Yahweh."

Who is Yahweh? It would be simplest to say "Yahweh" is Dr. Jeffers' name for the being many people refer to as "God." However, the preacher would not be completely satisfied by that.

To define Yahweh pragmatically, Dr. Jeffers' pamphlet "Yahweh: Yesterday, Today and Tomorrow" (which is available from Kingdom Voice Publications for $1.25 or $2.95, depending on whether one looks on the front or title page of the booklet): "It is Yahweh who gives you health, peace, happiness, wisdom, knowledge, and it is the power and vibration of the Name Yahweh and its exclusive use by all mankind which will finally bring peace, happiness, perfection and brotherhood in the Golden Kingdom on earth."

The pamphlet also deals with E.S.P. (extra-sensory perception), reincarnation and gives a bit of Dr. Jeffers' background.

"The most controversial religious figure of the 20th century!" the back cover says about Dr. Jeffers.

A discussion with the prophet-preacher revealed how he indeed might stir up heated debate among uninitiated listeners. He believes thousands of Russian spies are roving the countryside and leaving bombs planted near airports and that Dr. Arthur "Burnstein," head of the Federal Reserve System, is part of a plot.

Discussion with Dr. Jeffers reveals traces of his training as a Baptist preacher. He explained he attended Southwest Baptist Theological Seminary and was licensed as a preacher in 1914. Yahwism, however, is not a Christian religion, he said. Traces of his experience in vaudeville are also present in his conversation, which weaves together topics such as health, religion, history, current events and Yahweh.

It was a desire "for something real" which led him to begin a search eventually ending in telepathic communication with Yahweh, Dr. Jeffers said.

"I trust everything to Yahweh," he said. "He takes care of us. The other day a woman called and said she had misplaced an important check. Yahweh gave us inspiration to find it and later the woman was able to give us a donation. That's how we keep going."

A telepathic message from Harry Truman, the late President, was responsible for bringing the preacher to St. James. Dr. Jeffers said he had been Truman's pastor in Washington years ago and the President had always said Missouri is the center of everything.

"The reds of Russia, the blacks of Africa and the yellows of Asia are going to band together against us. Not even Canada will stand up for us. I've seen that the Capitol building is going to blow up and New York City is going to turn into a great bottomless pit," Dr. Jeffers predicted.

The National Star, a weekly newspaper somewhat similar to the better known *National Enquirer* and published in that city which is soon to be a great smoking pit, carries several of the St. James prophet's predictions in its "Predictions of the Week" column for July 6. Among the forecasts are:

- Henry Kissinger will have requests from both Democrats and Republicans to run for President.
- Mrs. Kissinger will continue to experience abdominal disorders.
- There will be a black revolution very soon.
- The weather will remain extremely difficult to predict.

Dr. Jeffers' home is outside St. James in a large residence he shares with his two children (his wife is deceased), helpers and offices where materials for Kingdom Voice Publications are prepared. Commitments to travel, in order to make guest appearances, interviews, lectures and other obligations, keep him away from St James most of the time, he said.

"We're not out to reach people in St. James or Rolla in particular," Dr. Jeffers explained. "We're searching only for those who are searching for us."

—*Rolla Daily News*, July 19, 1979. When I last drove by the Reverend Jeffers' compound, his corrugated metal pyramid seemed to have been converted from a worship center to a hay barn.

18

From Birch Tree to the Battle of the Bulge and Back

Bill and Trudy Reed

> Weekly newspapers can be a great place to learn a lot about a rural place. Sometimes they're boring but often you can read between the lines and see what's really important to people.
>
> This profile was written in part because I had a chance to know Mr. Reed over many years. He was not a talkative barber; he was in his late 70s when I first starting going to his place on the square in Birch Tree. I was usually the youngest person there. Trudy has one of the most active businesses in Birch Tree.

* * *

What's it like to live in frozen mud with only irregular access to food or warmth? Bill Reed remembers. You do not forget things like that. Times are a lot easier now. He can relax and enjoy his memories. He has finally, definitely retired.

It has been a long career with some tough battles along the way. Mainly Bill has been the barber for Birch Tree and hills and hollers round about for 62 years. At 87 he has finally decided to hang up his clippers. He celebrates his 88th birthday on January 26.

"My knees just aren't cooperating any more," Bill explained when tracked down on a snowy December day at his wife's shoe store, also in downtown Birch Tree. Bill had a sturdy metal walker parked near an armchair where he enjoyed taking it easy while Trudy got ready for holiday business.

"I cut my last head of hair in November. People still ask me if I can do one more for them, but I just can't," he said. "I still remember cutting 60 heads on a good day. My biggest was 65 guys. I was the best flat-top cutter in the area back then."

Some folks may have mixed feelings about going to a barber. Maybe they see it as an expensive waste of time or somehow unhealthy.

A visit to Bill's barbershop offered most of his visitors a chance to relax. Bill won't talk your ears off. Or cut them off either. His knees may have become a little wobbly but his hands have been steady and his mind sharp.

Mr. Reed also has more tales than a highway has armadillos. He has opinions too. He keeps most to himself. His memories of growing up near the Irish Wilderness south of town echo some amazing stories about his World War II service during the Battle of the Bulge.

His barbershop at the west end of the town park offered the perfect setting for his buddies to share a tale or two. One big old barber chair, two long wooden benches on either side of the 25-by-25 or so room with a window looking out on the park and a generous mirror on the back wall, it felt like a tavern, coffee shop and a history museum rolled into one.

When I first started going there during the 1990s, Bill kept a guitar in the corner by a coat rack, but during recent years it's been in a case. He's given up playing though still goes to music parties. Even though Bill slowed to working six mornings a week for the last few years, the shop seemed busy enough. He enjoys telling about working in the timber as a kid.

"I started hacking ties full-time about when I turned 16 years of age," Bill begins one story. "Hacking ties" means using a crosscut saw and axes to turn hardwood trees into railroad ties, a big industry in the Ozarks for more than a century.

"My dad hurt his back one day when I was a teenager. I had to go to work doing whatever I could."

"How did he hurt himself?"

"George Walter Reed, that's my dad, was not a tall man. He was born in 1892, never weighed more than 168 pounds, but he feared no kind of work.

"One day he was helping on a threshing crew for a neighbor harvesting his wheat. He got to betting his friends he could lift the rear end of a fully loaded grain wagon plumb off the ground. No one else could do it. But he did. Some of those guys must have had trouble believing he really did it. So he tried it again.

"Well, he tore up all the muscles in his back. Dad could never do a day of hard work after that. That's why I had to go to work."

Hacking 10 to 15 railroad ties in a day in the early 1940s could make Bill up to a dollar apiece. Good wages for a kid born in 1926, but then he was drafted in 1944.

All his five brothers would also serve in the military. Bill may not have been too unhappy to leave the farm. Growing up, the boys each shared one of three single beds in the kids' bedroom; his three sisters shared one single bed. The parents had the other bedroom in the house.

"That's how most people lived back then, close together. We didn't have electricity, that didn't come until the early '50s. We all helped on the farm. We all played music. It wasn't bad but it wasn't easy.

18. From Birch Tree to the Battle of the Bulge and Back

"Mom had two big vegetable gardens. We helped her, and we had livestock and chickens. That was our food. We didn't buy much but coffee. We were all born at home, and my mother also worked as a midwife. Ora Brawley Reed was a very intelligent woman who went through the 10th grade at Winona. I was lucky to get through 8th grade."

One major illness Bill remembers from his boyhood was typhoid fever. "I was in bed a long time for that. Several in our neighborhood had it too. It gave me a heart murmur. Because of that, doctors tell me they can't operate on my knees."

Added to this health issue, Bill has to deal with his injuries from the war, such as losing all hearing in one ear.

"I had finished my infantry training just after the D-Day invasion of Europe. So they sent me to the front lines. We were closing in on the Nazis.

"On December 16, 1944, the Germans counterattacked with everything they had. This was the beginning of the Battle of the Bulge. They knew it was their last chance, so they even sent out young, untrained boys against us.

"I was on the front line for 128 days straight that winter. It was one of the coldest, most snowy winters they ever had. We couldn't get any of our air cover. That gave those Nazi tanks a pretty good advantage for a few days. They even went past us so it was hard to know where we were or get supplied with food or ammunition," he summarized his view of the battle.

"Have you ever tried sleeping in a freezing wet foxhole?" he asked.

"No, I did my time in Vietnam."

"Well, you can't sleep much. I got frostbit on my feet. Later in the war I was in one foxhole with my buddy Brown. We both ducked down because we heard in-coming artillery. I had a slight wound and slowly stood up. That man hunkered down right with me was killed by the shrapnel."

By the time spring came Reed's unit was back in Germany. The bridge at Remagen—the last standing on the Rhine—was captured by soldiers of the U.S. 9th Armored Division in March 1945. Bill's unit, Company L of the 309th Regiment of the 78th Infantry Division, was able to cross the river before the Germans destroyed the bridge in an ultimately futile effort to prevent the American advance. Cut off from any reinforcements or supplies, Bill saw more action there with nothing at all to eat for a three-day stretch.

After the Nazis finally surrendered, Bill was assigned to be in charge of prominent Germans who stood trial for war crimes.

"I remember Axis Sally," he recalls. "She was on the radio with all kinds of propaganda against us. I mainly remember how glad I was to be able to go home after 19 months overseas."

Bill has remained active in his local American Legion post and has held many positions in the community. You can't talk with Bill for very long and not realize he has done what he can for Birch Tree and the area.

The same is true for his family. He married the former Shannon Klepzig of Winona in 1947. They had three children, all of whom are alive and make Bill proud as do his six grandchildren. Five grandchildren have gone to college and one is a nurse.

A year following his first wife's passing in 2005, Bill married Trudy Carter, who was then a widow living on a farm south of Birch Tree. Her daughter Anna is a teacher and overseas missionary. For anyone who has had the pleasure of meeting either of these two, it is not hard to see they bring out the best in each other.

Maybe it helps that Trudy grew up in Germany. She knows how to handle this tough Ozark survivor … barber, father, tie hacker, hunter, musician, fisherman, grandpa and storyteller.

—Originally published in November 2014, in the *Current Wave*, Shannon County's weekly newspaper, published since 1874 in the county seat, Eminence, Missouri. Bill died shortly after the article appeared.

19

Exposé from a Newbie Election Judge

> This piece was an op-ed, inspired by an elderly lady, on the first time I worked at the polls rather than covered the voting as a reporter. It ran in the *Springfield News-Leader* in November 2014.

* * *

Probably it was her daughter helping this elder with a metal walker. Slowly they rounded the barricades toward us 16 election judges squirming on hard seats. She didn't want any help voting.

It could have been her neighbor. Several neighbors came together on Election Day.

She shooed her helper away. Then she bent over the notebook where I pasted a label giving her address and what ballot type she should receive for her neighborhood and electoral races.

Her companion reached over to help steady this lady's hand. The elder brushed that assistance away too.

She used both hands to hold the pen. As gnarly as hawks' claws, her fingers guided the pen to sign for her ballot. Her letters were as clear and sharp as the skies last Tuesday were nippy and rainy.

A brief smile flashed across their faces when I reminded the two women to be sure to take their stickers. Then they slowly made their way toward one of the dozen round tables to cast their ballots.

Everyone gets a kick out of that. Remember to wear your sticker saying, "I voted."

"Awesome," they'd say. Or, "Cool!" Wear your stickers. Be proud you took the trouble on a bad day to come out!

Not that many folks did come. Less than half who registered took the trouble to vote. I spent almost a year in Vietnam in a stupid, illegal war so people could vote. Millions were killed. Why do our politicians make it hard for people to vote?

It should be a national holiday. No one should be required to work on

Election Day. It's that way in other countries. It is hard enough to make a living these days. It shouldn't be hard to vote.

We toiled mightily in the guts of American democracy last Tuesday at one of the busiest voting places in Missouri. This was my first visit to the innards of elections. It's the last time that Richard Struckhoff, Greene County clerk, oversaw this process. He and his staff did a great job from what I could tell.

"We rented Remington's for the 2012 Presidential election. It was then the busiest election site in Missouri," Struckhoff said when he visited our site. "We only had eight poll workers available then to handle four times as many voters as you will likely see today. The line stretched out the door and all away around this building at 6 a.m."

One of my co-judges told me a friend had been one of those poll workers in 2012.

"She said the line never stopped, they hardly had a chance for lunch, which she took when using the bathroom," he said. "She said this was her first and last time to work an election."

The co-judge and I agreed God must have been out there assuring several hundred people would visit us each hour. We were never bored. We were always amazed with the gumption from at least some of our fellow citizens.

20

A Day with the Rainbow Family

Ted Berger and Ronnie Jones

> This story developed by chance after I formally left the Rolla newspaper. Editor Steve Sowers had always been open to new ideas. His family sold the newspaper long ago, but I sense the new owners seem to hire enthusiastic writers when I have a chance to visit Rolla or see their website.
>
> A few years ago the Ozarks had a Senate primary candidate who won more than 30,000 votes speaking out for legalized marijuana. It seems Chief Wana Dubie must have gotten all the votes plus some extra from the Rainbow Family, which has some regional groups. Too bad the Chief did not live to see legalization in his day.
>
> Marijuana powered the Rainbow Family, but remains illegal in the Ozarks, except for alleged medical issues.

Drumming Up the Hollow; A Soulful, Dusty Day with the Rainbow People

"I am a little concerned," said Ted Berger, the brawny veggie farmer, as we begin our visit to the Rainbow Gathering a few miles from here. "From all I've heard, I feel we're entering the outer ring of hell as Dante described it."

Lots of folks share his apprehension. About 200 miles due south of St. Louis, this Ozark town near the Arkansas line has joined the media circus. Some 15,000 free-spirited celebrants have been camping in nearby forests and fields since June 28.

The town's schoolhouse has become the U.S. Forest Service's command

Many followers of the Rainbow Family adopt Native American ways for their annual gatherings in the Ozarks and elsewhere. This sketch illustrates a talking circle where "holding the feather" allowed speech (illustration by Anna Bolt).

post to monitor the gathering, which is being held by permit, a first in its 25-year history. Gatherings have occurred in National Forests all over the nation for two weeks centered on Independence Day, a holiday of special significance for the freedom-loving Rainbows.

"We agreed on an operating plan to minimize environmental and public safety problems," said Randy Moore, supervisor of the 1.5 million acre Mark Twain National Forest, which is headquartered in Rolla. "They seem to be sticking with it. They've done a pretty good job of policing themselves so far."

Moore was back in his Rolla office last Wednesday after several days of Rainbow pow-wows and town hall meetings with concerned local residents. Additional meetings are planned until the gathering officially ends July 10.

Unforeseen Expense

By then special law enforcement and related services could cost the agency up to $700,000, an unexpected budget item according to Charlotte Wiggins, spokesperson for the Mark Twain National Forest. Last year's gathering cost Kit Carson National Forest in New Mexico $181,000; about $200,000 had already been spent here by early last week, Wiggins said.

The Supreme Court has ruled that the federal agency must allow all groups, including the Rainbows, to use the forest. As a follow-up, Congress last year mandated the non-commercial group use a permit system now in effect for groups of 75 or more.

Last Monday Forest Supervisor Moore had a chance to display his listening skills. Cool reckoning with some 1,000 Rainbow campers—wearing bright, outlandish clothing or a few pieces thereof—contrasted with their sometimes windy rhetoric.

Squatting, sitting, cuddling up or standing as tall as Moses on the rock, they surrounded Moore and two other uniformed Forest Service officials in what seemed an eternal confrontation between order and anarchy, youth and maturity. Horses used by the rangers fed in forest shade. Except for an occasional hawk overhead, the grown-up field centered on this ring of dialogue.

"I just tried to reason with them, plant a seed about how and why we have to do things. I explained our law enforcement officers have to keep their sidearm when in the gathering. It's part of their uniform," Moore said. "But we've compromised some. We're not using our motorized four-wheelers anymore because of noise, nor a neighboring ranchers' horses because of their droppings. We'll be sticking to mountain bikes for patrolling; that's how I got into the site yesterday."

At one point, Moore asked the circle what else he could do to explain the Forest Service's position on maintaining a checkpoint into and out of the site, a 20 mph. speed limit on the access gravel road and related matters.

"Thank Mother Earth"

A young woman in a flowing dress, holding a feather which gives a speaker the floor in Rainbow tradition, responded, "Every time you eat, every meal you take, thank Mother Earth. Every time you take from the Mother, please put something back." Moore nodded his assent.

But this exchange of views came late in the day. Our visit began about 2 p.m. We had loaded up on canteens, food, bug repellant and emergency rations.

Rumor in the area had it, "They're a pretty wild bunch," as the owner of Al's Photography in Willow Springs, remarked. "The food and water is supposed to be unsafe, and who knows what else goes on?"

We were joined by Ronnie Jones, an organic grower known for his and his wife Heidi's ornate dried flowers. As we drove in past brush coated thick with red clay road dust, Ronnie's son from a previous marriage, Jonathan, 21, told of some of his adventures at previous Rainbow Gatherings here and overseas.

"The Europeans don't seem to be so entranced by drugs," Jonathan said. "They're a little more serious."

Welcome Home

At the check point Forest Service rangers waved us on—could grey hair look that docile?—but a Rainbow welcoming committee stopped us.

"Welcome home! We love you, brothers." The first of many similar such greetings we were to receive as we entered the campground. The Rainbow greeters offered hugs and a simple map with gathering guidelines.

We joined a young man in immaculate blue jeans and still ironed shirt who said he had just flown in from New York City, rented a car in Memphis that would remain with thousands of others in a rutted, sweltering field. But we lost him on the other side of the road. We paused in A Camp, for alcohol drinkers, to watch folks pay a $1 a blow to smash an old Mazda as a fundraiser for more booze.

Once we entered the woods things slowed down. Dakota, using a made-up handle as do most Rainbowers, explained recycling was a big part of the group's self-policing effort. His one-man stand had an efficient, but overwhelmed appearance.

The further we walked down the old farm road, the more tents, improvised shelters and signs hanging from trees we noticed.

20. A Day with the Rainbow Family 149

"If you love us," someone had scrawled on a piece of cardboard posted by one camp, "please find a latrine."

The few of these we noticed were hand-dug slits designed for squatting. Privacy? Forget it!

But maybe there were other facilities. The more we walked, the more camps we noticed and the more elaborate many became up on the hillsides. Needless to say, much of the gathering we didn't see or fully understand.

After a mile or so, we reached the first of several old fields that provided meeting circles or large tent kitchens for organized groups such as the Hare Krishnas, better known for proselytizing at airports and bus stations.

At the first crossing of Spring Creek, the Rainbows had built a crude bridge out of old logs and clay. Maybe 75 people, most of them about 20 years old, rested in the shade or knee-deep water while a young man, holding a feather on high, recited the first amendment to the Constitution. Two uniformed Forest Service rangers paused to listen, then carried their bikes across the bridge and continued on their way, with wary smiles.

"Leery distrust" is how Wiggins describes the relationship between the agency and the campers. Several Rainbows visited a recent Thomasville community meeting to help explain the gathering, she noted.

In this first mile of old roads and fields, the beauty of the site becomes apparent. No one could argue the area couldn't handle a few thousand folks. But 20,000?

Considering the volume of foot traffic, it was lucky not many of the campers had set up trading operations on blankets or rugs to display their crafts, crystals, cigarettes, Snickers, cult books of all kinds, including James Joyce's *Dubliners* and *The Adventures of Huckleberry Finn*, and whatever else you might need.

The combination of hot sun, incense, marijuana (in the air and others' nervous systems), and the dusty trail made an information booth at roughly the half-way point a natural stop. But the folks weren't too friendly.

Variety of Activities

Was it the grey hair, our sweat or our lack of gold rings or pierced ears, nose, lips or nipples? Plywood billboards nearby posted details about all kinds of activities—healing seminars, UFO groups, Libertarianism, massages, etc.—but my impression focused more on psychedelic tunes among milling throngs as if a Grateful Dead or some other concert were about to start. Endless small talk, but fun for most, it seemed.

Bosnian War, endangered species, the federal deficit, gun control, the death penalty or other current political issues seemed non-existent for this crowd.

"They're a lot younger than the group we had near Salem ten years ago," said Wiggins. "There's no way we can police their drug violations or indecent exposure in the gathering. Our ranger's job is to protect the forest and related public resources. If they had some kind of major health problem due to the water or bad food, we would of course try to help out, but their safety is their responsibility."

Luckily out in the next field, folks seemed more focused. A wedding was about to transpire. Ganja cake for everyone. But, false alarm, it's an hour off still.

We drifted over to a trail appearing to go up a steep hollow vibrating with apparently dozens of echoing drums. But we were too lazy or wary to take off our boots and cross the creek. It was time to start heading back.

At three miles the camps had dwindled. Both Rainbows and rangers maintained barricades to mark the end of the public use area.

Group Kitchens

We visited several large kitchens sponsored by groups such as Om Kaloma (a Rainbow group from Oklahoma) which had elaborate ovens made of two oil drums stacked—the lower one for the fire, upper for cooking—which can produce everything from bread to wedding cakes.

As we neared Dakota's recycling station, the crowds coming in became heavier and more disorganized. Some kids just dragged their duffle bags and stuff through the heavy dust to reach a campsite while others used little red wagons left over from not-too-distant childhoods.

Bearers shouldered sacks of pinto beans or potatoes for the kitchens. A few of the brave were barefoot, but they winced at each stone in the path.

At one point we stopped to admire a fine stack of fresh-cut bamboo poles a couple had brought from North Carolina for a teepee framework. All of a sudden the woman looked closely at Jonathan and said intently she knew him from some place.

They embraced and started laughing. "I could never forget those eyes," she said, and introduced herself as Rainbow Weaver. She and Jonathan had been at a gathering in Poland.

"It was so beautiful," Rainbow Weaver said. "Poland was just opening up after all those years of communism. It must have been '89. Everyone was so enthusiastic. Then Jonathan and I and someone else went hitchhiking to Denmark. I knew I recognized those eyes."

They exchanged addresses, and we eventually headed west with the sunset with two Rainbow hitchers who needed a ride into the town just north, Birch Tree, for supplies.

"Isn't this incredible," one of them said. "People will share everything with you. Me too. It's one huge party. If you need food, I'll give it to you. But this beer I'm going to get, that's something else. The beer is for me."

20. A Day with the Rainbow Family

At Birch Tree the two asked to get out at a service station they knew sold beer. To a car with two women in it pulling away from a gas pump, they hollered, "Let's party," and roared with laughter on their way inside toward the cooler.

—Thomasville, Missouri, Summer 1987. From the *Rolla Daily News*, July 1987. Most Rainbow Gatherings are in western states.

Memoir: Holding the Feather
Reflections on the Rainbow Family

> This was written and published by the *Rolla Daily News* shortly after the July '87 gathering described earlier. It stands as a statement for tolerance. This is a rare opinion piece. I was trained to keep my opinions out of writing, and still have reservations about sounding off. This is part of what attracts me to oral history. I'm fascinated with the variety of experiences and opinions from others. The more the better; just keep it peaceful and respectful.

* * *

So, what's the big deal about these Rainbow folk? Who cares if 15,000 or so scruffy old hippies and their younger devotees camp out in the woods down near the Arkansas line?

That was my attitude. I had limited desire to see what and who these Rainbows were. From what I had heard about their previous gatherings, the main focus of things seemed to center on running around bare naked in the woods and doing lots of drugs. That seemed about as interesting as viewing a bunch of rusty, tie-dyed Volkswagen buses having a demolition derby.

By chance, I happened to be in West Plains at the Old Time Music and Heritage Festival the weekend before Independence Day and heard lots of amazing stories from a variety of people, reliable sources all. A couple of these friends said, why not go see for yourself. So, being a true "Show Me" Missouri mule in basic personality, I did.

As a writer, I loved it. These folks are what journalists call "great copy." Lots of them have a few grey hairs and kicked around life enough to know how to tell their stories with élan. The younger ones too tended to be bright with a creative streak. Anarchy is always more amusing than authoritarianism. What most interested me was how this incredible throng of people, a multitude larger than the population of Rolla, lived in the woods. (Eighteen thousand was the estimate as of July 5.) They had plumbing with fresh spring water and rudimentary sanitation systems, extensive kitchens, health care facilities, defined neighborhoods for bartering and trading, religious activities and a deep concern for the environment. Reportedly in a few days, Rainbow crews will clean up behind themselves, reseed and replant (they made a point of building bridges, shelters, everything, with dead wood so as not to cut growing trees). In a few months no one will know they were there, supposedly. The U.S. Forest Service, reluctant hosts, will have to check that out.

Having visited the gathering, I can see how people around Thomasville might well be concerned even if one should feel kindly about creative folks who want to vacation in the National Forest en masse. A fair number of Rainbows are what even the group knows to be losers, called "Drainbows": folks who come not so much to add something to the gathering, but to cadge free food, dope and sex, if not from fellow campers, maybe from the local welfare office or an unsuspecting merchant. At one swimming hole, I heard an impromptu gathering addressed by a young woman holding a feather, the Rainbow sign a person wants to be heard, who had stuff ripped from her camp. My friend Ronnie Jones said he picked up a hitchhiker near Mountain View who was leaving early to return to California because there was too much dope, dirt and dust at the gathering for him.

Of greater concern to the general public should be the cost of policing the gathering. The Forest Service reports it has already spent $200,000 mainly to bring in law enforcement. The final bill could be three times as high. From what I saw, I wonder why so much law enforcement is necessary; the Rainbows seem to be a reasonably calm bunch who try to make peace and love the center of their activities. Of course, there's always a few rotten apples, so the government is justified in taking precautions. But hassling the group isn't necessary.

What would make the Rainbows more attractive to the public perhaps is more responsibility on their part. Does the group make enough of an effort to cooperate with their hosts, the Forest Service? The Supreme Court has upheld their complaint that the First Amendment to the Constitution protects their right to meet. Getting a permit seems a silly issue to contest. Also, every meeting has costs. The Rainbows should consider helping meet those costs. The general public might drop by to see for themselves what freedom taken to near its limit can be. It may not be for everyone, but it isn't all that ugly, and can be fun if you don't camp in a poison ivy patch, which has happened at least once.[1]

—From the *Rolla Daily News,* July 1987.

Part VI

Making It as a Freelancer
Gigging—Community Culture from Diverse Angles

Freelance writing must be one of the most uncertain, stressful ways to make a living. Of course, I had to give it a try. For several years I typed earnestly as my first marriage gradually collapsed. Maybe being a prospector in Alaska would offer equal trauma.

I was lucky to strike a small lode and sell a few pieces. That was enough to make me keep mining for precious minerals far too long. Every work situation has its challenges. Each writer has his or her own approach to the craft. Maybe mine's a constructive cautionary tale of diverse opportunities on making a living writing as an experiment amidst controlled chaos.

I hit a small bonanza at *Audubon* magazine when the great Les Line was editor-in-chief long ago. He liked what I wrote on the Ozarks and commissioned a piece. The pay was almost enough to cover one month's rent in Philadelphia. I had moved east after working a year or so at the *Rolla Daily News* to understand urbanization's possible spread to the Ozarks. It was instructive appreciating culture along the mid–Delaware Valley while falling for an alluring local girl. I left Frenchtown, New Jersey, and we soon moved together to West Philly. In the attic above a two-story walk-up, we were cooking via an old electric wok and doing dishes in the bathtub.

Then we moved to Missouri after this Schuylkill River sojourn. We could afford a whole cabin, if I could cut the cords of firewood to heat the place. I labored away several months on spec writing about the pleasure of Ozark float trips. Nobody wanted these efforts. I gradually lost steam for prospecting in national publications. Too much time spent writing query letters and revising manuscripts. Boring and frustrating for a guy who was later diagnosed with attention deficit disorder.

After settling into the cabin, we splurged on a spring trip to see friends back in Philly just as an ice storm hit the Ozarks. The fish tank froze and burst, our marriage ended soon after. Luckily our ill-fated partnership proved good training for both of us. We each moved to more substantial affiliations, wiser for a score of months suffering uncertain marital bliss.

I soon discovered freelance opportunities for regional arts and humanities councils. These public programs seem rare in recent years as budgets have been slashed. I had learned just enough about oral history to lead workshops at middle schools. It's amazing how savvy fifth and sixth graders can be. I found I preferred the orderly approach of oral history projects to crafting query letters.

I also found local publications paid peanuts but were glad to have my quirky work. One of the best was an extraordinary magazine, the *West Plains Gazette*, the *Life Magazine* of what some consider the greater Booger County region: Howell and Ozark counties on the Arkansas border. Two talented brothers, Russ and Michael Cochran, published 30 issues of the colorful quarterly in the '80s before moving on to other creative projects. Luckily it introduced me to Booger County.[1]

I also landed a prestigious New York agent, Charlotte Sheedy, mom of a talented actress, Ally Sheedy. Charlotte's office seemed to be an archetypal Manhattan uptown loft lined with thousands of books written by her clients. I never added to that shelf for a variety of reasons: I was enthralled with writing articles I could knock out in a week or two; I had to bring in some income by various regular jobs; I felt I knew too little to write a book; and I lacked an overarching vision and rage at the world's injustices.

Since my all-inclusive tour of Vietnam long ago, I've gradually become more pragmatic, less a progressive pit bull. Politics fascinates me. I hope for a reasonable balance and some social fairness. Only dishonesty and egotism still unhinge me. As a writer I learned to appreciate multiple sides to a story, tending to be sympathetic with many points of view. This also corresponded with what I learned as a member of the Religious Society of Friends following my Vietnam tour. Quakers tend to be tolerant of diverse points of view. We believe each person must answer to their own Inner Light as much as to Christian tradition and the Golden Rule.

More than details of local politics, I tended to write what used to be known as human interest stories, especially on older folks who had done something unique and positive. As I learned more about oral history, working to document local culture and environments became my focus.

My advice for recording history in all forms balances a local focus with global acuity. It helps to bring as wide a perspective as possible to any project. Try different media, opportunities, even with scant prospect of renumeration. Local outlets can lead to unexpected openings. I've also learned freelance writing, as is true of the gig economy, requires a steady focus on an area of specialization. It also helps to be highly organized, to keep track of all expenses, to recycle past work appropriately and to engineer an indestructible ego while respecting one's curiosity. The necessary skills of freelancing have not been laid out as has Jack de la Vergne's thorough pro bono handbook for hard rock miners. The freelancer must mix the strength of a miner with the insights of an artist.

Diverse venues first published the pieces included in this section. Over the years, I have published local lore with the help of a variety of organizations. Many of those venues have sun-setted, but I appreciate and acknowledge the efforts of editors and diverse friends.

21

La Guignolée—Fiddling in the New Year

Kent Beaulne

French communities south of St. Louis and west of hills around Bonne Terre and Potosi have maintained spirited traditions. French fur traders and miners explored this part of the Ozarks in the early 1700s. Though not operational yet, one of the newest units of the national park system was created by Congress in 2018 as the Ste. Genevieve National Historic Park.

This article gives a sense of how this community maintains its French heritage. Reportedly many German residents, who followed the French in settling this area, deserve credit for preserving 200-year-old settlers' log homes, the basis for the new national park. Recognizing the structural strength of the old buildings, German immigrants put clapboards over local French homes and used them for decades, thus preserving unique architectural history.

This article appeared in the *Ozark River Fun Times*, a newspaper that promoted tourism and lasted a couple of years in Steelville, Missouri, during the 1990s. It did its best to create a lively forum for the northern Ozarks.

Fresh Start, Ancient Spirit: The Heart of Everlasting Joy

New Year's Eve and a bleary morning that began in 1980 still stand out. If any one New Year's Eve can be relived, that would be the one. I don't even remember if it was the moon, hard cider, a mild winter, nothing as wild as white lightning. Yet it was almost toxic crazy. By the end of that night I knew as much of what we did and said as I can remember now 13 years later.

These friends had a little factory making solar collectors in a hollow not far from Taum Sauk Mountain. It seemed like a good idea at the time. Jimmy Carter had the federal Solar Tax Credit in place. Everyone was going to buy a solar collector for their hot water if not a couple more to heat the whole house.

At midnight the moon was full and we howled like wolves then drove around the back roads in pursuit of women or wisdom. New Year's morning we hiked up Taum Sauk to skinny dip in Mina Sauk Falls to begin what we assumed would be the Solar Decade. We were going to save the environment from polluters and oil companies. We started the year right, eating a big mess of black-eyed peas.

Nevertheless, mortgage rates rose that spring. Not many Missourians bought into solar. The collector factory went back to being a barn, the guys got regular jobs and families. These days I find myself agreeing with my wife's idea of an agreeable New Year's Eve, something quiet and safe. Too many amateurs heft bottles then. Still, there's this streak deep down in me saying this one night has to be different, somehow new.

New Year's Eve and Day can haunt you for the rest of the year. Thus it was with considerable curiosity a couple of years ago we joined friends in going to Prairie du Rocher, Illinois, just across the river from Ste. Genevieve. Both towns have won attention lately for battling the flooding Mississippi. They deserve distinction for maintaining some of their heritage as well.

These French towns of the mid–Mississippi valley are the oldest European communities in the Midwest. Generally that would have merited a big yawn from me a few years ago. Have we Europeans done any better in the new world than our ancestors did in the old? A few worthwhile traditions from the old world hang on in odd corners of America. Drinking too much booze is not one of them. *La Guignolée* is.

Though it is just across the river, the ferry wasn't running then so we had to drive for an hour or more from Ste. Genevieve to cross the Mississippi then backtrack upstream to Prairie du Rocher. There we found two signs of civilization, a friendly bar and a palatable restaurant, amidst a few scattered houses.

"A lot of the old French families in Missouri got their start here. This is where my people are from," said my friend Kent Beaulne, a carpenter who reveres the old ways. "For all I know they've been celebrating *La Guignolée* here since the area was settled in 1700."

About 10 p.m. people in the restaurant suggested we go over to the Old Creole House, one of the ancient, one-story homes now protected by a local group. Snow was beginning to fall. It had gotten much colder since we

21. La Guignolée—*Fiddling in the New Year*

had left Kent's house with the last sunset of the year. No one was moving, no cars or trucks, not even a stray dog or cat. Only a few more cars huddled near the bar and a faint plaint of the jukebox suggested this was some kind of special night, a festive moment in the depth of winter.

We entered the yard of the Creole House through a low wrought iron gate, crossed a generous porch and knocked at a heavy front door. A timid voice invited us in.

Luckily a huge fire was roaring in the small grate in one corner. Coffee and introductions were made as we began small talk.

Kent explained we had heard the *Guignolée* singers would be stopping at the Creole House. Yes, our host said. They had been doing this for years and years. They will stop here, just as they will stop at the restaurant, the bar, American Legion and many homes in town.

We don't know exactly when they will come, one of the ladies said. Her granddaughter from out of town was visiting and she wanted to be sure the girl wouldn't miss *La Guignolée*. A blizzard was blowing snow almost flat along the ground when a big tour bus pulled up after what was probably an hour more of visiting. Maybe 30 people piled out laughing as they entered and filled the tiny main room of the Creole House and began singing: "We ask you only for the oldest girl of the house/ We will make a good girl of her / We will warm her feet." It's a long song they sing in French. My friend Ray Brassieur, a folklorist, says several different versions are sung in different communities along the Mississippi.

The tradition dates back to Medieval times before it came with the early French settlers down the Mississippi: "Nightingale of the green bower, Ambassador of love, Go tell my lover that She has a heart of everlasting joy." Most of the group were in costumes from the Ozark frontier of 200 or so years ago.

We shared punch and cookies that the historic society had prepared. In a few minutes the singers finished their snack then piled back into the bus. The snow had slowed down. "The lead singer was a German," Ray said. "I think he had his French down pretty good. They all did good as Cajuns."

As we thanked our hosts and left, we could see the bus open its door at the restaurant and the singers come out. The faint wail of a fiddle could be heard again across the frozen streets of the old village. The New Year was starting well once again.

—*Ozark River Fun Times*, Steelville, Missouri. 1990

22

Good Sports: A Burnham Sunday Tradition

Gini Webb Scudder

This is one of the first articles I wrote for the *West Plains Gazette*, a quarterly magazine described in the section introduction. I hadn't been back to Burnham or seen Gini Webb Scudder in decades, which is regrettable. I've learned that Gini died in 2019. Does her family's croquet grounds and its tradition continue?

Occasionally I encounter Gini's former boss, Wendell Bailey, who has become one of the greatest boosters of Willow Springs, Missouri, one of the old timber towns along U.S. 60 west of Poplar Bluff. Wendell, family, friends, and the local arts council have done everything possible to help Willow Springs thrive.

One of their greatest accomplishments has been creating the Star Theater as a venue for a local symphony orchestra, theatrical productions, bluegrass concerts, movies and more. These kinds of community projects don't happen without incredible effort and appreciation, which can be seen as necessary for a place like this old croquet grounds as well.

* * *

You know how Gini Webb is. Once she gets onto something, she won't let you forget it. She's a little like a puppy worrying a bullfrog and gives up only when she's got your attention right where she wants it.

With Gini on his staff, Congressman Wendell Bailey has a secret weapon, better than anything the Pentagon has produced. I almost feel sorry for any well-meaning Democrat in a discussion or debate with Miss Webb about this fall's candidates. Almost, but not quite. Most anyone who has met Gini knows she means well. Could a Baptist youth education director, choir leader and semi-professional clown mean otherwise? I had no doubts about taking up her offer to see where her stepdad plays croquet every Sunday.

22. Good Sports: A Burnham Sunday Tradition

"Oh yes," Gini said over and over again last winter and summer, "after church and Sunday dinner the men always go to the croquet grounds. Leonard will excuse himself even from company to play croquet. That's understood at our house. Mother never schedules anything for Sunday. They play 'til the snow hits. In the fall they build a fire to warm up with 'til they really get going."

All and more of Gini's description of the croquet grounds near the little community of Burnham proved gospel true. Especially what she said about the grounds itself.

Every sport has its classic home, the playing field where the records have been set, where great performances still live to challenge each generation and hold our imagination. Tales of the wily skills of the best players aggregate to sanctify the land itself. For all I know of croquet, the grounds near Burnham have rightful claim to be St. Andrews, Wimbledon and Yankee Stadium all rolled into one for this game of gentlemen.

As far as you can see, rolling country in the distant shadow of Blue Buck Mountain soothes the players' eyes. Overhead, huge hickory and oaks block the heat of the day. When we visited, the blackberries just beginning to ripen in the bramble hedge around the court gave the place a privacy as comforting as any cricket club must offer. But Gini said on some Sundays there's a capacity crowd of consultants and spectators. Everyone's welcome to look on, visit and even try a game with the old pros.

When we drove over after Sunday dinner at the Duddridges' a number of older men on a bench were concentrating on their checkerboard as hard as some do on the stock tables. James Newberry, West Plains auto mechanic, was whipping everyone. "He's as good as there is in the country," said Jack Spence, who was introduced as the senior member, at 78, of the croquet players.

During the course of the afternoon, Jack and his brother Stanley "Peck" Spence explained no one really knows how old the croquet grounds are. They do remember for certain, though, that their father had a grounds a little north of the present one in 1911.

"There were other croquet grounds around here for sure," Jack said. "I've heard that Walnut Grove had one and quite a few other towns too. We even used to have lights on this one. It used to be a much bigger thing."

Leonard Duddridge agreed. "I don't know of any more croquet grounds around anymore, but I do know we used to have one at the CCC camp when we were building Noblett Lake. It was a bigger thing back then for sure."

"We all take care of the grounds," Leonard said. "Somebody comes by early in the afternoon and uses the metal scrapers to push the sand and dirt into the low spots. It's a very level grounds. It doesn't vary much more than an eighth to a sixteenth of an inch so it doesn't take much upkeep. In the spring we'll bring in a quarter yard of sand to fill in any bad spots left over from the winter.

"We follow the standard rules. Sometimes we bend them a little. It's okay with us if you use your handle to bat your ball out from behind the stake. That's one of the objects of the game, to roquet your opponents' ball behind the stake. It takes a while to get out from there unless you know how to use your mallet handle to flip your ball up from behind. That's okay with us but I tell you, it's a hard shot to do right."

Games last half an hour to 45 minutes at the most. Teams of two switch off all afternoon so that everyone gets to play in between checkers and visiting.

Leonard said the regular bunch is some eight to ten players. All but two or three are over 60 years of age. "In some ways this is an old man's game because it's not all that strenuous," he said.

But I doubted that as I watched. The club's style usually involved choking way up on the mallet. Players bent down over the ball almost like football linemen.

The second Saturday in September this year, the players got together for an all-day session at the grounds. Gini's brother Ron Webb recently told me. Though Ron works long days all week driving a soda truck, he said he spent most of that Saturday with the group. Ronnie Bryan, the only other regular player still in his 30s also works long hours driving a quarry truck, but he makes it to games whenever possible.

"We're still not as good at the old pros," Ron Webb said. "And it took us a year to get halfway decent compared to them. These guys play pretty hard croquet. There's two brothers from one family and three from another, so they don't take much off of each other. I love playing with them. Over the years they've developed terrific companionship that's hard to describe. They get a lot of fun out of beating each other, but the main thing for all of us is coming out to the croquet grounds just to play."

—Published in Autumn, 1982.

23

A Visit with Bob Holt and Venae Heier

> I did several projects with the Traditional Arts Apprenticeship Program in the late 1980s. As part of the Missouri Arts Council, this group sponsors master crafts people to pass on their skills to (usually but not necessarily) younger apprentices.
> It paid expenses and an honorarium to interested observers to report on each partnership.
> Is this a good use of tax dollars? I'd say so, since part of the arts council funds came from a small tax on video rentals. They've funded everyone from storytellers to duck call makers.
> The whole process of naming someone a "master" in the partnership can be a benefit in itself. Who do you know who is a master? Bob Holt took this opportunity to show skills that can now only be heard on recordings.

* * *

I was late in arriving for this lesson and apparently the two expected me even earlier in a mix-up about the appointment, so I was apprehensive. Luckily Bob Holt is a man of great patience. And Venae has a heart of gold. If an average pupil could learn as much as she has in the last six months, the world would be gilt.

That must have been one of the songs, "Golden Slippers," the two played together during their lesson that afternoon. In addition to their regular lessons, they also make cassettes for Venae's later study. As Bob had been sick over the winter, they said they were a little behind on lessons. But hearing Venae, one couldn't tell she had "started from nothing," as Bob put it. Her playing was smooth and clear, lacking only the assurance of a polished player and perhaps tempo and speed control. At least a dozen songs were played in the afternoon's visit.

During the lesson Bob spoke several times about the importance of square dancing in this area, and Venae said attending the dances was one of the first things that attracted her to the traditional fiddle. "It amazed me how no one could sit still during these dances," she said.

It seemed to me that Venae will soon be ready to sit in with local bands and play for square dances. Bob mentioned a number of bands play regularly in the community. Probably several of these groups would be glad to have another fiddler back up their regular members. Venae seems to have a strong appreciation for the square dance tradition of Douglas County and Bob's teaching has helped build her enthusiasm and skills.

If I recall correctly, Venae is Bob's first pupil. Like Art Galbraith, he was reluctant to take a student because his time is valuable and he does not want to waste it on needless repetitions. Both master and apprentice have been happy with this relationship as both are natural musicians.

Certainly, Venae could progress with more lessons, but perhaps she could progress just as quickly by playing in a variety of situations in the area that would increase her self-confidence and repertoire. If Bob could find another student as gifted as Venae, his patience probably would be rewarded again just as surely as it would if he continues working with his first pupil.

—Ava, Missouri; April 23, 1988

24

View to the East: Country Folks Will Wave

> When I moved East to get a change of scene, I kept in touch with a few old friends and publications. I hoped to return eventually to the Ozarks. For a while I wrote for Edd Jefford's short-lived *Ozark Digest and Access Center* in Eureka Springs, Arkansas. This column, slightly edited, for Edd's semi-monthly newspaper, describes one local environmental leader in what remained of rural New Jersey.

* * *

Vincent Abraitys[1] began working as a chicken farmer in Hunterdon County, a region he describes as still rural. It lies upstream on the Delaware River from where Washington's army crossed at night on Christmas, 1776, to surprise hungover Hessian mercenaries, one of the rebels' first big victories.

"The egg business in the East pretty much went downhill about 15 years ago. The big retailers realized they could raise chickens in places like Georgia and Arkansas a lot cheaper than they could in New Jersey. It's the labor costs which we can't match," Mr. Abraitys said.

Vince attended Brooklyn Polytechnic Institute briefly but had to leave due to the Depression. He still lives on his 12-acre former poultry farm with his wife Rose. He has been his township's tax collector, and a member of the regional high school board for 20 years, the only Democratic freeholder in a strongly Republican region for four three-year terms in office. A recent *New York Times* article described him as being "as close to a folk hero as anyone in Hunterdon County."

Vince laughed about that. His main interest is directed to nature rather than politics. For 16 years Vince has been writing a column in the local paper on his observations of the natural world. The former farmer has seen his 24,000-acre Delaware Township change from a community dependent on agriculture to one where only three families now depend on farm work.

Yet, more than 300 local residents enjoy low land assessments for tax purposes because a New Jersey law gives a low rate to those owning more than five acres and run a few ducks or polo ponies. Mr. Abraitys doesn't think much of so-called preferential assessment for agriculture as a means of encouraging it. He says that lower assessment of any open space would, "stop making liars out of so many people," and would have the desired effect of preserving open space. Agriculture, he suggests begrudgingly, will probably become centralized in the Midwest.

Can farming be carried out successfully in the East? Population pressures and demand for relatively high wages makes it unlikely that ag, excepting specialty items, will thrive here, Abraitys believes. He's not bitter about these developments and takes the influx of population as a source of amusement.

"City people don't know how to live out here," Vince says. He describes a friend who has counted song birds every spring along a certain road for years as part of an Audubon Society census. In recent years this friend has been questioned by local police who wonder what he is doing stopped along the road every half mile.

"Years ago," Abraitys says, "when somebody came down my road I threw up my hand and waved, and they would do the same," he recalls. "Today if I were to do that, they would think, 'What kind of deviate are you?' One just doesn't stop along the road or enter a wood these days, because the first thing you know the local policeman chases you out."

How can a place like the Ozarks keep what makes it unique? Abraitys is not one to try to form barriers to people. He says planning zoning would best be arranged on a regional or state basis, with geologic and soil boundaries forming a basis for determining what can be developed where.

What determines a region's character? Abraitys says agriculture is basic. Food and eating, who can argue with that?

25

Route 66: African American History Along the Mother Road

> Missouri State University's Special Collections and Tom Peters, an inspired librarian, sponsored this program. I did several video interviews for the project available on their website.
> As chief funder, the National Park Service is incorporating some interviews for its Route 66 Corridor Preservation Program as part of national trails promotion. The Mother Road may never be a national park as generally understood, but may become more a regional heritage and tourism venture. That's what it is now, a steadily growing phenomenon.

* * *

As did many in the Midwest, I grew up with Route 66 being a popular song, television show and old highway evoking pleasant memories of vacations and escape from a city. My dad favored this highway to take us fishing.

He had special places to stop, especially a 2,400-acre private arboretum 20 miles outside St. Louis. Now called the Shaw Nature Preserve, these old farms have matured over a century to become a showplace for ancient pine stands, open prairies, woodland gardens, bottomland forests, demonstration projects of all kinds. But when going fishing, we usually beelined it to the late Cow-Mo Inn in Lebanon for cheeseburgers. Then to Charlie Brown's fishing camp on the Niangua, which I've written about in a memoir in Part I.

The interstates began under President Eisenhower in the 1950s as high-speed corridors. Route 66 was officially ended as a federal project in 1985. The old pavement sometimes became local roads or gradually fell apart. Interstate highways took the place of 66, the Mother Road.

Route 66 was the opposite of a superhighway. A narrow, mainly two-lane concrete roadway rarely with shoulders, the Mother Road connected little towns along the twisty route between Chicago and Los Angeles. Somewhere in the Oklahoma Ozarks, the highway stops going southwest and changes to head due west. Tulsa, Texas, panhandle and Albuquerque, here we come!

* * *

I won new appreciation for the Mother Road in the early 2000s. That's when the oral historian David King Dunaway said he was working on a major Route 66 documentation project.

"You'll see, Route 66 will be the star of a big new movie by Disney!" Dunaway said at the Oral History Association's annual conference when it was in Oklahoma City, October 2006.

I've traveled the Mother Road enough to know the highway does have an unusual, powerful vibe becoming stronger each decade. An early oral historian and professor at University of New Mexico, David often attends the conference and remains an active researcher in popular culture. (David's recently been researching an oral history of eye glass wearers.)

In 2006 Disney did release its Route 66 film, *Cars*. The studio has continued to release sequels and spin-offs of this travel epic. The highway represents the values of local history and culture. High speed interstates do not have the soul of the old Mother Road. Thousands of foreign visitors come here to cruise the Mother Road. They're attracted by the chance to see a slice of real America. In *Cars,* the animated film features talking automobiles happily enjoying soda fountains and friendly service stations.

I've been amazed by the popularity of the film and Route 66. The highway has become a 2,400-mile artifact with a variety of meanings for different audiences. For much of the world, Route 66 has become a symbol of American freedom to travel and enjoy an open road with endless possibilities. I've seen the Route 66 shield logo all over China. Like flashing a "V", Route 66 means freedom.

But, can a highway be a legitimate focus for historical research? I was skeptical. The hype about Route 66 felt lightweight, like weekend antiquing or beer can collecting.

I learned the value of transportation history shortly after moving to Springfield in 2011. It has the drama of military history, big bucks of corporate history and a cast of characters to keep biographers busy for decades. Luckily, I had a chance to sit in on lectures by Roger Grant, the dean of transportation historians.

Totally fascinated by rail lore, riding Amtrak, the history of the railway crosstie industry, and travel all captivate me. Route 66 is a big Ozark industry, especially in Springfield.

* * *

This city attracted Cathy and me to move here after living in the woods of Shannon County for three years. Ticks and chiggers, using a community well and limited solar electric drove Cath nuts. Despite both being St. Louis natives we fell for the friendly, Ozarky openness of the Queen City of the Ozarks.

At 160,000 population, as of 2020, the town has everything, especially a revitalized downtown, great biking opportunities and three universities to bring in diverse culture. Missouri State University offers a huge variety of courses and resources, including a focus for oral history projects.

Years ago I searched out Dr. Katherine Lederer, an historian on campus who focused on African American history. She encouraged me to develop a proposal to do an oral history of black communities in the Ozarks. Three towns other than Springfield had small but historic African American populations: Lebanon, Potosi and Rolla. A partnership with the former public radio station in Rolla, our proposal was turned down by the state humanities council.

"You really have to grab funding agencies with something unique," Katherine warned me. "I've been battling for years to get people to pay attention to Springfield's black heritage. You have to focus for the long haul to get attention for anything that's out of the ordinary."

Dr. Lederer was an inspiration because she did not give up. Her collections of local African American history have resulted in new appreciation for the heritage that remains despite difficult decades following a lynching of three young black men on the town square in 1906.

Racial issues hit a low point a century ago everywhere, especially in the Ozarks and elsewhere in the South, as research on lynching has documented. Several Ozark towns had black residents driven out. But some cities were more progressive and open-minded. As during the time after the Civil War when the Exodusters began migration from the South to Kansas, local as well as federal support for African Americans was sparse to non-existent.

Self-reliance has been necessary for new residents in any community. It took several years for Cathy and me to be comfortable living here. Some people were particularly welcoming but fitting in takes time even for the most gregarious. Springfield has a reputation as a "Buckle of the Bible Belt," but a more distinguishing feature may be a panoply of self-made entrepreneurs, such as Tom Peters wrote about in his recent biography, *John T. Woodruff*,[1] one of the founders of Route 66. (Cyrus Avery from Tulsa, the other major promoter of the Mother Road, also is the subject of a new biography.) Agriculture and the Ozark hinterland underlie wealth here.

* * *

I was glad to do interviews for MSU's project on minorities on the Mother Road because I grew up with the highway always nearby. I learned the Mother Road had much more to show than cheeseburgers and cruising in a Thunderbird.

The Park Service sought more than sunny vacation stories from Route

66. The agency had also contracted with researchers at the American Indian Alaska Native Tourism Association (AIANTA) in Albuquerque to highlight the influence of 25 tribes along the highway in Oklahoma, New Mexico, Arizona and California.

The MSU project may be almost as colorful a report as the AIANTA project. The interviews have been archived and are available as digital audio files and transcripts at cdm17307.contentdm.oclc.org.

Results of this collection may not be readily apparent. These interviews carry forward research supporting a variety of new and on-going projects such as the city's African American Heritage Trail begun in August 2018 and the restoration of the beautiful stone Timmons Temple in Silver Springs Park.

We discussed possibly including other minority groups in the Route 66 project. Latino-Americans are relatively recent arrivals in Springfield as are Asians. We agreed Wing Yin "David" Leong should be interviewed as he had a major influence on the city. "Springfield Cashew Chicken" developed in his restaurant here in the 1950s, an establishment which almost failed to open because it was firebombed by unknown local malcontents. Now some 50 Chinese restaurants in Springfield offer Mr. Leong's unique dish and other Asian creations. Mr. Leong died a few weeks before his 100th birthday in August 2020, and unfortunately had not been interviewed. His son continues Leong's Asian Diner and serves his father's famous chicken.

Food was one of the highlights of the interviews that were recorded. Several speakers had stories about Graham's Rib Station, a Southern barbecue restaurant near Route 66. James and Zelma Graham emptied out their bank account to buy supplies a few days before their establishment opened in 1932. A few days later a run on banks during the Great Depression resulted in most bank customers losing all their savings.

The Grahams were lucky to have cashed out. Their barbecue was active serving all races for 60 years here. Nat "King" Cole and many other celebrities ate here before local concerts or while traveling. It was one of the only places open for African Americans locally.

Their daughter, Elaine Graham Estes from Iowa, has donated a restored version of the restaurant's sign to the new History Museum on the Square.

Another historic Route 66 sign was redone as the MSU Route 66 oral history project was on-going. John and Alexa Schweke restored their antique sign for what had been the Greystone Heights Motor Court ten miles west of Springfield.

John Schweke, who is restoring two of the cabins, said they were inspired by the movie *Cars*, according to Route 66 News. Seeing the film inspired John to think about the importance of his property's history, including the demise of little businesses like Greystone Heights after interstates replaced Route 66.

25. Route 66: African American History Along the Mother Road 171

"It didn't really hit me and hit my heart until I saw that movie," he said.

I visited the Schwekes as they were preparing their floral business at the former motel for an event in 2017. They had sponsored a barbecue, country band and car show which brought many neighbors to stop by for a visit. I was impressed by the care and enthusiasm the family had for carrying out an accurate restoration of their buildings. The old highway casts a spell.

Many other facets of Route 66 have been restored in Springfield and elsewhere in the Ozarks. Luckily the archived Ozark oral histories show the highway helped pave a way for more diversity in community culture, foodways and racial harmony.

Sidebar

Hard Traveling in the Ozarks

> Do you think two men and one horse could cover 150 miles in two days? Can you guess how they did that?
>
> This is a story I heard while doing storytelling as Nathaniel "Stub" Borders, a famous Ozark timberman and river rat. I did storytelling for church and other groups because I was amazed by Stub's stories, as retold in George Clinton Arthur's *Backwoodsmen: Daring Men of the Ozarks* (Boston: The Christopher Publishing House, 1940).
>
> This story describes how two men walked the old White River Trace, originally a Native America trail, that became U.S. Route 66.
>
> You have to put yourself back into the early 1820s, when timbermen set up the first sawmills on the Big Piney River. They could raft pine timber down the Piney to the Gasconade into the Missouri River then sell their raft at St. Charles for cash and a horse. This is how I heard the story, and retell it:

Well, let's say there were two guys, Daniel and Joseph. Daniel would start down the trail riding that horse. After a few miles Daniel would tie up the horse and keep walking down the trail.

In an hour or two Joseph would come up to where his friend had tied up their horse. Joseph would untie it, jump on board and ride down the trail and after a short while would catch up with Daniel and then keep riding for another mile or two. Then Joseph would tie up the horse and keep walking down the trail. Eventually Daniel would come up to where Joseph had tied up their horse and he would get on it for a second ride. After a short while he would pass up Joseph, then tie up the horse again so his friend eventually could have another ride.

They would take turns like this all day long and could go 70 or 80 miles on an average day. Do you know what this process is called? Hitch hiking.

Usually in our times, "hitch hiking" refers to drivers picking up riders alongside the road. This method of long-distance travel is a little different than the modern meaning. It allowed both men and their horse a chance to take a break and still cover a lot of territory and describes this process that must be centuries old.

> Gerry Cohen, who taught linguistics at the University of Missouri–Rolla for many years, told me once it would be worth researching how hitch hiking may have developed among early timbermen. Check out your online etymological dictionary for other derivations of the term.

26

Celebrating the Ozark Highlands Viticulture

Mary Codemo

One of my more entertaining freelance jobs involved helping the half dozen wineries that make up a district near the upper Meramec River.

This job meant drinking a lot of wine, listening to talk about making wine and figuring out how to get the world interested in their wine.

I wrote a newsletter and press releases for the group, attended their regular meetings and was paid in wine. This was in the '80s when they were just getting started.

Now Missouri has more than 100 wineries. Each is a little different; some have regional distribution, most sell locally or at the winery.

Officially known as the Ozark Highlands Viticultural Area, my group had one big deal going. People had been growing grapes around St. James for more than 100 years. The state highway department allows local growers to sell fresh grapes at stands along Interstate 44 because it's such a well-established tradition. Many of the growers have Italian ancestry. This is what we published about one of the families.

Mary Codemo is our link to the Old Country and to the traditions of early winemaking in this region. She is the last surviving local immigrant from Italy, the rural Bologna area that she left when she was five.

Ninety-two years of details about her childhood and the early days of the Rosati community color Mrs. Codemo's remembrances today. She lives with the vigor of a woman half her age on a farm north of Rosati with grandchildren and great grandchildren and keeps her own house on the place.

"I've given up canning tomatoes," she said recently. "When I was just

26. Celebrating the Ozark Highlands Viticulture

Mary Codemo came to Rosati, Missouri, as a little girl from Italy (illustration by Anna Bolt).

married I would put up 200 to 300 quarts of different vegetables. All we did then was work, except when we had dances at different neighbors or in the church basement."

Before canning jars were widely available, Mrs. Codemo would preserve tomatoes by boiling and pouring off the water until the pulp was thick enough to place on a board.

"Then we'd dry that on the roof till they were as thick as dough. We'd form them into small sticks then cover them with olive oil so they'd just slide into a corn shuck," she said. "We'd tie the shuck at the ends to keep out the air then store them in the cellar till we needed tomatoes."

Wine was also made on nearly every farm in the community. Everyone had an acre or more of grapes for wine, juice, jam or pies.

"We used to drink wine in our coffee. There are so many things that we did for ourselves then," Mrs. Codemo recalled. "Everything is so different now. Why, my husband never kissed me until we were married!"

> Several others told me they like red wine in their coffee. They call it Café Royale. It's got a good wang, maybe better than my friend Martin Spanevello's preferred cream substitute, Wild Turkey Bourbon, his favorite morning eye-opener.

27

Visit with an Ozark Swamp Queen
The Nature Conservancy

> This article ran in a newsletter from the Missouri Chapter of The Nature Conservancy long ago. This organization seeks to protect unique biological resources for long-term conservation. My dad volunteered for TNC over many years, as is described in Part VIII.

* * *

The house sits on a low ridge looking south over an Ozark valley. Hay has been cut. One patch was left standing. "You must have come to see the queen," the man said when I finally found his farm on a gravel road above the West Fork of the Black River.

Gary Botkins looked like the kind of guy who can do it all on a farm much less chaperon a queen. He's a pine tree of a man. His face lit up with pride when he handed me a pair of binoculars.

"I can see them blooming with just my bare eyes," he said. "You might need these."

Finally I recognized at the edge of some unruly grass the clumps of pink tufts that Gary was talking about. The Queen-of-the-Prairie, a wild flower that grows here and few other spots in the Ozarks or anywhere else in Missouri, rules this stretch of the valley.

Thirty-seven acres of the more than 500 that make up the family farm have been part of The Nature Conservancy's Natural Area Registry Program since 1989. The program gives special recognition to landowners who protect unique environmental features on their properties.

Susanne Greenlee, who handles TNC's volunteer registry program, had said a visit to the Botkin Fen might be worthwhile. I've walked the deep muck, prairie and other types of fens that make up the TNC preserve in nearby Grasshopper Hollow, which is managed in conjunction with the Department of Conservation, so was curious what made the Botkin Fen unique.

Driving down to what Gary calls his swamps, he mentioned working closely with Dr. Nevin Aspinwall, professor of biology at St. Louis University, to improve the fen.

"He's encouraged me to burn these four acres and the other two acre swamp in the spring. That's made a lot more flowers," Botkins said. "I have fenced off a thirty-foot square and no one but Dr. Aspinwall gets in there."

Later I had a chance to talk with Tim Smith, a Department of Conservation botanist, who said Botkin Fen has the largest population of *Filipendula rubra* in the state. Only seven other sites in Missouri have the plant. It is most common in wet areas in Ohio and Indiana and states to the east and west of there, but Missouri is its western-most range. The Queen is available commercially as an ornamental plant.

"This is what we call a relic species in Missouri," Smith said. "It has been left over from previous climatic conditions, which most recently was the era of the glaciers 18,000 years ago. The northern part of the state was covered with ice and the Ozarks were probably much cooler. Now only fens meet this plant's needs."

To help understand the genetic makeup of Queen-of-the-prairie and the diversity of the state's natural heritage, the Department has sponsored further research on the plant by Dr. Aspinwall.

"One thing I've learned that makes Botkin Fen unique is that most of these approximately 1,000 flowering stems are part of one individual plant. There are five other individual plants, but they are on the periphery," Dr. Aspinwall said.

"The fen also has other rare plants such as *Phlox maculata*. What makes this site truly unique is Gary and Veronica Botkins. They're not draining the area or mowing it. They're doing a very good job for the plants."

When I asked Gary why he protects Queen-of-the-Prairie, he said he was just continuing conservation practices on the farm instituted by his grandfather, D.C. Miner, who first showed the spot to the famous botanist Julian Steyermark in the 1950s. "Besides, we both enjoy flowers a lot. We like helping people like Dr. Aspinwall," Gary said. "And we've got something here no one else has."

28

Video with Ralph "Treehouse" Brown and Others

Audio and video naturally support local history projects. The secret to success involves extensive planning. Audio interviews in advance will pinpoint information and stories to be featured in final production. Our videos may seem folksy and loose but all required lots of advance planning.

Once the cameras are rolling, it's rare unrehearsed material will make the final cut. Here's an overview of my work on local videos, all successful projects, but with limited distribution and financial benefit. They were labors of love from all involved in the Oral History of the Ozarks Project.

* * *

While freelance writing I met the singer/songwriter Tom Shipley, one half of the Brewer and Shipley folk-rock duo. Tom had retired to Rolla sometime after the group's gold record, "One Toke Over the Line." Tom had an outdoor shop in town, then worked for a short-lived local TV station. As the largest town in the northern Ozarks, Rolla has a technological university and government research offices, which have made it a lively, brainy place.

Tom liked the nearby fishing. He also loved shooting video. After I did my Ozark rivers oral history project for the regional planning commission, I sensed Ralph Brown merited a cinematic treatment so I enlisted Tom.

"You gotta meet Ralph," I told Tom one day. "He's the real thing!"

Tom was impressed with the old Scotia bridge and the rough and tumble campground with all its stuff. Ralph himself totally blew Shipley away.

"The camera is going to love Ralph!" Tom said after that first visit.

I asked him exactly what he meant about a camera loving anyone.

"There are just certain people who translate onto a screen," Tom said. "It's not just the physical appearance of their face, but how they speak and hold themselves and their body. Their whole being comes across as someone you want to see more and know because he or she is so damn vital."

Float trips have been the most popular way to beat summer heat in the Ozarks for centuries (illustration by Anna Bolt).

Several days later I told Cathy what we were planning. She couldn't believe Tom and I had decided to feature Ralph Brown in what we planned to be an educational oral history video funded by the state arts council.

"He's one of the most ornery, repulsive old hillbillies I've ever known," Cath said, or something to that effect. This mirrors exactly what Tom saw in Ralph too.

* * *

Tom and I agreed from the beginning that we wanted any of the videos we'd make to be as immersive as possible, with people telling their own stories. We didn't want any so-called experts or talking heads explaining things. We wanted direct storytelling with video images providing context.

To win $5,000 from the state arts council—how we planned to fund the whole project (but not ourselves)—we had to submit, among other materials, a 5-minute pilot video to show we had technical abilities to put together a larger project. I had met Ralph Williams, who was one of the early fishing guides on the Current River, now a National Park, south of Rolla near Salem. Tom knew a cameraman, Gary E. Jones, from Pacific, Missouri,

28. Video with Ralph "Treehouse" Brown and Others

who would work at cost, and Howe Teague, an old-time fiddle player from nearby Salem. Howe made a recording available for the soundtrack.

Can anything sound as sweet as a crystal-clear river in autumn harmonizing with a traditional dance tune played by a skilled fiddler? Unfortunately, those few minutes of our VHS video pilot tape are probably lost forever, except in my mind. This faint memory makes me want to pitch this computer and get on an Ozark river, ASAP.

As we began to develop the script for *Treehouse*, we realized that not only was Ralph Brown a great teller of his own and community history, but his neighbors could also help tell his and their stories. Our goal was to show how Huzzah Creek was important to the community, the Ozarks and the whole world. Farmers told about crops and livestock. Tom and his singing partner Michael Brewer wrote a song about Ralph and the river that brings all the local voices together. It's a masterpiece that also has LeVon Helm, the ultimate Arkansawyer, playing slide guitar.

We shot the video late summer 1988, the year one third of Yellowstone National Park in Wyoming burned in massive wildfires. We could see its effects in the late afternoon haze and brilliant sunsets. It was hot in the Ozarks too. Altogether we acquired more than 30 hours of video, which had to be edited down to slightly less than a half-hour—editing Tom did with great skill. Many people helped, especially Laura Nemi Gajda with fund-raising, Jim Bogan with editing, and many hillbilly friends living near the upper Meramec. More funds came from the National Endowment for the Arts, the local Pepsi bottler, Kerr-McGee Corp. and our own sweat equity. The video premiered in Steelville a year later to a full house at the largest theater in town. Eventually a local foundation hired us to produce a second, longer video on the community, *Don't It Feel Like Home*, about traditional qualities of life in Crawford County.

But Ralph was not able to participate in any local screenings for *Treehouse* or anything else we did. He was diagnosed with cancer and wasn't able to travel in '89. Luckily, he was able to enjoy the completed video every day for several months before dying in 1990.

Earl Halbert, his neighbor over the ridge in Cherry Valley, became the unofficial distributor of the *Treehouse* video in Crawford County. Earl sold over 2,000 of the VHS tapes in the years after its release. During this time, he and his wife Ada grew an almost equal number of watermelons, most of which had a friend's name carved onto the side. Visitors could check the growth of "their melon" over the summer and help decide when best to harvest. This kind of generosity is typical of many folks I've encountered doing oral history. Beautiful souls are enriched by sharing significant stories.

* * *

Why should anyone care about Ralph Brown now? Are we any different than residents of Crawford County who feel *Treehouse* represented an era gone by? The heart of that era was tough times that began with farming prices crashing following World War I, the Great Depression and the camaraderie of the so-called Good War. Ralph, family and neighbors survived it all on their own terms with little or no public assistance.

That's the message of *Treehouse* and *Precious Memories*, another video I did with Tom, on the Dillard family of Ozark bluegrass fame. It's also a 28.5-minute production from our Oral History of the Ozarks not-for-profit group. This video hits on the highlights of the Dillard family's history and features John Hartford showing how Homer taught him to jig while playing the fiddle. *Precious Memories* is a master class in how music can be passed from one generation to another.

The genius of all these productions depends on Tom's sense of timing as a musician. He didn't try to tell the whole family or community story. Music and landscape tell most of the story in the three productions we completed.

"I want the viewer to want more when it's all over," Tom used to say. He got that right; all our productions were extremely popular and are great with school and other groups. After seeing the videos, people tend to naturally want to talk about a basic issue: why can't we keep and respect the neighborly traditions of the Ozarks?

Were our videos simplistic and little more than local color? Maybe, but we never had budget or organization to do anything more.

Unfortunately another of our productions, *Saint of Stone,* about the French community in the hills west of Ste. Genevieve, never was completed. Tom said he was lacking one crucial minute. I never found out exactly why it wasn't finished; our communication fell apart. Tom got a job making video for the university and I started doing freelance projects on my own.

Video creation involves lots of ego and free time. Also the technology demands a large budget for a broadcast quality production. We were lucky to have made what we did. I feel the wisdom of Treehouse Brown, Homer Dillard and their families and neighbors may last to inspire new generations.

* * *

Also surviving to a somewhat similarly challenged degree have been Ozark rivers. A century ago it was rafting millions of railroad ties and logs downstream; now it's hordes of often drunk, hooting-n-hollering kids having fun. No Ozark streams have user limits. A few federal parks have horsepower limits on jet boats, but any discussion of limits causes friction. Ralph opposed any kind of limits on anything. Increased demands for water supply and recreation will surely bring up limits in various forms in the future. The Ralphs of the world won't be happy, but they see it coming.

What may survive most from Ralph is a love of language if not philosophy, his own unique tongue and thought. Luckily the whole video can

28. Video with Ralph "Treehouse" Brown and Others

be found now on YouTube. Our production has many great lines: "I never found my limit, I just got frogs…"

"I don't care if you call me a hermit," he says about his campground. "That doesn't sound like a bad name. There's no way I want to live in town with the big crowds and the luxuries. I want to stay out here in the country."

The ultimate truth of the video: "You can't run a dog away from his home. If you get a wolf and run him under the porch, the dog won't leave home. It's the wolf's time to go when he gets under the floor."

29

Voice as Fast as a Fiddle

Dancing at a Country Music Club

> This was a column I wrote for the *Ozark River Fun Times*, a Steelville–based tabloid published in the early 1990s. It's the story of a guy who shared all the joy he felt.
> James Springer did all kinds of work--iron mining, highways, farming--and he was an artist at living life to the fullest. Luckily, I still have a few folk art birds and tin raccoons created by James.

* * *

It's not hard to find Jim Springer's place at the edge of Bourbon on the road to Japan. Birdhouses, dog pens, whirligigs, gardens and flowers surround Jim's house in the shade of huge old oaks.

A sign trumpeting traps, birdhouses and feeders invites you to come on in and see what's all the stuff for sale. But no sign, no matter how big, could prepare you for all that Jim Springer has to offer.

You needn't worry about the safety of your wallet because, even though Jim is a fast talker, he's not a slick operator. He's sly enough, but not slippery. He won't try to sweet talk the money out of your wallet.

James' biggest operation gets even more attention than his artistic creations, hounds or garden. He and his wife Bernice put some of their best licks into keeping the Bourbon Country Music Club, one of the liveliest spots in Crawford County next to the Pole Bridge Tavern.

The music club holds forth at the new Bourbon Community Center behind the roller mill on the first and third Fridays of each month, 7 to 10 p.m. Everyone's invited and you won't be disappointed.

That is if you can dance. If you can't, you're going to be left in the dust. The Bourbon area has a lot of vigorous dancers, and they all love the Bourbon Street Jammers, Jim's group. Visitors are welcome at $2 a head.

"They call me the head man," James said the other day. "I line up the jobs. We play for free, but sometimes we'll take donations. I've found money can mess up a band." He should know, he's been playing music for much of his 75 years.

He learned from neighbors in Blue Spring Hollow when he was a boy on the farm. Farming, dogs, music and his two daughters have been a good bit of his life since.

Tenor banjo keeps Jim busy, Kathy Summers plays fiddle, Bill Benthal's on guitar, Stanley O'Neal handles bass and guitar and sings, Fred Pinkston, mandolin, and Cecil Goforth sometimes sits in on fiddle or dobro.

"I still just play by ear," James said with pride. "We play it all, gospel, country & western and bluegrass, which is what I like the best."

It is best to get there early and be well rested. I learned the hard way that the crowd who follows the Jammers keeps moving.

A couple of years ago Cathy and I stopped by the Sullivan Community Hall to hear the Jammers. Most everyone was white-headed, a few grays and Steve and Laura Hausladen, infectious dancers from the Vilander area, all smiling at this start of a warm October weekend.

We're the token representatives from the Baby Boom just beginning to wrinkle and trying to shake it as good as the seniors who fill the dance floor with every two-step, waltz and polka. Two dollars pays for everything, all the coffee and juice you can drink, the band and a potluck for which we brought along okra pickles. Maybe 50 people talk softly and soberly, Jim's neat sign by the front door warns all: no alcohol or drugs at the Country Music Club.

Inspiring me almost as much as the dancing is seeing an older gentleman in a brown suit who comes up to sit in with the band on fiddle. By the way he holds the bow, I can tell standing gets tiring for him. The more he plays, the more he lags and becomes a little out of tune or tempo, the more energetically he hops around, screeches the bow a little wildly across the strings. He becomes the reckless fiddler of his youth who would play all night if the dancers were willing.

It was the best music of the night but by 10 p.m. everyone in the place was getting a little tired. Jim had put down his banjo and danced with his wife who had handled tickets at the door and set up the potluck.

Mr. Reed, who has sat next to me on and off this evening, more off than on because he has danced with every lady in the place, lets us know we're always welcome to come back. He says he's 80 and skips rope 150 times without stopping whenever he's feeling a little slow.

"My doctor told me to stop jumping rope because of my heart, but I would never do it. I won't let myself stop." His mother taught him to dance at 16 when he was on the farm and would dance all night and work all day whenever there was a dance anywhere in the county within an hour's ride on the plow horse.

Seeing all the people watching or dancing, playing music or fixing food somehow restores my faith in this crazy world, and my expectation that being a senior citizen can't be any worse than being a teenager when the most exciting thing we did was drive over to East St. Louis, lie about our age to buy beer, then drive around the back roads of St. Louis County listening to soul music. Three of us got high on a six-pack and being able to go anywhere in daddy's car.

Now I'll take a country-dance any day. Who could find anything better for Friday nights the rest of your life?

—*Ozark River Fun Times*, July 1993.

30

Deliberate Lives
A Celebration of Three Missouri Masters

> This is part of a brochure for an exhibit I helped organize that focused on self-taught Ozark artists. Their work has gone on to be accepted into museums, especially the John Michael Kohler Museum in Sheboygan, Wisconsin. This 1984 exhibit was shown at a space first known as First Street Forum that gradually morphed to become the Contemporary Art Museum, St. Louis. This kind of art may be much too low-brow for such a highfalutin institution now.

✶ ✶ ✶

A year ago the three men featured in this exhibit were involved artists. Now all have died, two in March—a somber experience for those who knew them. Their passing forces one to think of losses, both in a personal sense and in rural life, as much as to recognize what these men accomplished.

L.L. Broadfoot, Alva Gene Dexhimer and Jesse Howard shared an outlook still common in rural Missouri, an attitude as endangered as some of the wildlife. What's shared is the belief an individual can and must be self-sufficient. The difficulty of making one's own living, asking no favors and holding independent ideas gives these works rough patinas as worn as old tools. In their own ways they were artists as committed as recognized artists and they bare their souls, hopes and wily ways totally in their work.

The art of Alva Gene Dexhimer speaks to immediate needs. His death this spring at 52 is the most tragic. He was beginning to sell a variety of pieces to an increasing number of people who appreciated the gentle spirit his work reveals.

Dex could neither read nor write but filled his art with copied words to give the richest meanings possible. Handicapped by a farm accident as a boy, he began making objects and paintings for his own amusement as much as for passersby slowing on a sharp bend of a Morgan County highway to examine the bric-a-brac in front of an old trailer. Cedar chests,

Lennis Leonard Broadfoot traveled the Ozarks in the 1940s drawing and interviewing the early settlers of Current River country, in the central Ozarks of Missouri. A few of these folks hunted with stones and fished with their hands (illustration by Anna Bolt).

figurines, orotund crucifixes, found object flowerpots, gun racks, bird houses, whirligigs and more were available for whatever you were willing to pay.

Jesse Howard's work shared Dex's concern for writing and religion. His signs, painted gates, windmill blades and most anything available all seem part of a larger work: his 8-acre home on the outskirts of Fulton. Since the artist's death at 98 last November, eloquent new work has been located in sheds and an abandoned ice box by Willem Volkersz, a scholar, artist and collector at the Kansas City Art Institute, which maintains several major pieces in its collection.

A study of Howard's work by Rusty Marshall of the Missouri Cultural Heritage Center in Columbia shows the artist has been one of the most publicized in the state in recent years. His fiery inventiveness deserves it. Disagreements with the Fulton City Council, local police, those who vandalized his property, his reading of the Bible and newspapers—all inspired this artist's epic signs.

L.L. Broadfoot was also somewhat of an outsider. Residents in and around Salem did not often want to be reminded of their families' early days in the backwoods. In its fifth printing, his *Pioneers of the Ozarks* portrays root gatherers, tie hackers, herb doctors, even a "modern maid" with a cigarette.

Broadfoot himself struggled to make a living as an artist in the Ozarks and came to regard his book of portraits as his major work. Visitors to his Wildwood Studio a few blocks from the Dent County Courthouse were encouraged to buy a copy or more, but rarely would he consider selling his drawings or paintings. Loans to museums or galleries were out of the question. Urban museums had little interest in work that did not follow current trends, Broadfoot believed.

After their father's death in March at 92, the family has carefully organized his papers and collection. His correspondence suggests Broadfoot was a gifted draftsman from boyhood and a key member of an Ozark renaissance that helped create a growing folklore and tourism industry.

This show itself may be part of renewed regard for artists in rural Missouri who consistently produce art as sophisticated as any. Much good work could be disappearing as fast as wooden barns and hoot owls. Wise stewardship, empathy and hard cash is needed to conserve the land and those who celebrate it.

* * *

> Interest in self-taught, folk and outsider artists has continued to grow, but art museums in the Midwest still tend to look to East or West coasts in promoting new work. The Harlan Museum in West Plains, Missouri, has the largest collection of Mr. Broadfoot's work. Luckily, we have increasing cultural diversity, crafts and folk art being as accepted as fine art, and museums specializing in American art, such as the unique Butler Institute in Youngstown, Ohio, the Kohler in Wisconsin and the astounding Crystal Bridges in Bentonville, Arkansas.

Memoir
Hillbillies and Black Helicopters

> Big Dams are obsolete. They're uncool. They're undemocratic. They're a government's way of accumulating authority....
> —"The Greater Common Good," in
> *The Cost of Living,* Arundhati Roy, 1999.

My list of uncool jobs includes climbing rickety ladders for a roofing crew and late nights loading semis for Roadway Express. My most unprecedented gig involved a freelance job that sank before it started. I can't forget this opportunity because it could have been game changing for the Ozarks. A great possibility.

The Ozark National Scenic Riverways once considered establishing a Biosphere Reserve in Arkansas and Missouri. The U.S. has only 47 of these sites, all in cool, unique regions.

The proposal was to develop the biosphere program, then sponsor increased scientific research on the two national rivers in Arkansas and Missouri. I liked the idea behind this United Nations–inspired program because a secondary purpose was supporting traditional agriculture. I felt it might fit within the cultural traditions of the Ozarks. Earlier oral history work on the Current River involved collecting opinions, so I felt good about gathering information from local people.

This is what I proposed as a freelancer and what happened.

* * *

Once impoverished, now a booming home base for the Walmart Corporation, the Ozarks occupies a unique niche at the confluence of the Midwest, the South and the West. The French were our earliest settlers and still refer to this region as "l'Amerique profound," which suggests the region's complex cultural heritage. Curtis Marbut, founder of the U.S. Soil Survey in the 1920s, grew up here and observed how progressive, market-oriented agriculturalists bypassed the Ozarks for better, less rocky ground in Kansas or Iowa.

The Scotch-Irish arrived in the early 19th century. They were herdsmen who thrived on hills similar to Appalachia where many of their ancestors had settled after leaving Ulster. David Hackett Fischer's *Albion's Seed: Four British Folkways in America* follows linguistic patterns in what he and others call Southern "backcountry" settlement. In the early 20th century these people were dubbed "hillbillies" in joke and scorn. Now the name is used with pride. After 40 years of various oral history projects in the Ozarks, I appreciate how dominant and complex this backcountry heritage remains.

Rivers, streams, and rocky hills are notable natural features still. Even before the Great Depression, hydroelectric projects were developed along the White River, which snakes back and forth across Arkansas and Missouri. Yet our region does not have quite as many impoundments as the southern Appalachians' Tennessee Valley region or the Southwest in general.

Disputes over federal water policy led to the creation of two early Ozark national public riverways: 150 miles of the Buffalo River in northern Arkansas became a national park in March 1972; and earlier, in 1964, the Ozark National Scenic Riverways (ONSR) was established, encompassing long sections of the Current and Jacks Fork rivers in south-central Missouri. The U.S. Army Corps of Engineers had designated all of these streams for multiple impoundments. Regional opposition to dams led to the creation of these popular riparian parks instead.

From their beginnings however, these national parks along rivers presented challenges. The great Ozark author and angler Harry Middleton floated the Buffalo River in 1985 with Dr. Neil Compton, an Arkansas physician who founded the Ozark Society to protect the river. "The trick is to learn to enjoy the river without abusing or harming it," Dr. Compton is quoted as saying about the Buffalo in *Southern Living* (August 1986; pg. 88). Striking a balance between responsible public use and resource preservation lies at the heart of continuing debates about these rivers' futures.

*   *   *

Cultural rights and traditional uses of these Ozark rivers have presented political issues to legislators from the early days. For example, both trapping and hunting are allowed in the ONSR; few other national parks permit such activities. But some traditional uses had to be limited to accommodate thousands of typically urban visitors on river floats. This meant converting scores of farms to wilderness and some eminent domain takings to create campgrounds. Outboard motors and country gravel roads providing river access became limited: unpopular changes for local residents. Gradually federal park administrators and locals have reached wary accommodations in part due to new revenue from tourism.

In 1989, a new proposal tested this uneasy understanding. A committee of U.S. National Park Service, Forest Service, and state conservation administrators decided to determine if the United Nations' Man and the Biosphere (MAB) Programme might work in the Ozarks. Mainly biologists, they had been attracted to the U.N. program in part because it offered a framework for increased scientific research as well as support for traditional, sustainable agriculture outside the core park regions. The Buffalo and the ONSR have similar riparian ecosystems and surrounding hill-based farming. The Ozarks produces most of the calves that eventually end up populating smelly Western feedlot operations.

Because I curated an agriculture museum and completed an oral history of 20th century farming's impacts on the Current River (see Part III), I became interested in MAB. For years, local people complained that the rivers were "filling up with gravel." Oral history was one tool geomorphologists used to examine this problem. Changing Ozark land use is best recorded in the region's collective memory. I appreciated local residents' strong feelings for the importance of rivers in their lives.

*   *   *

One of the most unknown, in the U.S. at least, cultural and environmental conservation efforts, MAB created, as of 1989, 440 Biosphere Reserves in 98 countries. (As of 2020, 124 nations have created 701 biosphere reserve projects.) No new reserves have been created in the United States since 1991.

Talking with Department of Interior land managers, I could see the potential benefits of the program. In 1988, I applied for an advertised position to conduct a public opinion survey on an Ozark biosphere reserve. My approach was to interview regional public officials and opinion leaders as well as inform interested citizens via local newspapers, meetings and a short video. The application was a lot of bureaucratic paperwork. The person who won the contract took the more traditional approach of focusing mainly on opinion leaders and promoting little public information.

This approach did not work. What the regional MAB committee feared might happen did happen. Long established networks of local people mistrustful of government programs in general heard of a "potential U.N. program" and fanned public fears with innuendo and half-truths. Public meetings were called to castigate federal and state bureaucrats. Some claimed U.N. "black helicopters" would transport noncompliant landowners to secret concentration camps. To put it simply, the MAB proposal created bad vibes that endure. A year or two after MAB was dropped, a Missouri effort to lessen duplication of federal programs, Coordinated Resource Management, met a similar fate. Again, tales spread of black helicopters carrying off private property defenders courtesy of the state Department of Conservation, a.k.a. the pesky game wardens. More recently, a landscape-scale restoration project in the Ozarks developed by a prominent NGO, The Nature Conservancy, had similar problems in regional public opinion.

"They never tried to build support for the project" seems the view of sympathetic conservationists on the short history of the Ozark MAB. The proposal appeared to be "a harmless bureaucratic idea a committee was trying to sneak under the radar, and because no one really knew what a biosphere was, no one saw any need to support it." Doomed from the start, MAB was never explained and ultimately helped fan latent Ozark xenophobia, which probably lurks in our Celtic DNA.

This was also the conclusion of a 1998 University of Missouri study on the proposed Ozark Highlands biosphere reserve. Carried out by Theresa Goedeke and Sandy Rikoon, their 100-page study concluded that neither Arkansas nor Missouri officials at any level of government developed interest or support for the MAB project.

* * *

Failure to understand the culture of the Ozarks has a long tradition. In the 1830s, one Eastern settler commented on his frustration hiring local people:

> I had always paid them as soon as the work was done, and I knew all they had to live on was daily wages, for they had not a foot of ground under cultivation nor a cow or pig or chicken. At last the man said, "No, we can't go today, it will storm by three o'clock." And they all walked back to the fire, and the old man took up his fiddle and began playing "The Arkansas Traveler" and as far as I could hear, that old fiddle was just raking out the music.

This memoir[1] suggests persistent perceptions of Ozarkers as lazy and unreliable.

The cultural divide between tradition-oriented groups and modernizers remains wide. Over time, the importance of private property rights and hunting to local people have added to these differences. Hunting and gun ownership remain important local rituals which outsiders have difficulty appreciating culturally or emotionally. The importance of the clan-based structure for Scotch-Irish families has been well documented.

Will a public agency in the United States ever again attempt to establish a biosphere reserve? The current political climate and budget shortfalls suggest that it may not happen soon. However, perhaps a significant segment of the public could demand such land-use management if these projects can be shown to offer great public benefit. Fewer than a dozen state and federal officials made up the committee led by the ONSR in 1989;

broad representation of many local officials would be necessary for future success.

Maybe we'll elect some environmentally responsive local officials before the Ozarks burns up like the West Coast. They say it can't happen here because crown fires are rare in deciduous forests, but I am truly spooked by what increasing global temperatures might mean for us. I lived through the infamous 2009 Ozark derecho and don't look forward to another climate catastrophe. Neither does Joplin, Missouri.

* * *

> I wonder if part of the reason I didn't get this job was basic confusion about what a biosphere is. After all, isn't there the futuristic Biosphere 2 out in the Arizona desert? Is the whole biosphere concept just too far out for the Ozarks?
>
> Probably also, I didn't win this job because my credentials weren't quite right. This is a problem all freelancers face. I learned over the years to apply for lots of possible positions and accept I will not win them all. The Ozark Highlands MAB sounded exceptional as a way to inspire research on our two states' national rivers. I just wish I had been a little more aggressive in applying for the job. It was won by the typical milquetoast approach. The Ozark Highlands MAB could have inspired new protection for Ozark traditions along our rivers. Now research in our National Parks remains minuscule. It shouldn't be.
>
> In 2009, long after the MAB went down in flames, a local chamber of commerce came up with a plan to establish a National Heritage Area in 13 Missouri Ozark counties. With support from the National Park Service, heritage areas had been established in unique historical regions all over the U.S. But not here! The Ozark Property Rights Council opposed it, stating on January 26, 2011, "This will be a gradual takeover of our area by the Park Service and its global goals." It never happened. One man got a broken arm at a public hearing for voicing his opinion.
>
> While an anti-government attitude and devotion to land rights are common in the Ozarks, to me, extreme fear of government can be unnecessarily paranoid. The rapid pace of change in our society makes everyone a bit nervous, especially in rural areas. Suspicion of government shows a skeptical outlook, which I share after my time in Vietnam. Yet, I appreciate people working together to protect and support what most of us agree is important.
>
> Biospheres are growing elsewhere. It takes a while for these new agreements and purposes to be worked out. For example, six years were spent developing an agreement between the Frontenac Arch Biosphere Network in Ontario, Canada, and the

Champlain-Adirondack Biosphere Network in New York state and Vermont. These two biospheres are united by geography and close ties in the Great Lakes and St Lawrence River watersheds.

Could concern about increased environmental degradation and global climate change result in support for programs such as biosphere reserves? In my interviews with Ozarkers, some have shown concern for less land available for hunting due to urbanites buying property and not allowing local uses to continue. Thus private property rights can "hollow out" traditional rights, a loss that long-time residents of this region rightly interpret as rural gentrification.

To be effective, a campaign for community conservation must show it respects local knowledge. Ozark people can determine who benefits in the long run from public projects and know their hesitation is often justified. More public discussion can result in change that local people understand and accept. Cultural rights, paired with respect for local heritage, forms a viable historic continuity.

Diverse users of our natural resources should be able to agree on some common ground for a shared, sustainable future of land, river and community. We all have to live here together; can't we respect one another? Could the failed Ozark biosphere reserve be just a misstep toward eventually realizing the full benefits of protecting sensitive rivers and wildlife?

Part VII

Profiles, Portraits and Champions
Likeness—Capturing an Essence

A year before being drafted into the Army, I spent two months at a summer school on a highland lake Down East in Maine. A serious art student at Colorado College, I won a scholarship to the Skowhegan School of Painting and Sculpture.

But Vietnam got in the way. Luckily I met talented folks and figured out how to benefit from that summer on my own terms. I did a lot of drawing, hitch-hiked to Monhegan Island with a friend one weekend, fell in love with a Maine girl, did my first oil paintings, and got to know the artists Elmer Bischoff, Larry Rivers and Mercedes Matter, who had recently started the New York Studio School and brought her favorite models to Maine. We could do all the figure drawing we wanted. Maybe about 60 students, we were all wowed by the surrounding landscape. We wanted to work and create every moment possible. But it was 1966. Hundreds of our generation were dying in Indochina every week, and we were dropping tons of bombs on innocent people.

Luckily a painter named Walter Murch was on the faculty that summer. He did meticulous paintings based on intricate scientific apparatus. I appreciated his quiet reserve, feelings for people and the unique objects that mattered to them. Named for his father, his son has become a well-known film director and editor. A man with that kind of steady focus helped me get through the 1960s too.

One other guy that summer also made a big impression: a fellow student named Richard Mock. As confronted many of us in 1966, the draft was breathing down our backs. Dick was living in Soho or the East Village then. He knew his city Selective Service Board would draft him immediately. Wisely he requested a transfer of his military induction physical to the Skowhegan draft board that summer. The night before this crucial medical exam he stayed up and drank a ton of coffee. As hoped, he flunked the test: 4F, physically unfit or something like that. Later I ran into Dick when he was involved with friends who made a film on the Winter Soldier Investigation about the Vietnam War. Dick became one of the renowned printmakers of our generation.

The painters I particularly studied did portraits, especially George Caleb Bingham, Paul Cézanne, David Hockney, and Alice Neel. I kept drawing after the military, but gradually writing has kept me more than intrigued. I learned a lot about perceiving details and structure from drawing.

These interests also developed from family influences. My mother had studied art as a young woman before becoming a housewife and active volunteer in worthwhile efforts. My father worked all his life in journalism, assisted the historian Samuel Eliot Morrison while in the Navy and had been friends with the writers John Hershey, William Burroughs and the activist David Dellinger in college. I was lucky in my direct and distant influences.

I was free to figure out on my own what to do, what kind of career to follow. Everyone has choices, but Vietnam was then an existential snag. Luckily my parents paid my college fees. I found summer jobs. Art seemed like a career that would eventually end up with some form of teaching. I couldn't follow that direction because the war in Indochina left me with too many questions. Luckily studying art helped me to step back, use Ben Franklin's moral calculus I learned about as an English major and trust in the Inner Light as Quakers teach.

The pieces below haven't appeared elsewhere because I started these out of pure fascination with no idea where they might be published. They are like drawings, exercises to see where they will go. These folks are doing something spectacular. They are artists in living on their own terms.

The war naturally led me into politics to try to understand how we could get so deeply involved in a terrible mistake. I still draw when I have free time because it's fun and helps me appreciate details of experience. I remember the painter Kenneth Callahan, one of the "Northwest Coast Mystics," saying that summer at Skowhegan to let personal style develop naturally. Don't rush in following current trends; find out what inspires you first, the market later. Good advice for most fields, except farming. Farmers got to know what people need first. That's real realism.

These appear here roughly in the order I've been able to dig them up in the wilds of my diverse files, still in recovery from recent relocations.

31

Healing the Waters on an Ozark Frontier

> Barbara Harmony came up with the phrase "We all live downstream" thirty years ago at the National Water Center that she helped begin. Her community must be one of the more dynamic, fun places in the Midwest if not the nation. Barbara helped make it that way.

* * *

Eureka Springs continues to attract an astonishing array of sightseers and pilgrims as it has for nearly 150 years, and millennia more considering the Native American heritage of Arkansas. This deep mountain valley in the northwest corner of the state lured Victorian era multitudes for healings credited to dozens of natural springs. The water's polluted now. You're not supposed to drink it, though some still do. The place has a spell; folks do wacky things here they don't do back home.

The town has harbored all kinds of cute, surprisingly elegant shops including one specializing in hand-stitched old-fashioned quilts. My friend Barbara Harmony said the quilt store in town now is not where she worked for a decade or so.

"We had a unique way of selling quilts. Our goal was to sell at least two or three full-sized quilts every day during the busy season," she explained.

I wanted Barbara to tell this story again when I visited the spring of the big floods, 2015. It's one of the best Ozark survival tales I've heard over the years. She was willing to go over parts of it, but Barbara's presence in Eureka Springs ranges wider than this tale suggests. Her life in the hills has become a true epic. The town inspires life on a grand scale, so individualists of all kinds can thrive here.

"The owner of our shop was very smart at marketing," Barbara said quietly. Always reticent, she did not want to go into details. This is what she told me in May: "Every winter the owner looked over the home decorating and style magazines to see what colors and themes were going to be 'in.' He knew the Mennonite community in the area and commissioned hundreds

31. Healing the Waters on an Ozark Frontier

Barbara Harmony helped to make the National Water Center a vital force in the Ozarks, and popularized the observation, "We all live downstream" (illustration by Anna Bolt).

of quilts to fit his designs. They had to be ready by spring. Forty quilts hung from the ceiling of our shop. Every summer and autumn tons of Texans come here to cool off. Dallas is only a few hundred miles away. I tried to be nice with everyone, we knew most of them were just looking and having fun with their girlfriends.

"But when one woman would bring in a man, we knew that was special.

"The sales bell was chiming! This is always a big purchase. This New Jersey girl knows how to sell quilts on a sultry afternoon in the Ozarks! It was fun and paid us all well. I worked there 11 years and my boss went on to develop a successful, fun business in Branson Landing."

This is another tourist hot spot in the Ozarks. There's a long tradition of poking fun and making money off tourists here.

When Barbara speaks now, she's much slower and more careful than when we met some 30 years ago. We were idealistic back-to-the-landers; she's still battling for the environment and has victories to recall. She also is dealing elegantly with disease, Parkinson's, which has slowed her down. Her mind and soul still seem broad as ever.

"I've been shocked to enter the pill world," she said with a laugh. "I need someone to help me make sure to take a certain pill four times a day. I had been too lax in the past, so I have to pay someone to remind me about this and help with other things. What a change from living alone out in the woods! I have embraced my old age."

She's my first friend to choose an assisted living residence. We're both War Babies, not Boomers, which may give us a slight edge. A priest told me once he finds two kinds of people in assisted living: the complainers, and the steadfast survivors. Barbara is steady, no rush about her. Barbara put up with my questions with dignity because she knew I would write something fair, maybe of use or inspiration.

"What has been your main employment besides selling quilts?"

"Oh, I've had lots of jobs. Many paid nothing," she paused to reflect. "Most recently, I have been an astrology reader and wedding officiant. People can be generous if the time is right."

* * *

The summer Bill Clinton won the Democratic nomination for president in 1991, the *Wall Street Journal* datelined its story from Eureka Springs and highlighted the then gay mayor's pink Cadillac leading a town parade. They knew how to sell newspapers. The *WSJ* naturally led a story about Democrats nationally with the "town where misfits fit."

"When I got here in '74," Barbara said, "within a week I had ten new best friends. This is a magic community!" She had just turned 21 years of age.

When I first visited Eureka Springs in the early '80s I couldn't believe the springs. Barbara and her friends were working to renovate the flowerbeds, making signs to tell the history and role of each and seeking to render the water drinkable once again. We had met earlier at a nearby bioregional congress, a gathering of inspired dreamers.

This city had an amazing vibe for a small-town daily newspaper reporter when first visiting. Eureka Springs had fallen on hard times because modern medicine in the early 20th century downplayed water-inspired therapies. Automotive-based tourism had bypassed Eureka Springs until the 1960s with its folk culture and music revival. Also, an associate of the late Governor Huey "the Kingfish" Long of Louisiana, Gerald L.K. Smith, brought his organizing skills to begin the annual outdoor

31. Healing the Waters on an Ozark Frontier

Passion Play, similar to one in Oberammergau, Germany. Mr. Smith is buried by one of the town's most prominent monuments, a huge Christ of the Ozarks statue, which hovers over tourist hordes from atop Mt. Magnetic. At 65 and half feet this sculpture is among the largest works of art in the U.S. This concrete Christ presides over Eureka Springs almost as a divine folk art god to assure peace reigns in this valley of health and healing.

In the 1960s and '70s, back-to-the-landers and hippies began migrating to the Eureka Springs area. The poet Frank Stanford[1] reportedly wrote sections of his epic poem *The Battlefield Where the Moon Says I Love You* at the New Orleans Hotel in the heart of the old business district, which twists up a ridge lined with restored Victorian architecture as colorful as the poet's sumptuous imagination. Staying in the weathered but wonderful lodging with Cath for a couple of days, I was knocked out to see on a third-floor bookshelf a copy of Frank's first chapbook, *The Singing Knives*. The small book has been reprinted in toto in the Copper Canyon Press's new expertly edited collected poems, more than 700 pages of mordant Ozarky murkiness. Clearly inspired by the poet's early days growing up in Arkansas levee drainage camps with his engineer father and an assorted crew of tough guys doing the grunt work, Frank's first poem in the 1971 collection ends:

> There was Jimmy
> He had the knife like night
> He was white
>
> I had the hands like dragonflies
> I killed one white man
> He was a midget
> I did it with a frog gig
>
> It was the summer of the Chinese daughter
> I danced on the levee

This was the end of the Vietnam War and all the craziness that the Doors, the Stones, the Kinks and other bands celebrated. As the work of Frank Stanford suggests, the Ozarks share these dark energies too, but Barbara was not attracted by frantic delirium. She has focused on herbs, water and healing.

Near the historic New Orleans Hotel, I vividly remember a spooky bar that offered the best rock 'n' roll in the Ozarks. I forget the name, but we happened to be there for its closing night long ago when the pub was packed, and the music echoed up and down the icy main drag with its slippery stone slab sidewalks. Harmonies yowled from the packed tavern like coyote calls in a dark hollow. So many incredible folks came out of the backwoods for this final party, it was nothing like Rolla, Missouri, a four-hour drive to the north. I'll never forget this one guy who had bedsprings twisted into his long locks and danced with anyone and everyone, man or woman.

It has long since become a t-shirt shop or something equally lucrative. Luckily there's still a great bookstore on Spring Street and lots of surprising art and crafts in numerous galleries all over Eureka Springs. But maybe not so much craziness.

One career has been surprisingly lucrative for Barbara. It has made her famous. She has worked as a fortuneteller at Basin Springs, the main park at the heart of Eureka Springs. She would sit on one of the benches surrounding the spring fountain with a politely worded sign and attract plenty of business. Honeymooners and families were natural customers. She has amazing rapport with people, true insights into what is driving them forward. She has also been an astrologer, group facilitator, non-denominational wedding minister, and community organizer.

My wife and I visited Barbara with both of our foster daughters in earlier years. Of course, she had good things to say about the teenagers, but she could see each as a unique individual with challenging pasts and futures. Not telling them everything she could see in their futures intrigued both girls as much as her accuracy for what she said about their character.

Our oldest still remembers Barbara predicted she would go to college. Thirty years later, Teresa graduated from college while working full time. She still recalls this prophecy.

Barbara's own son Ben, a law school graduate, has enjoyed a productive career in public service, and is the father of Barbara's first grandchild, a daughter named Harper.

* * *

What makes talking with Barbara Harmony such a pleasure? I like the way she makes no elaborate claims, no sense that she has saved the world or if that's even possible. Yet, she's totally committed to her life-long vision of health and balance. Having graduated from Goddard College in Vermont then working in Philadelphia and New Jersey as a social worker, she realized that she needed a change of scene when she found herself obsessing about parking places in the city. Luck brought her to Eureka Springs.

"I thought I was going to the southwest. That was my plan. But I came through the Ozarks. All these green hills just opened my eyes to something totally new. There were many people here committed to healthy lifestyles. Isn't this why Eureka Springs began a century ago?"

One of her early volunteer efforts developed alternatives to a large sewage treatment plant to be built near Lake Leatherwood, a city park. However, this is not just any city park. At 1,600 acres this is one of the largest municipal parks in the U.S. It also features a massive hand-cut stone dam built during the Depression by the WPA.

"Our campaign against the sewage plant and the problems with the municipal water system as a whole has been successful over the long haul," Barbara believes. "We haven't been able to deal with all the infiltration affecting our springs from leaky old sewage pipes, but we have seen people become more aware of these issues. We started the National Water Center in 1979 here. It's been active for decades and now has a dynamic new executive director.

"There used to be a 'flush and forget' attitude here as there is most other places. Now we are a part of the city government. The springs committee works with planners to protect our spring recharge zones. We live in a karst area. Most of the Ozarks is like Swiss cheese. If you have sewage systems that don't work, our soils here cannot clean effluent. The sewage from anywhere nearby will come up in our springs and easily ends up in people's wells and drinking water. That's what karst is all about."

She attended the 1995 U.N. International Women's Conference in Beijing; she remembers it as an amazing opportunity to connect with some of the 35,000 women attending.

"Most of the sessions were in English," she recalled, "but I wanted to get away from my national bias and learn what was happening elsewhere. The conference was often minimalized in U.S. media, but I think meetings like this helped women rise to leadership internationally. The number of female leaders around the world is a phenomenal change in my lifetime. And it is only going to improve."

* * *

She hasn't looked back. She's still surprised a New Jersey girl could thrive and harmonize with nature in the countryside around Eureka Springs. Her old house/cabin 10 miles out of town has a magic feel to it because she lived in the little place so long, saw clients there and kept gardening. Soon it will be passed on to a deserving person.

She's comfortable now at a small, assisted living center outside the historic downtown. She has her own room, and many of her books. Mostly Barbara has a lot of friends. She's on the phone, on the Internet and her website, talking with people much of the time. She even continues to consult as an astrologer and is available to officiate at marriages.

When l saw her a couple of months ago, she was sitting with a group of women. They were talking when Cathy and I came in. It made me think how in the end it's the women who are going to be the survivors, the longest lived and maybe the wisest. Men have a hard time getting old, as Tracy Kidder documents in his oral history *Old Friends*, about the last years of two gentlemen in an assisted living center where he too lived for a year to write this classic.

Barbara seems to have known how to slow down, how to accept change, how to value what is most important, every day, every season, all her life. She likes the small things. She doesn't dwell on herself or her accomplishments or her family. She must see the stars have aligned themselves right for her times.

—Autumn 2015, Eureka Springs, Arkansas.

> Barbara died in August 2020. Her family plans a memorial service once the pandemic has subsided and suggests friends honor Barbara's life by doing something kind for another person. Nothing could be a more fitting tribute to the life Barbara lived than making the world a little better even in the simplest of ways.

32

Organic More Than a Century

Frances "Nana" Yeary

> Friends urged me to visit Mrs. Yeary because she helped make her family farm one of the most beautiful along the Meramec River. Several of my friends have parents over a century old, but I hadn't actually talked with anyone over 100.
>
> Mrs. Yeary was remarkable for more than her age. She saw the Ozarks and Crawford County change and remained positive about much that she experienced.

* * *

Nana turns 105 years of age this July. She was born in 1910 in Bourbon then grew up nearby in Cuba, two Ozark landmarks along the old Frisco railroad.

Happy birthday, Mrs. Yeary!

Several friends urged me to interview Nana, as they all call her, so I will too for this communiqué. My friend Anne Jacobson, an artist who lives in Columbia, joined me in this Saturday visit on a sweltering summer afternoon. We are going to one of the most beautiful stretches of any Ozark river to see one of the loveliest ladies anywhere.

"If I had met her on a street in town or at a friend's house, I might have thought Mrs. Yeary was in her 70s or 80s," Anne said as we drove back to a friend's big ol' summer party outside of Leasburg. "Her skin was so fair and unwrinkled, but most of all her mind was bright and lively. She seemed to have so many interests and was so happy. I think we could have talked with her for two or three hours. She would have worn us out!"

Doing oral history projects for almost forty years, I'm occasionally told I ought to interview someone. Of course, I enjoy talking with different folks anywhere in the Ozarks, but usually it's not feasible. It takes time to do interviews right.

Most of all there has to be a reason to record someone and preserve a few of their stories. Now I'm bringing together interviews and profiles done over the years with excerpts of recordings.

Nana asked me right away why I was interested in this interview. She didn't want to waste her time. I told her about this book project. I assured her that she and family members could look over what's written and recorded to make sure it's fair and accurate.

I wanted to talk with Nana because I knew her son Milton when I was a reporter in Rolla. He was a mover and shaker in the farm community. He had an important job at the regional Production Credit Association but is now deceased. Also, I had floated by their farm on the Meramec and knew it was one of the most placid, beautiful stretches of this or any stream.

* * *

Driving over to Yeary Farm, Anne and I cross the Meramec outside Onondaga Cave State Park. The river has been flooding in recent days. I still remember the old wooden hog-trough bridge there, and then a metal replacement destroyed in a flood shortly after being installed.

Next we cross the concrete low-water bridge over Huzzah Creek around the bend from Onondaga. The scene at Scotia is total craziness: rattly school buses haul hundreds of canoes and floaters, mostly well lubricated and roasted pink by the hot sun. Rose Brown, who runs her famous late father's old canoe outfit, is directing traffic and laughing with the county sheriff deputies who help keep order.

It's neat to see so many young folks cavorting in wild water, but disconcerting too. Party time more than mellowing out on the rivers seems all too common. Craziness vs. calm, but I understand city folks need to hoot and holler on the river.

As we drive down the main drag into the old county seat of Steelville, Anne says her friends Merrill and David Horner, who run the venerable Dairy Isle and Grill downtown, said part of town had flooded earlier in the week.

"They are doing so great here," Anne said. "A dream come true for them. The Dairy Isle's open nine months a year; they get some vacation in winter. Steelville has a great local arts council and there's lots of music in town. They stay pretty busy with all the floaters coming on the weekend."

* * *

We continue ten miles west on Missouri Rt. 8, one of the oldest highways in the state and one route for the Trail of Tears through the Ozarks. All the activity of town and the floaters fades as we drive a mile down the old Yeary School Road. Everything's bright green. Not much hay cut yet because of all the rain.

32. Organic More Than a Century

This is where Nana came during the Great Depression to teach 22 children, first through eighth grades all in one room with a big woodstove in the middle. She was 18 and had recently graduated from high school herself. The bigger boys helped with the fire, but she did everything else.

At the bottom of the ridge a ranch house nestles in trees, shrubs and flowers mostly all in bloom. We knock and Nana answers. We talk over an hour.

"I met my husband here," Nana says at one point. "Milton Bonaparte. He rode by the school most every day on a big white horse. He was so handsome."

They were married after two years. She taught two more years in the Yeary School then helped manage the farm and raise their two children.

"We had just enough savings and credit to buy our 600 acres during the Depression. We didn't inherit anything but our good families. My grandfather Hertlein came from Germany when he was 14. My father was one of 14 children. He became a businessman and a miller in Cuba, which was such a busy place. I was the oldest of six kids. How I loved to see the men fire up the boilers in mornings for the steam engine at the mill! Then watch the shimmering white flour as it flowed down to be bagged."

Nana's stories flow like freshly milled flour. Just as shining, endless and eternal.

* * *

Behind us Nana points out above her couch a print by Jean-François Millet, the pre–Impressionist nature painter. It's one everyone may have seen, "The Angelus," 1858, one of the most famous paintings of rural life. Also known as "The Potato Harvest" or "The Blessing of the Crops," a young couple bow in prayer. Near their heavy wooden clogs a few potatoes they've managed to wrestle from the field rest on the furrows. This print sets a peaceful tone, especially for a country school packed with children.

"We had so many pie suppers. That's how I made a little extra spending money for supplies and bought this framed print for our school. So much fun! Milton could recite Mother Hubbard for the children. We had kerosene lamps, but I was able to buy a good propane lamp later on.

"You know we had some tough men working on the rivers back then, rafting railroad ties downstream. Once a whole bunch of them got liquored up and came to the school to see what was going on. I helped the children jump out of a window and run on home, they were so scared by those big men!"

* * *

As we talk I sense Frances has strong German characteristics, just as does my wife, Cathy, whose German grandparents farmed north of here on Little Tavern Creek in Maries County. They spoke German at home on the farm when they wanted a bit of privacy from their children.

This northern section of the Ozarks was heavily German. I remember once teaching a workshop in St. James, and the school librarian said that in the 1930s shops had to have at least one clerk who could speak German. Now it's rare to hear German in the Ozarks, except occasionally at parish picnics in places like Frankenstein, Hermann or Vienna.

Nana was born Frances Emma Hertlein, July 15, 1910, at Bourbon, Missouri, to Frederick Hertlein and Emma Katherine Biller Hertlein. In 1929 she was united in marriage to Milton B. Yeary. They had a daughter, Lorna Reasor, in North Carolina, and one son, Milton Frederick Yeary, who lived on the farm and passed away at 75 in 2010.

"I love the farm and all the land we have for its beauty and what it has brought us," Nana said. "My whole family manages it together, but I own it. We are lucky to all get along so well. I have trouble believing many of my great grandchildren have now graduated from college! That makes me feel a little ancient!" Nana says. Like their son Milton, who had five children, their daughter Laura also had five.

"Most of the family are like Milton," she says. "They love horses. I'm not so big on riding. I think it was sort of a Southern thing with my Milton. My job was to see to the cooking and do the books. I liked to see the numbers come out right. I was good at that! And good at doing the flowers too. I have been organic almost my whole life! When I grew up in Cuba, there were flower gardens and orchards everywhere. I still need to see flowers every day."

We get an idea of what a good administrator Nana has been when she tells us how she saved the library in town.

"The Odd Fellows lodge had given the town their brick building some years ago," she recalls. "It was a big old building. The library board voted to let the city use part of it too. After a while we needed more space. But the city didn't want us to have it.

"There was talk about the library having to shut down, then I went and looked up the deed. It said the library could use all the space that was needed to provide for an 'adequate library.' That was it, the city had to look elsewhere, not us."

A decade ago, the library did build a new building near the spring that attracted the first settlers and helped Cherokee survivors on the Trail of Tears.

As Anne and I say good-bye and thanks for our visit, a neighbor from the area drives down the hill in her pickup. She carries in Nana's dinner right on time. Everything is organized so she can maintain herself living alone in the ranch house overlooking the bottomland pastures.

32. Organic More Than a Century

"I love my family. I feel safe here. I wouldn't want anyone else here at night. There's plenty of help nearby. Sunsets here can last hours and hours."

> Nana's living room is neat and quiet with a few bookshelves, family pictures, artwork, antiques and a birdfeeder with one-way glass. We can see cardinals hopping onto a platform for sunflower seeds, but they can't see us. It's better than any television show. Mrs. Yeary died Saturday, October 10, 2015, at the age of 105 years.

Sidebar

Is It True?

> This was for Jim Bogan, who taught art history at the Missouri University of Science and Technology in Rolla. Besides organizing the university's free film series for many years, Jim has created a sculpture garden at Moonshine Hollow along the Little Piney and has written several collections of criticism and poetry.

You were floating down the Big Piney in moonlight summer night by yourself just lying down in a canoe. It must have been a gentle section of the river you knew well enough to put down an old quilt or something and stretch out, legs resting over the gunnels.

Only an occasional stroke of the paddle would keep the boat twirling downstream with the current and out of the backwater eddies. Over-hanging sycamores and big river birch play against the night sky, soft summer breezes, towers of bluffs silvered by moonbeams, bats circling, hoot owls echoing up and down river.

Was it easy to just drift through the riffles with katydids and whippoorwills singing? Did you feel as if you had found the Land of the Peach Blossom Spring and never would return to the troubles of the post-modern age?

Did you drift under a huge white oak where wild turkeys were roosting then hurdled into the night squawking and splattering your dreams with dark green droppings of the day's grasshopper harvest from fields and glades dappled through the river-hugging forest? Or is this just another one of those stories you hear around here?

—Summer, 1998, written near Ross Bridge, Missouri.

33

Visiting Moondog in Manhattan

> This memoir sketch helped me recall aspects of living in the East for a few years. I enjoyed Philadelphia, especially some of the small Quaker meetings in town and out in nearby rural areas.

Trouble sleeping this evening, having just read a review of "Moondog: On the Streets of New York."[1] I had a brief visit with the blind musician long ago when in the city. Many times in the early '70s I was able to hang out in the Big Apple.

I had a friend trying to break in as an artist. My father once invited me to join him on flying in the Pulitzer company plane to LaGuardia. One of my strongest memories is of saying good-by to dad once he had reached his midtown hotel and walking down to a subway for the Village on a pleasant winter afternoon.

"What are you smiling about Sunshine," a bummy-looking guy scowled at me. I had no idea that being a Midwestern rube may have been all over me.

Moondog was not that kind of old guy. He didn't look like a bum as he stood by a Midtown modern office building on Sixth Avenue. Wearing a cape and his Viking helmet, he had a sign asking for donations and some kind of instrument to offer a musical interlude. I forget what we discussed but he made an impression as a happy creative soul, not a freeloader, in the heart of the city.

Manhattan rang with creative energy then, before real estate became too expensive for young artists. I was on the board of Vietnam Veterans Against the War about this time and went to plan Dewey Canyon III.[2] Some of our members were making films about the war. Using a radical, minimalist approach, the most important film focused on the Winter Soldier Investigation, which let recent vets tell about horrific war crimes they had experienced. The sculptor Richard Serra and other artists were affiliated with the group.

My friend Charlotte from the Skowhegan School of Painting and

211

Sculpture had moved to Brooklyn. We had a deep connection, but I couldn't commit to any kind of a relationship because the war was still raging. Also, I hadn't developed a career and was undecided where I was going.

Another friend had moved to SoHo in lower Manhattan because his paintings began selling at the nearby Ivan Karp Gallery. A former assistant to the artist Ernest Trova in St. Louis, Richard Jouharian had discovered something totally new.

Richard used automobile enamel to spray abstract designs on one side of a clear vinyl sheet. Because he learned how different colors interacted, once the vinyl was stretched over a white canvas, incredible layerings of colored glazes seemed totally fresh because the viewer was seeing through a clear, shiny surface into vibrant designs. It was encountering an Ornette Coleman saxophone solo brought to life as a dazzling painting.

Richard was selling everything he could paint. Unfortunately, sudden success caused problems. Richard became paranoid. The Mafia wanted to kill him because his work would make their investments into other recent art worthless. His neighbors were fascinating: the artist Alan Saret, and a guy named Daffy who played loud music all night. But Richard lost his SoHo loft and never was able to get back his groove.

This didn't happen to Moondog. The recent review pointed out Moondog also had Ozark roots, from Batesville, Arkansas, also elsewhere in Missouri and Kansas, where he was blinded by an accident as a teenager. After high school he went to music school briefly in Memphis then on to New York, which harbored him until his Viking heritage led him to finally settle in Europe.

Eventually I lived near the city for a couple of years and occasionally enjoyed the downtown art scene. I remember hanging out at Max's Kansas City with Richard, hearing Susan Sontag hold forth at an opening, Gilbert and George from England doing a mysterious, ghostly performance and other boundary-pushing events. But I always had at the back of my mind getting back to Ozark folks and rivers. Everything else seemed like a sideshow.

34

Magic Quartz Near Mount Ida

> This visit occurred on a typical trip through Arkansas. Not hard to find something cool in Razorback land.

These mountainous ridges create rolling farmland where two-lane highways follow forest coves in twisty curves. We're behind a semi going slow across Arkansas.

All of a sudden, a big black pickup passes on our right going maybe 70 mph. Up a hill the highway breaks into two lanes, one for passing. The pickup roars by us, charges the semi on its blind side and sprays gravel back towards us from the ditch.

For a second it wobbles as if the driver has lost control.

Frightening. Close to losing control, he could flip his truck over the hill. Luckily, I tend to drive our new Chevy Volt slow to recharge the battery as much as possible. That and the semi creeping uphill must have angered the ol' boy.

We slow down even more. We're on our way to Texas on backroads. It's getting on toward dusk. Some folks get squirrelly and impatient, especially after maybe eight hours on the job.

I try to keep out of the way. I'm an old guy now. No rush to get anywhere this evening.

* * *

A filling station comes up on the right as we get close to town. Been driving almost two hours from Crystal Bridges Museum of American Art, founded by Walmart heiress Alice Walton.

Instead of gas pumps, this old service station has tables covered with mineral samples. Lots of bright crystals catch the evening light. I pull in to catch my breath.

A man comes out of a house next door. "Howdy," he says, "I'm Jay Manley, been hunting crystals most of my life."

We get to talking. This part of Arkansas is famous for all kinds of minerals. There's even a diamond mine in a state park where people often find valuable specimens.

"Lived out on the river 25 years," Jay says.

"You must have a few stories," I comment.

"Sure do. Four boys and four daughters. Boys are even better than this old guy at finding crystals."

Inside the former service station, counters and tables gleam with dazzling geometric shapes. We can't help ourselves. Too beautiful not to buy a few for gifts. We start looking as Jay tells us a few tales.

"My boys even sold a good load of rock to Alice Walton, who started that art museum up north of here. You know what that's called, don't you?"

"We had just stopped by," Cath said, "quite a collection, but no minerals on display."

"Well, the boys went to her house. Said she couldn't be any nicer. What a place, they said. Crystals everywhere! Never seen such a house...."

"People say Miss Walton knows a bargain when she sees it."

"Yes, the boys had a real good time at her place. Mighty nice sale. We had 74 folks at our house for that Christmas. A house full for anyone, especially us in Gibbsville!"

35

Selling Ties in an Early Blizzard

> I met Doyle Faubus in the late 1980s at the Shiloh Museum in Springdale, Arkansas, after I presented a program on the explorer Henry Rowe Schoolcraft. As the brother of former governor Orval Faubus and the youngest of three boys and four sisters, Doyle had poignant stories about growing up in rural Madison County during tough times.
>
> One story stuck. I've retold versions at several swapping events. Oral historian Roy Reed wrote that Doyle, who inherited his mother's voice and love of music, "would become a writer and singer of ballads and earn a local reputation as a singer."[1] He gave me a cassette of his songs, which is hiding out in my tape collection Cathy threatens to recycle any day.

* * *

Doyle Faubus lived with his folks way up near the White River in the wilds of the Boston Mountains in the deep Ozarks. Doyle had just graduated 8th grade in December 1932.

That was as far as most country kids went in school in those days. It was the hardest times of the Great Depression.

On a cold winter night a neighbor came by to ask Doyle if he'd haul down a dozen ties he had cut high up on Standley Mountain. They'd be worth $3 at the Pettigrew store. Doyle would be given a $1 pay to do the job and another dollar for use of his dad's pair of mules and big wooden wagon. Doyle said he'd do it. He was glad for the work. Not bad wages for a 14-year-old.

So at 6 the next morning he had the team hitched up and drove out of the farm yard in the early light. The ground was frozen, but his last piece of cornbread still warmed his belly. The road went up past Greasy Creek School then followed uphill.

By 9 a.m. he had the wagon waiting in a clearing and the two mules hitched to the tongs so he could skid those 200 lb. ties out of the brush where they had been cut. Just before dinner time he had found all dozen ties and wrestled them into the wagon.

Turning oak and other hardwood timber into railroad ties with a crosscut saw and axes was a major industry in the Ozarks after the Civil War into the Great Depression and beyond (illustration by Anna Bolt).

35. Selling Ties in an Early Blizzard

Doyle had a bacon grease and cabbage sandwich for his noon-time dinner, then started down the trail. It was warming up. The ice in the ditches was starting to melt, so he had to be careful to keep up on the high part of the road. All of a sudden, he felt the wagon skid a little and slide into a ditch. Then there was a sucking noise and he felt the mule pull hard, but there was a loud "snap" and the wagon stopped dead.

Several spokes had broken in a rear wheel in a frozen mud hole. Doyle at first didn't know what to do. He could look across the valley from where he sat and saw the farm of old friends way across on the other ridge.

It was early afternoon when he got his team unhitched and rode the two mules several miles over to this other farm. "You can use our wagon for the day for $.50," the farmer said. Doyle said that was more than fair.

The sun was dipping close to the ridge when he finally reached where his father's wagon had broken down, drove up around it and backed down so he could more easily load the 12 ties into the borrowed wagon. Snow was coming.

When he started down the trail the sun had fallen behind the ridge. The ditches were freezing. Doyle went as slow as he could; he couldn't break down.

Dark had nearly fallen when he left Greasy Creek Road and got on the main state highway along White River. He had to go slow onto the side of the highway; the team might slip on the icy pavement. Finally, he got to the Pettigrew general store. A kerosene light was on. The man had stayed late for him.

Doyle thanked him for waiting. He was glad to get that $3 for the load of ties. Luckily he had brought along a little sack of corn to feed the mules something at the end of their long day. He remembered what his father said.

Just a few days before he'd been out hunting with his dad and shot a squirrel. His old hunting dog was so hungry that he didn't bring the squirrel back like he had always done before. The dog ran into the bushes to eat that squirrel. His family had to have cornmeal mush again for dinner that night, almost like going hungry. His father was very embarrassed.

So Doyle was careful to take care of those mules he had left tied up by the hitching post. He brushed the snow away from the frozen grass to pour out the shelled corn. Back by the hitching post he noticed a little green paper. It was a dollar bill. Doyle brushed the ice off the money and took it back into the general store.

"Some of them old drunk tie hackers must have dropped the note when they were in here a day ago," the owner said. "Why don't you keep it? You found it!"

Doyle said he appreciated that. The dollar would go to repair the wheel on his father's wagon and help pay for part use of the neighbor's wagon. If he was lucky he might be able to keep half of the dollar the neighbor had promised him. Doyle said it had been a good day to end up with a piece of good luck like that.

> This story is not oral history. It is based on Doyle Faubus' recollections, but I shaped it for each audience, once at the Swapping Grounds at the National Story Telling Festival in Johnson City, Tennessee. Storytelling seemed like a natural outgrowth of collecting local history.

36

A Man Who Loved Copperheads

Ken Carey

> This profile describes an Ozark visionary whose writings won praise from Ram Das, Elisabeth Kübler-Ross, Marianne Williamson and other New Age healers.
> The Ozarks often receives attention for militant militia and other anti-government groups. But independent, environmentally inspired dreamers have been attracted to our region for centuries. One of the first was Daniel Boone. Their varieties are fascinating. This profile is just one of many that could be done on Ozark visionaries, though, aren't most of us visionaries to some extent?

* * *

Ken Carey always stirred strong feelings. Still full of celestial harmonies yet reclusive in his last years, he formed a powerful presence for me and many others inspired by his books. He created the Greenwood Forest Association, an early land trust in the Midwest, a project that has grown into a community of about 1,000 acres and a score of households directly involved.

Maybe now is the time for Ken's message to be heard. His vision for a new ecological millennium seems prophetic and necessary as we approach the winter of 2020:

> Toward the last days of the historical era it may come to pass that a few fearful cities will be quarantined, that in these places, certain dramatic presentations might take place.

This is from page 30 of the second edition of Ken's 1995 *Vision: A Personal Call to Create a New World,* published by Harper Collins.

Not many folks were talking about quarantines back then. While not mentioning pandemics, Ken Carey's vision seems more relevant now.

His introduction explains that this 90-page text came largely through channeled transmissions or a mystical experience such as the 16th-century Spanish poet and priest St. John of the Cross popularized in literature. Ken Carey's visionary experience first occurred in 1978 while he was recovering from a fever and "drifted into a calm, meditative silence," he explains in the introduction to the book. He slowed down on his carpentry work to write his first book, *The Star Seed Transmissions*, in eleven days. Others followed. He says his inspiration came from help of intermediary forms of intelligence, which he refers to as "informational beings." These voices speak to him directly and form the basis of *Vision* and other writings.

Usually such material may seem overboard or bizarre. Ken's book sat gathering dust on a shelf for many years; I just picked it up in the process of revising what I had written about him earlier. A few minutes ago, on this lovely autumnal afternoon of October 8, 2020, six men have been arrested and charged with an attempt to kidnap Michigan Governor Gretchen Whitmer while plotting to attack the state capital with 200 armed men. Our current pandemic has inspired a rash of "dramatic presentations," as Ken describes, which may yet, "stimulate the required change of heart. Hopefully, this will not often be necessary. If you help me now in the work of education, it may not be necessary at all," as he continued this passage.

A change of heart and education seem to be a basic message in all of Ken Carey's writing and teaching. Maybe now with 4 million acres burned this year in California, an almost equal amount last year in Australia, and more than 1 million killed by the pandemic, maybe this is the time for some healing as called for by this Ozark visionary. What may have seemed over the top millennialism, now appears necessary if the world will continue to add billions in population and trillions in national debts. What follows gives some background to Carey's life and teaching.

* * *

Ken's memorial on a gorgeous mid–May weekend in 2017 brought together a diverse crowd of a hundred or so Ozarkers and others to the farm where he and his wife raised seven children. Everyone seemed to glisten as if transforming into heavenly beings in late spring golden sun.

A potluck, square dance, concert and computer-based photo-remembrances of Ken's life ended with a burial of ashes. All his children participated at the farm neighboring the land trust. Maybe the only oversight was a flaming Viking warship to float down Flat Rock Creek, rather than a handcrafted wooden urn, to see Ken onto his berth in the heavens.

Mr. Carey had a robust avatar side to him. He wrote several spacey books which I tried to read, but these went way over my grits-clogged chakras. One of his last books seems a whole other kind of parable. Check out *Flat Rock Journal: A Day in the Ozark Mountains* on GoodReads.com. Not everyone likes it, but lots of people are still reading it, which is amazing for a long-ago, 160-page memoir. One day in the author's life becomes a natural history epic that received little attention when Harper & Row snuck the new release into bookshops with scant fanfare.

The *Kirkus* review in 1994 called *Flat Rock Journal*, "a model of moss-velvet nature writing, quite possibly a classic." With its author's passing it seems time to anoint it a true classic, one that needs to be reprinted. Appropriately the author's final resting place is in a rock cairn near the highlands over the creek he immortalized and helped preserve.

During the sunset memorial circle many shared memories. I spoke to recall reading how the Careys left a nest of copperheads to grow under their home out of respect for native wildlife. This was the one major aspect of the book that stayed with me for some 30 years. So many other books I've totally forgotten. *Flat Rock Journal* still has a powerful aura.

Everyone had wildly different stories and memories of Kenneth Xavier Carey at his memorial. There was lots of laughter in that circle of family and friends.

I was most impressed by his oldest son Bill who produced a limited-edition CD of 19 songs Ken wrote and then performed in various local venues. Thirty of the discs were given away during the afternoon, and Bill and his brother Pat are working on preserving more of their father's music.

"Ken had been working on a new book, but no one knows much about this yet," said Patrick Houser, an old friend, writer and jack-of-all-trades, who drove up from Austin, Texas, for the weekend event. "His ex-wife Sherry has the material and many people are curious what this work might be.

"His last years were tough. Bad health, divorce from Sherry, a pacemaker and a quadruple bypass. He had some loss of brain function, painful arthritis. It even was hard for him to get dressed. I wasn't too surprised when I learned in March he suffered a fatal heart attack while living alone in West Plains public housing."

Nearly 40 years ago I had a chance to interview this carpenter and environmental hero of the Ozarks. His work impressed me at the time, but I moved on, and didn't know how his plans developed. Then ten years ago I met Ken Carey again. Things were changing for me. I remembered I wrote about Ken's plans as they were developing. This is part of my long-ago article:

Man Develops Unusual Plan to Save Forest

By Alex Primm of the [Rolla] *Daily News* Staff; 12/20/1979

MOUNTAIN VIEW—Looking for an unusual Ozarks-related Christmas present, and money is not a consideration?

Three families near here have developed an innovative real estate scheme—to use a word they would not—but a deadline of February 6 threatens to kill the project before it can get off the ground.

The project calls for 600 acres bordering the Ozarks National Scenic Riverways, on the upper Jacks Fork, to be broken into approximately 20 small parcels with most of the land, about 450 acres of forest, to be owned in common as a forest preserve.

"As best we know this has never been tried before," said Ken Carey yesterday on a tour of the property. He is a carpenter and strong-willed individual who is devoting most of his time these days to what is officially called The Greenwood Forest Association.

As he talks, Carey looks the part of the stereotypic "environmentalist": young, longish hair, plaid work shirt, jeans with holes and utter sincerity.

But his opinions don't quite fit the stereotype.

"In the last few years there's been a lot of talk about wilderness," he said. "I've got nothing against setting aside a certain amount of wild land, but our preserve won't be a wilderness. We probably will decide that a certain amount of the land held in common can be thinned and cut every year."

When asked about his background, Carey declined to say how old he is and if he went to college or not.

"That kind of information just categorizes people," he said. "It's not important. What is important is reaching the right people, purchasers and donors by the middle of January."

Carefully Selected Missouri

Carey did say that he and his wife moved to their homestead in 1973 from California after extensive research on climate, proximity to nuclear power plants and other features. The choice narrowed to Nova Scotia, northern Minnesota and here. The mild climate made the difference, he said.

However, the main selling point for the project, according to its promoter, is that the purchasers will have access to and control of some 450 acres of beautiful land. They will also know that others who purchase property from the association share at least a certain degree of appreciation for natural Ozark forest. Restrictions on deeds to individual lots will limit timber clearing to 40 percent of the lot, prevent use of firearms or hunting (because of children), specify non-polluting, composting toilets be used and that most utility lines be underground.

Two Options Available

Two options are available for those who want to purchase land from the Greenwood Forest Association, a not-for-profit organization. These are five-acre tracts for $8,500 and 10-acre parcels at $12,500.

"We don't have anything against cutting timber or logging," Carey said. "We just feel that this particular piece of property can be better used by people for recreational homes or residences. The land is bordered by the federal scenic river, a Missouri Teachers' Association summer camp and smaller private owners.

"It has numerous springs and two year-round flowing streams. There are caves and a 10-acre sinkhole pond which has several rare and endangered plants. Most important though is that we are showing that average people, without the government or major foundations, can both save and use beautiful land."

* * *

Greenwood Forest in 2020 and Beyond

One fascinating thing about Ken Carey's vision for our land trust is that it follows the same ideas he and friends developed in the late 1970s. What he called for in the interview above has all been realized. More land has been added to the project over time; more people have become involved.

Of course, many folks have moved on. Ten acres along rocky Ozark ridges has proven a nearly impossible place to raise a family much less a worthwhile garden or to try to farm on just 40 percent of your cleared ten acres of land.

Several persistent growers have nevertheless created amazing green spaces. Families have raised a talented new generation. Over almost 40 years, Greenwood has created a compelling micro-history.

Probably the most important feature involves the land trust becoming a diverse, vibrant community. An opposite tendency would have been lots gradually being bought up by wealthy folks from urban areas who visit occasionally on weekends and holidays. That could be GFA's ultimate fate, but several trends keep diversity healthy.

The strongest core of the community is that half-dozen households are occupied full-time by a collection of intelligent people who don't mind getting their hands dirty. Some of these are professional folks, often teachers and counselors; others make a living doing various manual jobs. All have something of the dreamer or the loner in them. Most are comfortable with a chain saw.

You may be a bit touched to live 12 miles from a town of 2,000 plus three miles further out on a gravel road, which washes out regularly. Cathy and I lived in these woods for three years, but finally she said, "The ticks and chiggers are driving me nuts. And not having air-conditioning has done me in." Though now we're basically part-timers, I still appreciate the forest as endlessly fascinating and challenging. We have 300 watts of solar power and all the water we can haul from a community well.

"People were so great when we moved in after we sold our Rolla house in the Great Recession of '08," my wife Cathy recalled as we recently discussed our tenure in the woods. "My mom had just died, and we had a few weeks to move out of Rolla. We stored things in people's barns and sheds, there was a welcoming party. Every Friday night Debbie Larson had a soup supper and invited everyone who was in the woods to share, especially wine and opinions."

"But things really changed after the tornado of May '09," Cathy said. "That was a defining event for us and GFA."

The storms changed everything for the land trust, surprisingly not all for the bad.

The basic facts can be found in a Wikipedia entry on the May 2009 Southern Midwest Derecho. It is defined as:

> An extreme progressive derecho and mesoscale convection (MCV) event that struck southeastern Kansas, southern Missouri, and southwestern Illinois on May 8, 2009. Thirty-nine tornadoes, including two of EF3 strength on the Enhanced Fujita Scale, were reported in addition to high non-tornadic winds associated with the derecho and MCV.

The end of the entry shows the federal government provided several billion dollars to help rebuild affected regions across four states. (Illinois and Iowa suffered an MCV event earlier in 2020 with even greater losses.)

What this storm meant for Greenwood involved thousands of trees dropped or torn out of the ground in a few seconds that May 8 morning. Luckily, Cath and I had a basement where we could take shelter as trees smashed into our roof, solar collectors and Prius car. No loss of life

36. A Man Who Loved Copperheads

occurred in this sudden, un-forecasted event across the Southern Midwest uplands.

Trees across our gravel roads made travel impossible for days.

Immediately after the wind and rain stopped, each family crawled out into the eerie silence, fired up chainsaws to go find out who suffered and clear our roads, basically old logging trails following ridge tops. If you didn't cut toppled tree trunks, you hauled cut branches back into the woods. One family offered their home for lunches. We shared food, gasoline and showers where possible.

People really got into helping one another. Bill Echols, the solar carpenter/architect who built our cabin, spent three days cutting his way in to help us and others.

Many neighbors came into Greenwood to help us clean the roads. We can never repay this, just pass on the spirit. When disaster strikes, drop everything to help!

I still remember going down Bear Ridge Road riding on the bucket of a friend's tractor hoisted all the way up. I had to reach as high as possible with the chainsaw to cut blown down tree limbs while avoiding my own. Not OSHA-approved, but necessary.

This storm-spawned spirit of helping one another translated into another aspect of Greenwood's recovery over time.

For the first time in decades, a forest committee went to work to develop a forest management plan. Many Greenwoodies had been committed tree-huggers: let nature take her course, she will heal past wounds as the forest naturally restores itself. We agreed to be more proactive in management. (Our region had been commercially logged during the Ozark timber boom of the early 20th century.)

Luckily, we were able to find consulting foresters who helped us develop plans and goals for all the different forest conditions within Greenwood. Everyone agreed we had to harvest more as most red oak species have relatively short life spans. Native Ozark Shortleaf Pine does not regenerate well without bare ground and some disturbance to allow pinecones to spread their seed into soil.

Our goal is a sustainable, selective harvest of about 20 acres a year to recreate resettlement conditions. We have more designated days to work together to improve the forest.

As a result of active forest management, personal feuds seem less common. No one is building fences, so they don't see their neighbor, as happened in the past. There are no freaky types living in the woods as in the early days. For example, the ancient history of Greenwood includes one resident who flashed floaters from bluff tops above the river.

I've heard some local residents complain that Greenwood has taken away access to the river that folks used to enjoy. But most Greenwood landowners seem willing to invite local people to use the river access if they call and ask. This is rarely done, however, as the closest access is a rough walk through tick territory, a mile or more.

Management of the Ozark National Scenic Riverways has had little effect on the land trust. We don't allow ATVs to go down to the river. We protect the federal land as much as we do our own.

* * *

Following the May 9 Derecho, Ken Carey joined the forest committee and tried to help where he could. He occasionally joined some of us for Quaker meditation or music jams. His energy seemed low, but it was clear he still cared for Greenwood.

At his memorial weekend, Sherry told me Ken always regarded the land trust as his finest accomplishment. Both he and Sherry spent hundreds of unpaid hours to get word out about their vision. While such lengthy effort is no longer necessary, many on the board and the forest community volunteer to keep the project running smoothly.

There are many collective social events. Parties and potlucks happen many weekends. Jim Ryan has been teaching square dancing. Some guys have camped out in the woods to learn primitive skills and howl at the moon. River floats are a regular Greenwood activity.

For a decade one couple has hosted a Martin Luther King, Jr. Day weekend memorial party and peace celebration. This year local musicians resurrected a song, "Leaves and Moss," that Ken Carey wrote.

We all sang with awareness that the songwriter had paid his dues and left us with a legacy that we must protect and grow. Will others be more proactive to protect forests everywhere? Will the pandemic teach us anything? Will we learn new respect for nature and wildlife? Is this a time to look for new visions to inspire necessary change?

—Mountain View, Missouri, October 2020

37

An Ozarker in His New Kentucky Home

George Marshall Smith

> Visiting Louisville, Kentucky, during its famous Derby the first weekend in May 2016, Cathy and I enjoyed a bourbon-infused weekend with old friends. We had a calm time, with a surprising highlight: meeting a local doctor who said her father had grown up in Puxico, Missouri. She has only visited the town a few times, but said her father had great memories of growing up in this historic Ozark community.
>
> "He loved growing up there," she said. "And he was part of that famous basketball team."

* * *

On the Sunday after the Kentucky Derby 2016 as things in Louisville quieted down, Cathy and I cruised to a nearby apartment complex to meet George Marshall Smith and his wife Wilma. It's not often you have a chance to visit with a native of Puxico. There's only one Puxico in the world. The logging boomtown began in the late 1800s, but that's about all I knew before our visit.

"Call me Mark. That's what everyone calls me. Actually, I wasn't on that famous basketball team. I was on the B squad," Mr. Smith said. "My twin brother was on the starting team that won the state championship."

I'd heard bits about this team over the years. His senior class had some 70 students, Mark said. Their gym was made from logs. The town's also unique because it's on the eastern edge of the Ozark mountains near Swamp East Missouri, one of most wild, bodacious parts of the Midwest.

"My father was a wonderful businessman. He owned 13 farms near Puxico at one time, often just buying them for the timber. We were a family of seven brothers, no sisters. We all had to work all the time, especially my mom.

"She was a miracle worker and quite a lady. She had gone to a finishing school and had a cook when we lived in Alabama, but when dad moved us to Puxico all refinements were limited. She cooked and took care of all of us boys. If anyone did anything wrong, he wouldn't eat, get any laundry done, or have a place at the table until he apologized and changed his ways."

Mark helped his bothers run fish traps in the nearby Mingo swamp, now a national wildlife refuge, among other chores as a boy.

"They were wire and wood traps with three interconnected chambers. Fish can't swim backwards, so I could reach in the third zone to pull out any catfish we needed. Once a water moccasin crawled into the boat. I grabbed our shotgun, blew him away but that boat quickly sunk. Never did that again."

* * *

The Puxico team toughened up by logging and farming all summer. That was part of their secret, Mark said: top conditioning. The more he talked, the quicker the words flowed as he relaxed back in his comfortable armchair. Most of his friends and family had heard these tales; to me it was a world of wild frontier living. The words flowed, he hardly paused, and his eyes grew large as his spoke. Most older gentlemen are more reserved, but Mark has so many good memories he just moved from one story to another as William Faulkner wrote in his epic novels.

"How big was that gym?"

"To us it was a castle, one of the biggest buildings in town with big double doors and operating windows above the bleachers. The ceiling was maybe 40 feet high, but its floor was just a little bigger than a regulation court. We had to have mats on the walls at either end so anyone doing a lay-up wouldn't crash into the logs and get hurt."

Built by the community and the federal Works Projects Administration during the Depression, the gym also had a stage for school programs. The basement held the heating system and a kitchen. Lunch was served on the court during school days. It burned down by accident long ago, as did the WPA log school and railway depot, but the log library is still standing and used by the town.

* * *

How good were the Run-Shoot-Run Indians? The year—1951—they won that state championship: 40–0. Most games were won by huge margins.

Not only did they have an amazing record, the Puxico boys changed the way basketball was played everywhere.

You can read about them on the Internet: totally amazing even for marginal hoop fans. Mark's twin, Astie Welborn "Leb" Smith, was a starter for all four of his high school years and was named to the All-State team for each of four years. The record for those teams? 149–10. Nice to start off life as winners.

37. An Ozarker in His New Kentucky Home

What was it like to be in that high school then?

"To us it seemed the whole town was part of the team. Everyone got involved, stores closed early if it was an away game. Lots of our home games were actually played at other schools' bigger gyms because we couldn't hold crowds coming to every game. Harry White's drug store stayed open late so the team could have burgers and shakes afterward," Mark recalled.

"One Friday afternoon a neighbor's mule walked up to the high school. He came in a back door like he belonged. Some of the boys closed the door. He stayed in all weekend, eating textbooks and leaving his calling cards up and down the hall. They never found out who did that."

* * *

Mark died in March 2018 and remained a Puxico Indians fan. The town was named by historian/entrepreneur Louis Houck for Pucksicah, a Shawnee tribal chief who had lived in this area.

38

Clyde and the Recycled Chairs

Cathy means well, sometimes too much. She and our friend Cay picked up two old lawn chairs some neighbor had pitched.

"Rebuild or recycle!" Cath said proudly after lugging this plunder to our bungalow in Rountree.

Luckily, I had the sense to see this as "not my job." It's someone else's. Someone who needs cash. For me it would result in levels of frustration. I'm not so great at working with rusty metal, though I did a great deal of this kind of work at the agriculture museum. I'm almost as big on recycling as Cay and Cath.

The newly rebuilt chairs will make everyone happy whatever the price. How complicated and costly can a few coats of paint and plastic seats be?

* * *

I won't go into all the calculations, only aspects offering some levity, some enduring inspiration. I just wrote off the money, a big step.

The first blacksmith I knew said the chairs were rusty junk, the metal's rotten out, save your $$ and buy new chairs.

This is where Clyde comes in. He's the kind of blacksmith who takes pride in doing everything, even the simple challenge of bending metal to match another piece. A friend told me about him: three tours in Afghanistan.

* * *

Every week for over a month I went by. His shop is near the old Springfield downtown airport in a neighborhood Clyde watches closely. He likes talking, showing off his work, no rush. Whenever you can get to it, I said. Once a neighbor stole his prize-winning Chihuahua. It didn't take Clyde too long to figure out where she went. Some neighbor.

The next day he went over and demanded the dog back. "If you ever do that again, I'll kill you," Clyde told the woman. Three tours in hell.

"The other night a cat jumped on my car hood, had me reaching for

230

38. Clyde and the Recycled Chairs

my rifle when I finally realized I was back stateside, and I turned off the light."

After several visits he had put together some pieces of old tubing to make our chair back. He said it would be $35. I said I only had so much cash and could write a check. He said that $27 in greenbacks would be good enough.

* * *

It's been a year since I've seen Clyde. I stopped by yesterday. His place is all cleaned up. A sign out front, "FOR RENT," and a phone number which I called.

"Clyde just left out over the winter," claimed the landlord. "Clyde said I could have all the tools and everything inside. It's a mess. The city got on me to clean up outside and get all the old metal hauled away."

What are you looking for to rent the place?

"The shop was $300, and the house next door was $500 a month. It was great for him and his wife, very convenient."

He really did like the place, something must have blown up for Clyde, the landlord and I agreed. Not like him at all to leave so quickly.

Clyde—not his real name—kept some kind of pellet gun by the shop door and an old rusty lawn chair out front. He'd shoot starlings. Didn't like them at all. It seemed almost like some kind of recreation from the old days to sit there and blow away those noisy birds.

I was going to invite him and his wife over to see how our recycled chairs turned out once painted. But his old landlord has no idea where Clyde could be.

"Give me a call if you find him. Just like to talk with him."

—Springfield, Missouri, March 2016

39

Woodcarvers
Harold and Elaine Enlow

> Today was going to be extremely productive thanks to a well-organized list of errands. I got delayed like a Frisco freight caught behind a milk run.

* * *

I ran across a convention of carvers who had filled the Springfield Knights of Columbus parking lot with their trucks and RVs from Texas to Canada, Pennsyltucky to Colorado. John Engler, an expert carver from Branson, organized the gathering.

Cathy had a coupon that would be good for a catholic lunch at this spot. Instead, it became a chaotic end to my errands. No lunch today, almost.

Inside the hall hundreds of productive crafters buzzed like a nest of baby rattlesnakes. There were some reptile carvers on hand. Lots of fuzzy critters created as well. Cowgirls and mountain men. Pigs. Hillbillies. Horses. Etc.

Most of all, Santa Claus. No Trump or Obama figurines. Nothing off color or over the top weird. Just lots of fat men with white beards and red jackets.

At long folding tables the carvers worked and gouged, chatted and listened to the experts who offered classes. All seemed productive folk who focused on learning new techniques from each other while building up their inventories for upcoming summer craft shows and visiting grandkids.

The first person I met while wandering the aisles was Elaine Enlow, who had grown up in nearby Nixa. What a smile Elaine has! She and her husband Harold, a native Springfieldian, have lived many decades about 100 miles due south in Marble Falls, Arkansas.

"Our town had another name," Elaine said. "Dogpatch."

Wow, everyone's heard of that!

"Really it was called Wilcox in the olden days," she said like a historian bent on accuracy. "It was halfway between Jasper and Harrison, so people

39. Woodcarvers

used to stay over for the night because it was such a long trip in a wagon. Then it became Marble Falls, for our beautiful waterfall.

"Then some investors got the idea of creating Dogpatch, a theme park based on the cartoon strip. It did pretty well for a while. They even changed the town's legal name. That's where Harold and I had our craft and wood carving shop. It did well for a while."

I had to ask, "Did you ever know Orval Faubus?"

Roy Reed's great biography of the late Arkansas governor describes him ending up as a ticket-taker at the theme park.

"Oh yes. He was a nice guy. So friendly with everyone. People really enjoyed him and his pretty young wife."

What finally happened?

Harold had come into the booth as we talked and listened in.

"The investors got greedy and squabbled," Elaine said. "The place began going downhill. They tried to sell and ended up going broke."

"It was tragic," Harold said. "The place eventually closed up. We had to abandon our shop, then I think some squatters must have gotten into it. Our place and two other buildings burned down. The whole place is a mess now.

"Some investors from California supposedly bought it, but they haven't been able to do much to get it going again."

I sympathized, thanked them for visiting and went on the prowl for dinner. Sitting at a bar waiting to order something, I asked a fellow how the food was.

*   *   *

"Here, you can have half my billy beef," the man said. It smelled terrific. How could I turn that down?

We started talking. Great barbecue; thanks, David Gulley! I owe you one. It turns out David's a student at the gathering and a retired coal miner from southern Illinois. He took time to show me his work on several Santas based on a pattern his instructor had developed. He also demonstrated several carving tools Harold Enlow had made from band saw blades, umbrella supports and other recycled hard metals.

"Harold is like the grandfather of all us carvers," David said. "He not only hand makes quality tools, he carves, writes books and can draw like a real artist."

That got me thinking. Carving like this is a true craft. I learned it has roots in Scandinavia and traditions that go back generations. Many of these carvers are carrying on what they learned from grandparents. The goal is not creative original designs but assembling three-dimensional design to delight. The more I watched David carve, the more I could see it's not all that easy. I went back to look at more of the Enlows' work.

*   *   *

"I do the painting," Elaine explained. "Harold does the carving. I also help with the books. This is how we've made our living for forty years."

Junior Cobb, the great deceased carver from Three Brothers, Arkansas, was one of their friends.

"Junior used to bring his whole family to Silver Dollar City when we were working there," Elaine remembered. "People loved him; he was such a natural storyteller!"

I couldn't help but notice a basket of antique, wood-handled kitchen tools for sale nearby. Each had a tiny smiling face carved into its grip. I couldn't decide on buying a handmade tool, something for our kitchen or gifts. Maybe later? I had to get a handle on these craftspeople. They inspired me.

These must be some of the most successful of my generation, the Depression and World War II Babies. They get to travel and do something they love. The longer I was in the room, skipping my errands, the more I wanted to whittle myself.

Then Burley Henson came by. He's another of the Enlows' carving buddies. Burley said he has worked 32 years at the local Olive Garden as a dish washer and rides his bike everywhere. Doesn't own a car. He pulled out a chunk of wood he has been sculpting into an Indian chief.

"I've been doing the MS 150 bike ride lately," Burley said. "Not bad for a 62-year-old guy. I paint, crochet and carve. The Enlows got me going and I haven't stopped since."

That reminded me of my errands. I wanted to get home, grab my bike and peddle by Drury University to hear Dr. Brandy Schillace give a talk for the state humanities council. Medical ethics, cloning, artificial intelligence, tech dread and steampunk, topics maybe not removed from shaping tree parts into living memories.

—Springfield, Missouri, Winter 2018

> Dogpatch made the 2020 news: Springfield entrepreneur Johnny Morris has purchased the site and has big plans for the place, none revealed as of this writing.

Memoir

Portrait of my Father as an Eminent Hillbilly: A Cautionary Tale

> When I was growing up my father was a god who survived naval battles in the Pacific, swung corporate business deals and identified migrating warblers. He saved me from having a tracheotomy when I was five or six with a chicken bone caught in my throat. By telling me stories about an Indian boy named Rookie, he calmed me down so the physician was able to dislodge the obstruction. As I age, I realize it was not easy living in the shadow of a distant sovereign.

* * *

Befitting his classical name, A. Timon Primm's style could be regal. Down deep he was a farmer and a good ol' boy as much as a newspaper executive and a public citizen supporting many causes. He loved nature and being with people, doing business and being with friends and family.

This is almost impossible to write, but I need to share this stuff. I need to laugh and watch out now that I'm the age a sudden heart attack took this champion of Fremont Leather Flower one summer morning.

Helping to preserve this rare native Clematis and some of the Ozark glades where it lives are among his proudest accomplishments. My purpose is not to dwell on these, but more on one incident, a rare fiasco for a man used to winning. Finishing ahead had been inculcated from his earliest days.

Just as much as he strove to win, he loved kicking back with friends. Once he went west with his neighbor Leonard Hall, an Ozark author and fellow former newspaperman. They stopped at a Kentucky Fried Chicken in Arizona.

Timon went in first. "I've brought the Colonel with me," he told the young woman behind the cash register.

"You mean our founder, Col. Harland Sanders?"

"Yes indeed, we're taking a vacation in the Southwest. Just don't let on you recognize him. The Colonel doesn't like people to make a fuss."

Needless to say, Leonard, with a striking white goatee, looked just like the world-renowned colonel and had a pronounced drawl from the hills. When Leonard, his wife Virginia—who enjoyed special treatment as a former dancer who performed with Fred Astaire on Broadway—and my mom walked in, the crew made a fuss. They'd set a table. Only after they were bringing out their order did Timon let on they were just folks from Missouri and that Leonard was often called Col. Sanders.

Timon grew up in the urban heart of St. Louis. As the youngest and only boy in a family of four children, he was gregarious and started working for the former *Star-Times* as a cub reporter while in college. After the war he moved to the business side of journalism realizing many reporters drink up their wages and rarely move ahead. The alley behind an upper floor city desk was thick with broken whiskey bottles. There was no air-conditioning and reporters had to fill new editions of their newspapers almost hourly. Whiskey could keep you cool and relaxed.

As a protégé of Joseph Pulitzer, Jr., Timon switched to the business side of the company after military service. During a 40-year career, he helped diversify the firm with other newspaper purchases, radio and television stations.

I remember him telling me once, "I was always an independent, but in the election of 1956 I decided Eisenhower would make a good president. Governor Adlai Stevenson of Illinois was probably the smarter of the two, but I was going to vote for Ike.

"As I walked up to the polls at Conway School one of my friends was handing out flyers. 'Here's a guy from that pinko newspaper downtown, don't waste paper giving Primm anything about Ike.'

"I laughed and shook his hand, but because of that crack I did end up voting for Stevenson." He supported the paper's platform the founder, Joseph Sr., set out in 1907 to fight for progress and reform. Loving nature was part of that.

* * *

Was it Timon's independent spirit, ambition, delayed hopes or his overarching love of life that led to his greatest disappointment? I searched through a file of his clippings and talked with a few people who knew him, but this mistake remains a mystery.

Actually, much remains a mystery about his life, but I have learned to live with that. We were never really buddies. He had a private side that I didn't know how to approach. His father Samuel died in his 50s, a semi-successful early automotive dealer. Timon never mentioned anything about him. Samuel had a brother, an antique dealer in Florence, who is buried in the Protestant cemetery outside Rome, Italy. His Uncle Alec also died without children. Another brother died as a young physician in St. Louis and their one sister, Minerva, ended up as a confused transient around the

39. Memoir

city after divorcing her husband and living in Majorca, Spain, for many years. Timon made a practice of helping manage her affairs. He was good with figures. But his family was somewhat scattered. Nothing like the clannishness common in many big Catholic families.

Originally, we weren't Catholic, but Protestants from the Picardy region in northern France who escaped to the Great Dismal Swamp after the Edict of Nantes was revoked. One of our relatives fought with fellow Virginians at the Battle of Yorktown, but neither Timon nor I have been inclined to know much more. I take my complex heritage for granted and know I could examine it more if ever I have the time. I am truly more interested in issues of people and places around me in the present. Details of my own family history seem a luxury for later. But I have been to Prim, Arkansas, once. Neat Ozarky town with a huge church right in the center! Still hope to go to Prim, Nevada, reportedly a lively casino town started by an African American relative.

Most every Saturday Timon worked at home in his small office, balancing his and Minerva's accounts while listening to the Metropolitan Opera especially for the emotional arias.

Another weekend habit was reading aloud the Sunday classified advertising section in his newspaper of "Farms and Land for Sale." Nearing his retirement, he and my mother Nancy bought property near their old friends Leonard and Virginia Hall in the Belleview Valley, one of the early pioneer regions of the eastern Ozarks. Calling his acreage Crazy Tree for a big old oak up high on a hill, Timon had a vacation home and enjoyed all the chores and friendly neighbors. Their place near Caledonia was a dream come true.

Nancy was a good sport going along to the country. Timon had deferred many dreams to be a successful business executive. Even before long hours behind a desk, ATP spent three years in the Pacific as staff to Admiral William "Bull" Halsey and others, including the naval historian Samuel Eliot Morrison. Two torpedoes hit his ship, the heavy cruiser USS *Northampton*, at midnight during the epic Battle of Tassafaronga. Timon swam through burning oil slicks to be rescued by a neighboring destroyer in the infamous Slot off Guadalcanal, November 30, 1942. Some 60 shipmates died. But amazingly he never expressed rancor toward Japan or its people, and was an early buyer of a Subaru. He managed to visit me in Tokyo when I was on R&R from Vietnam and he was traveling on business.

But we rarely talked about his war or mine. Early on I told him I was thinking of becoming a conscientious objector, but Timon said he would disinherit me if I did. I didn't know exactly what that meant, but I didn't want to force the issue. My Episcopal priest said I might consider serving my time then protesting the war if, on returning, I still felt it was a mistake. This seemed like a reasonable compromise at the time. I was lucky to be able to come back and join Vietnam Veterans Against the War. Timon understood why I had become an activist.

* * *

Timon was an activist most of his life. Nature inspired him most deeply. He, Leonard Hall and others in Missouri were members of a group started by the author and conservationist Louis Bromfield in Ohio called Friends of the Land, which was a predecessor to The Nature Conservancy. Earlier, Timon had summer jobs at ranches in Wyoming and Mexico. As a kid he went fishing with the Bakewell boys at the Sugar Tree Club on the Gasconade near the old railroad town of Newburg. Being in nature was his church.

He didn't get involved in controversial things like opposing the Vietnam War or the Civil Rights movement. But he supported integration. Some of the best sailors on the USS *Northampton*, he said, were the black stewards in the officers' mess.

The Navy was his standard of excellence. He chewed me out for not turning off the water, as he did aboard ship, after initially getting wet. "Soap up, then turn the water back on," Timon said. "You're supposed to be a river conservationist; show that you are!" To this day, I can't get in a shower without hearing his voice.

The Nature Conservancy (TNC) became the group that attracted his attention.[1] Near his farm in the Belleview Valley, Buford Mountain stands as the second highest summit in the state and forms a long ridge that attracts hikers and hunters. Timon, his neighbor Leonard and others in TNC were able to support a deal for the state Department of Conservation to acquire and protect the gnarly mountain.

They did the same thing with a group of local residents in nearby Jefferson County who wanted to preserve an archaeological dig that became Mastodon State Historic Site. This park and museum preserves the first site in the nation where evidence was found of early peoples hunting the giant wooly, elephant-like critters. A Clovis point, roughly 10,000 to 14,000 years old, was found among Mastodon bones here in 1979.

The kind of guy who could picture himself chipping out a Clovis point, Timon would have been right up front, chucking it at a charging Mastodon. He also loved the little things like Fremont's Leather Flower found on nearby Victoria Glade in Jefferson County. The Nature Conservancy and his friends help preserve that too.

For his last 20 years, TNC occupied much of his time. Many professional people, business leaders and scientists were attracted to the Missouri TNC because it focused on preserving unique pieces of real estate with rare or endangered natural features. The group tended to avoid environmental controversies in order to focus on buying sensitive real estate. The mission has grown and changed in recent decades with landscape-scale and international projects.

39. Memoir

Is this what broke his heart? Things got complicated. I've examined Timon's "Greer Spring" file of clippings and memos where this conflict from autumn 1987 unfolds. The second largest natural spring in the state, Greer, had been owned and protected by the Dening family as a retreat for most of the 1900s. Eventually the family wanted to sell the spring and its surrounding 7,000 acres in Oregon County. They almost worked out a deal with a giant brewing company to buy a small portion of the land, develop a spring water bottling plant nearby while donating most of the property to the U.S. Forest Service. TNC helped the Dening family work out some of these details.

A *Post-Dispatch* story about the issue begins, "The Nature Conservancy, a national conservation group, got a $10,000 donation last year from Anheuser-Busch Inc. before it helped the brewery buy Greer Spring, a designated national landmark." The appearance of under-the-table dealings! Environmental groups including the Sierra Club, the Wilderness Society and others raised questions in the press and a letter-writing campaign. Could a private company be trusted to develop sensitive real estate while respecting its essential natural characteristics? Would a bottling plant ruin the spring and its surrounding beauty?

Opinions were strong on both sides. "The Nature Conservancy is dedicated to the maintenance of the natural beauty of our state," wrote Andrew N. Baur in the *Post-Dispatch* letters column on September 21. (Drew was a part owner of the St. Louis Cardinals at the time and involved in diverse business projects.) "Its interest in our rivers and its dedication to preserving the natural habitat are well documented. On the other hand, the federal government has created a monster with the Current River. Greer Spring should be maintained, but I would trust Anheuser-Busch (A-B) and The Nature Conservancy before the Department of the Interior." This view did not prevail.

"Busch Drops Plans to Buy Greer Spring," a headline a few weeks later ran. The deal fell through. The story reads, "The company's brewery subsidiary had wanted to bottle water from Greer Spring for commercial sale. Instead, the company said it would make a $500,000 challenge grant available to any qualified non-profit organization to buy and preserve Greer Spring."

To say the least, my dad was disappointed. He believed the company would cooperate with TNC in good management, not damage the spring, and eventually create jobs and economic activity for people in Oregon County, one of the poorest areas in the state. Luckily a deal did develop. The Forest Service owns most of the property now. The old Greer Mill has been restored beautifully by a federal jobs program.

Initially TNC got rather a black eye from bad publicity surrounding the appearance of A-B doing a sweetheart deal. Lots of letters to the editor and editorial cartoons poked fun at TNC. Timon was mortified when the organization held a national meeting in St. Louis just as the bad publicity was peaking.

But more questionable things were happening in Timon's private life. He and my mom had a falling out. Timon wanted to be more active with environmental issues and be free to explore wild places. He found an apartment in south St. Louis that my mother graciously helped him set up. She didn't want a divorce. He seemed not to know exactly what he wanted.

I remember him visiting me in Rolla once for dinner. He wept during dessert: "I don't know what's happening with me anymore." I tried to be open and helpful. My own life was crawling out of a dark hole following a divorce from a marriage that had lasted barely a year. Then Timon was diagnosed with brain cancer.

With my parents at the Missouri Botanical Garden's cafe the day before the operation, I recall Timon looked as weak as a melting snowman, but he didn't let on anything was up to friends we encountered after lunch.

"Everything's fine," my parents both said, smiling and waving.

The surgeon had to split open Timon's bald cranium to extract a growth reportedly as big as a golf ball. Luckily it was benign. He had two more years after this and eventually moved back home.

My mom had played hardball. She wasn't going to agree to a divorce for a variety of reasons. She definitely did not want the stigma of being a divorced older woman. She lived in a judgmental upper middle-class society and had few friends she could talk with about her problems. It just wasn't done at the St. Louis Country Club. Talking about the weekly bridge game was as close as she could get to sharing her feelings. I doubt if her three children were much help. I think her Episcopal priest did some good as did marriage counselors.

Mainly she relied on her own instincts and common sense. She had ignored advice from various family members not to marry Timon at the brink of World War II because his family was questionable, Catholic and a bit chaotic. Her family was chaotic in its own way. Ultimately, Nancy took the train with a few family members to be married at Bremerton Navy yard near Seattle at a tiny chapel. Timon and Nancy had time for a brief honeymoon drive along the West Coast.

His new ship was in harbor for repairs. Some of the crew got word not to leave the St. Francis Hotel in San Francisco right away. Orders might change. There may be another night or two on shore for some. I appeared on the scene, summer solstice 1944, eight months after this last night stateside.

They both fell in love with Oregon. They looked at towns in the Willamette Valley that would surely grow fast after the war and need better newspapers.

But Missouri proved to have a stronger magnetic force when it was all over. As close as they got to living that dream was part ownership in a cherry orchard in the Yakima Valley with their buddy Paul Stark, the Missouri orchardist, and others. They tried planting cherry trees at Crazy Tree in the Belleview Valley. Deer gobbled them up.

* * *

Loving nature and growing things saved them both from far worse fates. If they had been true health fanatics like many young people now, they would have run and biked, done triathlons or practiced yoga. But their generation didn't do that. They were coming out of the Great Depression and had to secure a living for their family.

They both always loved growing gardens and fruit trees. As early followers of *Organic Gardening* magazine, nature and healthy living was always at the top of their to do list. Peter Raven, director of the Missouri Botanical Garden, was a good friend and mentor. Both volunteered and served on boards there.

Their friends ribbed them a bit. Once at a Christmas party they were given matching T-shirts: "Environmentalist" and "Environmentalist Wife" in bright red letters. At the country club, being activists was not encouraged.

Eventually, Timon spent less time at the club, duck hunting and playing golf as well. He developed a detached retina, so sports caused problems. He loved driving to his farm in the Belleview Valley or visiting environmental heroes he had met like Dorothy Leake along Crane Creek, Stone County, Missouri, and Eugene Perrot on nearby Ozark prairies.

I remember him chairing a TNC meeting after the Greer Spring ruckus blew over. He made grammatical slips and was not organized to discuss things. His heart didn't seem in it.

Looking back on his last years, I recall a friend who died of a sudden massive heart attack at an early age. John had been a partner in a small winery but differences developed between the two principals. He was forced out of the business. His wife told me later that John died from a broken heart that never healed following the failed partnership.

Is this what happened to Timon? Too many things going on around him? Things out of control?

My mom had a somewhat similar fate, but luckily she survived a stroke. She gradually recovered her ability to talk and walk but had given up gardening after moving to an apartment with an elevator. Not much exercise there.

I look back on these loving, intelligent people with such respect and admiration for what they did for their children and community.

Every day I thank the Great Spirit for blessings I've enjoyed and try carry on my parents' ideals of kindness and love of nature.

Now that I am about the age when Timon died, I realize how he struggled in his last years. Did he make a crucial mistake a few years before his fatal heart attack? Had he helped develop a poorly vetted plan to benefit private business more than nature? Only a more detailed examination of this dustup would answer that.

Was he right that a big firm like Anheuser-Busch could provide better protection than the federal government for sensitive environments? Does it matter that this local brewery has since been sold to a multi-national corporation? Will the American public demand our government and businesses support protection of clean air and water much less unique, sensitive places?

Is anyone really going to miss Monarch butterflies? I remember seeing clouds of hundreds migrating in late summer while fishing with dad on the river. Now Monarch have become rare. Other butterflies too, say goodbye! Are specimens preserved in museums good enough to remind the future what has been lost?

These issues swirl around us all, especially during a pandemic and collapse of natural systems in climate change. What a challenge Timon's many natural and spiritual grandchildren face to save the vital heart of our growing world.

Part VIII

Ethics, Activists and Timber

Hillbilly Ethics—Truth-tellin' and Rural Rapport

> This article was written for a 2020 competition sponsored by *The Oral History Review* for new views on ethics in our field. This did not make the cut for a special issue on basic principles, yet I appreciated the opportunity to think through the topic and suggestions by editor Janneken Smucker and two anonymous reviewers. How to get good vibes with people; that's what I seek.

Abstract: *Communication with rural residents can be problematic for researchers unfamiliar with these communities. This paper offers an overview of problems in establishing rapport. It includes a variety of personal anecdotes as well as discussion on sources of interview failure.*

Keywords: magical thinking, Ozarks, post-traumatic stress disorder, rapport, rural

> Well, then, says I, what's the use you learning to do right when it's troublesome to do right and ain't no trouble to do wrong, and the wages is just the same?
> —From Mark Twain, "The Rattlesnake-Skin Does Its Work," (Chapter 16) *The Adventures of Huckleberry Finn*, 1885

Every job has expectations. In some ways the hardest part of any kind of cold call sales pitch or oral research may be reaching people when they want to talk.

Isn't "oral history" something we all do all the time? How else can we appreciate what people close to us do and think? I tend to see oral history as a research method because I've had contracts with federal and state agencies to research developments not covered by official documents. However, oral history seems more vital than a methodology. It's essential for enriching what's possible.

When things go right in an exchange it's transcendental. You hear and learn things you never thought to ask. A good session lasts much longer than expected. To put it most simply, isn't this a form of love? How else can we thrive except through augmenting our empathy? This is the best part of fieldwork for research of any kind. While a shared give-and-take does not happen all the time, it's worthwhile appreciating harmonious understandings when they do happen.

Is this what makes communication a mystery? Is this the Indiana Jones of sleuthing? The usual explanation is the concept of "rapport," which I find somewhat foreign and complex. I want to explore a more flexible outlook on how to create good vibes and deep trust.

Rapport is connected with respect and affection, but it can exist among people who don't respect one another and who have little affection for one another. Rapport is critical to doing field work, but it's the only aspect of the entire enterprise I find so mysterious that I can only talk around it, not about it directly. And I do not know of anyone who can tell you how to make rapport happen.[1]

Creating a shared sense of agreement is indeed mysterious. It's the beginning of any worthwhile project. Is empathy basic to rapport? If a project begins well, it's much easier to keep it going in a way that benefits all.

Before becoming allured by oral history, I was a campaign aid and speech writer in 1980 for one of the most successful politicians from the Ozarks, the late Mel Carnahan. The job developed because I gave a talk at the local chamber of commerce to nominate my old Quaker buddy Professor George McPherson to be the "Rolla Christian of the Year." George always carried a tank of air in his truck in case he encountered a driver with a flat tire, among other charitable habits. He won the award in 1980. Appreciating my talk, Mel invited me to help him with his upcoming campaign to be state treasurer. Eventually serving two terms as governor, Mel enthusiastically did things with careful finesse. His first campaign for statewide office began from his efficient law office in Rolla where I worked in the basement:

> One of my first assignments was to make appointments for the candidate to drive 100 miles east from Rolla to Farmington and back, visiting local newspapers and radio stations. I gained tremendous respect for those who can labor on in public service, actually following all those statistics about Medicare, general obligation bonds, and testing of middle schoolers. Mel apparently loved doing this basic work that keeps society going. I still remember driving with him to a political breakfast in Lebanon, Mel at the wheel, me holding a list of local Democrats and quizzing him on names, occupations, spouses, and special interests. When we arrived shortly before 7 a.m. he greeted everyone by first name as if he had seen them yesterday.[2]

Part VIII—Ethics, Activists and Timber

This breakfast meeting allowed Mel to show his connections and rapport with community leaders in Laclede County. Benefiting from his father's two decades in Congress, Mel's passion for public life led him to prepare all details of meetings with voters. His voice inspired people and showed real love for reaching out to folks. His enthusiasm talking with new and old friends seemed totally genuine. This must be the vital heart of American politics: connecting with people, knowing how to win support, learning to listen. This form of rapport, or empathy, is basic to interviewing as well. I later completed oral histories of several family members, which is the basis of the article from *Gateway Heritage*, published by the Missouri Historical Society, quoted above.

* * *

Meeting a person who has a desire to communicate and share stories always inspires. Then good vibes are not the problem; it's a matter of keeping up with the flow. This was the case with Aileen Hatch who had her own way of doing things. At the end of her teaching career at the two-room Big Piney School outside of Plato, Missouri, she taught older boys:

> I had one boy who was badly spoiled. He didn't want to mind me. He didn't want to settle down and learn. So I asked his mother if she would come to school with him each day. She said, "I certainly will!"
> She rode the school bus with him every day. Came to school with him. We got that boy straightened out. So one day he came to me and said, Ms. Hatch, he said, I don't believe Momma has to come to school anymore.
> I said, John, you ready to straighten up? And he said, yea, yea, I'm ready to do like the rest of them.[3]

This is a typical story from Ms. Hatch. She loved telling it during our session long ago. She was the kind of teacher who bought boxing gloves so the bigger boys would work out their differences in an organized boxing match at school. Aileen had great pride in how she figured out how to do things. She had an infectious enthusiasm for life. Maybe Aileen was naturally an emphatic person.

Is this unusual? From my experience, a person with this strong sense of purpose or empathy is rare. Determination to do things in one's own way is unique, but maybe more common in rural communities. Being self-sufficient and tough are the basis of rural ethics. Most of us get distracted by various complexities and the search for the right, often polite, words. Rural people tend to just come out and say and do what they think. Is this simplistic? Maybe. But this is what I've found in the Ozarks.

One of the difficulties of doing interviews involves knowing the purpose and future uses of any project. Complications can begin even before a project starts. The equipment doesn't work right. Interviews get off to a bad start and never get quite straightened out. Logistical issues, such as travel, can complicate interviews. It often takes infinite patience to meet a person at the right time.

One particular incident has stayed with me for years. It was a head-on accident involving a man I had met and interviewed a few weeks earlier. After encountering the accident, I couldn't help but write about the event, and recently resurrected these notes:

> I park to walk toward what's left of the pickup truck where an older guy is lying on the grass. He looks like he's taken a .50 caliber round to the head, his face is so bloody. He says he's going to be okay, go help the woman.
>
> They must have met head on, both probably going the speed limit or better. This section of State Rt. 21 south of Ellington may be the most twisty highway in the Ozarks.
>
> Both vehicles ended up on the pickup's side of the road. All windows smashed, engine parts smeared back into the cabs or spread beside the still smoking wrecks. They stink of smoke, torn dirt and dripping oil.
>
> When I walk up to the van, another guy there says he was trying to reach the woman inside. He seems calmer than me. For two hours I've been driving on the far side of the legal limit and caffeine capacity.
>
> "Everything but the back door of the woman's van was locked," he says. "I had to crawl in over the seats to open the passenger-side door. Hated to do it, didn't want to bother her. I wasn't sure she was alive."
>
> Thick forest beginning to leaf out seems clean and silent this early spring morning. Only these two twisted remains of full-sized American-made machines seem foreign in the silent woodland.

Why has this accident stayed fresh for three decades? Travel requires certain risks on rural roads, heavily used highways or public transit. Risk may not be considered part of the dialog process. But the potential for things to go wrong can affect outcomes and creates a necessary tension in initial meetings.

This accident brought back memories of being in the Army in Vietnam and the random touch of fate. My military experience lies in my unconscious. The dehumanization of combat prepared me for random violence or injustice, whether it's street crime or the disorder of a pandemic. Life is crazy, unfair, only rarely bending towards justice. Political turmoil, whenever it occurs, recalls the slaughter of innocent Vietnamese by equally innocent American soldiers. Stopping to help during this near fatal accident sparked a personal sense of helplessness, psychological confusion and grief similar to post-traumatic stress disorder or a near-death experience:

> "Subjects with near-death experiences might differ from other subjects in being more open to unusual experiences (and also willing to report these) and being attentive to the so-called inner-states. It might also be that this personality trait is linked to the larger concept of 'magical thinking,' which has

been shown to depend on right hemispheric activity and affinity to 'paranormal' thought."[4]

Each interview represents a variety of risks, the main one being that a successful exchange won't take place. Oral history interviews normally don't involve stressful situations, but the initial phases of contact can be confusing and problematic. This can lead to "magical thinking" and irrational concern or worries. Taking time to explain a project helps assure confidence. A dialogue over several sessions creates a degree of trust. Gradually, important elements of life experience become shared by the respondent and often the interviewer as well. Usually showing up represents only a small part of the difficulties of connecting, but initial difficulties can result in future complications.

Bigger problems involve the interviewer feeling confident about the whole process and knowing how the process will benefit his or her project. Equally of concern may be problems with equipment. I had a hard time transitioning from analog recording to a digital format. What concerned me was the interface between the microphone and the recorder. I didn't trust mini-plugs; they seemed to be unstable and could pull out unexpectedly in some situations. Finally, I ended up with a big Marantz PMD 670 that caused another kind of uncertainty, this on recording levels and sound quality.

Technology anxiety affects people differently. As my wife Cathy points out I'm not so comfortable with information technology, while she lacks an innate sense of direction: maps confuse if they don't tell her when to turn. Gradually I've become more comfortable with what technology can offer. Embracing innovation is hard for an old country boy, but I try to keep up with what's possible:

> What I find most exciting in new modes of engaging digital information is the unfolding capacity to present such explorable spaces in imaginative, expansive ways, and the deployment of tools for their fluid, non-directed navigation. Both oral history and a range of digital realms are focusing more on creative exploration than on the dutiful provision of answers that can only be as good as the questions.[5]

Oral history research is going in many new directions; it's an exciting field as new technology makes sharing information easier. Anxiety over change can be a problem during interviews and may affect the process. Assuring all involved in a project understand how their information will be shared is essential. The Oral History Association has a thorough statement, a few hundred words on ethics in interviewing. It's actually a useful guide for doing interviews of any kind. Ethics develops from researchers' certainty that rapport exists, an irrational quality, but necessary. It's a balancing act to build mutual respect and understanding.

One early text in oral history, *Elite and Specialized Interviewing* by Lewis Anthony Dexter, discusses three possible sources of failure in interviews: contempt for the interviewer; undue desire to ingratiate oneself; and our "whole schooling system tends to teach people to give 'the right answers' as seen by teachers and textbooks."[6] These are all based on a failed or inadequate rapport.

As a basis of successful interviewing, creating good vibes often takes a sophisticated level of social understanding. Dexter discusses something as simple as how the wrong accent can affect interviews. I recall being given some inside advice when I was about to interview former mayor of Philadelphia Frank Rizzo: he won't talk with you unless you wear highly polished military-style shoes.

Appearances mean a lot in this field as well as in any kind of research or business. Body language means as much as voice in creating rapport and comfort.

> The passenger's door hung ajar enough so we could see the body of the woman slumped over the steering wheel splattered with her blood. Her skin seemed more grey than white. She didn't move or say anything when we called to her.
>
> Wet paint had sprayed over the whole interior. Off white, five or ten gallon cans. Parchment maybe, great for covering up layers of the past no matter how off-color.
>
> She must have been coming back from Popular Bluff, my destination too and the nearest big town. It was still early; she could have finished a painting job in time to surprise her husband.
>
> I stood with the other man at the van looking for several minutes. Is it a dead body? No, he said. She's moaned several times. Do you think the van could blow up?
>
> I'm not a medic. I don't know what to do. I don't want to mess up her tapes or van as I gently lean across to open the driver's side door. Death is almost like a disease that we don't want to be near. Everything else seems petty. You know what has to be done and what's the right time.

Thinking over some of the documentary fieldwork I've done, I feel the best projects involved time with people who usually have little opportunity to share their opinions and observations. For the oral history project at Ft. Leonard Wood, I had a chance to meet and interview Bud Massey who was born in 1927 south of Ft. Wood near the Big Piney River. His family had eight children. His father farmed and picked up odd jobs at sawmills and nearby construction. He and his brothers would cut a rank of wood, which is a half cord, and get a dollar for it during the Depression. Bud asked rhetorically: "What can you get with a dollar today? Not much, but back in them days, a dollar bought me a pair of overalls. I can sell a rank of wood today for $20, but I can't buy a new pair of overalls for $20."[7]

Mr. Massey had many observations like this, common sense concerns, especially on the changing quality of the Big Piney River. He knew the river all his life. Changing river channels were the focus of the project: how and why the riparian ecosystem has changed. Why there were more flathead than channel catfish and fewer varieties of fish in general, particularly concerned Mr. Massey. He spoke about the increased flow of gravel into the shallow channel but did not have ideas about how it developed. I only interviewed him twice, but I cannot forget his common sense and feeling that the environmental quality he knew as a young man has not been maintained, largely due to increased regional population.

Some of this oral history material has been preserved at the State Historical Society of Missouri in its Ozark Rivers Oral History Collection, #R-1430, including transcripts and seven CDs of interviews transferred from cassette tapes. While I appreciate the importance of archival conservation, I wonder about the significance of this material. In some ways it represents a grey area between oral history and journalistic interviews. Few of my interviews go into the depth of including life and career history. But my job was not to evaluate the worth of the material, just capture responses to specific questions. I did take time to understand how the oral histories would be used. I did not have to know all the details, just enough to know what was significant for the project. This kept me balanced and aware of what was really necessary.

> Still moaning, the woman slowly leans back against the seat, her first movements of life. We step back and decide it's best not to move her. "Did I do anything wrong," she asks. "Where am I?" She opens her eyes and slowly turns to look at we two witnesses standing by her van. "Did I hurt anyone?"
>
> I reach out to take her hand, bend down and say, "You're going to be okay. Everyone is going to be okay. Just lie back. There's been an accident and an ambulance is coming."
>
> Breathe deep if you can. I try to be reassuring and repeat these simple messages so she does not lose consciousness. After 10 minutes a state trooper pulls up and checks the woman's pulse.
>
> Blankets are brought over to cover her. Then a friend from Ellington comes up and says, "Don't worry Dorothy. We'll get you out of this in just a little bit." I'm still holding her hand and the other guy has gone out to direct traffic around us.
>
> All that matters is the regular flow of her breath. I tell her it's a beautiful day, that she's nice and warm. It will not snow again and soon you can make a garden. Vegetables make everyone happy. She breathes easy as I tell her how okra and tomatoes can heal anything.
>
> When the ambulance arrived with a flurry, an older woman and a young male medic seem pumped full of adrenalin while trying to do everything at once.
>
> Then I realized the other accident driver was Floyd Sutterfield, a local

historian and retired public official who had detailed information about Logan Creek. We had talked a week or two earlier. He had been driving the truck in the other lane. He had made a neat sign for the new general store in the town of Reynolds about the history of the place and the timber boom a century ago.

I called Floyd a couple of weeks after leaving the scene of the accident. He had recovered as had Dorothy, but I never had a chance to visit him again. His cousin Dan told me Floyd recuperated totally to live well into his 80s.

* * *

The transience of field interviews creates an inevitable sense of loss. What's the value of recording a few stories? One way to make personal sense of any exchange and validate short visits may be to see unanticipated encounters as a chance to "take the pleasure of a moment for some incidental friendship," the title of a fine art print by a friend, John C. Fernie, who made conceptual art as a young man before financial issues led him into a banking career. His appreciation for the varieties of human experience echoes what the farmer-poet Wendell Berry has written about the importance of personal experience:

> If the promise is serious enough, one is brought to it by love, and in awe and fear. Fear, awe, and love bind us to no selfish aims, but to each other. For when we promise in love and awe and fear, there is a certain kind of mobility that we give up. We give up the romanticism of progress, which is always shifting its terms to fit its occasions. We are speaking where we stand, and afterward we shall stand in the presence of what we have said.[8]

This type of direct, unselfish communication underlies what I have experienced in doing oral history in the Ozarks. It took years to be comfortable visiting all kinds of people in the region.

Part of my reluctance was fear of things going wrong, as suggested by the early morning highway accident I encountered long ago. I've learned that things can go bad quickly. Another aspect was fear of unknown, potential violence, as suggested in the 2010 film *Winter's Bone*, based on Daniel Woodrell's novel. I've visited with many people who share the outlook of Huckleberry Finn, who ends his adventures down the Mississippi stating, "I reckon I got to light out for the Territory ahead of the rest, because Aunt Sally she's going to adopt me and sivilize [sic] me, and I can't stand it. I been there before."

Twain's novel has been criticized for not dealing directly with the legacy of slavery in America.[9] My recent rereading of the novel suggests the relationship between Huck and his friend, the escaped slave Jim, is not the center of the novel. Rather it's Huck's growing maturity and realizing the limitations of adults and even of his old friend Tom Sawyer. Huck becomes a formidable, more confident individual when he acts on responsibilities to people he has met on his travels down the river. He has ample opportunity shown in the plot to realize life is not fair and often chaotic. Self-realization, such as Huck develops, may be a kind of "magical thinking" induced by unexpected events, rewarding relationships or other insights.

Empathy to understand interviewees may be a kind of magical thinking beyond rational thought. Rapport demands appreciating a wide set of variables and subtle clues. Rural people especially over much of the Ozarks, by necessity, have developed diverse values where self-sufficiency and autonomy remain the basis of personal ethics for many.

Rural people here tend to resist change and authority without understanding or rapport. Cities, industrial organization and urban life remain forces to be resisted.[10] Face-to-face conversation is the basis of in-depth communication. The march of the seasons and our crazy weather offers enough excitement to balance technological breakthroughs. When we talk in person, we share many visual cues that digital communication erases. Hillbillies tolerate a lot because we know we are going to be in our communities working long after any researcher has gone on to another project. We like to take time to visit, go slow, appreciate the chance to evaluate what's new, and laugh. No wonder President Trump had wide support here; Ozarkers distrust change. The canoe outfitter and ultimate hillbilly Ralph Brown just wanted to be left alone down on his creek. Like Wendell Berry, Ralph never had much use for progress.

What makes the most difference for Ozark people seems to be the quality of the story, the joy of the interchange, the depth and balance of what you have to say and ask.

40

The Sweetest Fiddler in All of Arkansas

Violet Hensley

Sometimes things happen just right, and usually at the Old Time Music Festival in West Plains, Missouri, lots does happen, mostly all great. This is one of my favorite Ozark towns, but Tropical Storm Bill about washed out the festival in 2015. Not many folks here for the first day, a rainy, sultry Friday.

* * *

Luckily I was able to listen to a living Arkansas Treasure. I didn't know it at the time, but at first glance this woman looked special. A tiny lady, her eyes had a spark I could see from fifty feet off. She entered the community center with several others who appeared to be family members. They helped her walk into the community theater and down a side aisle, her cane leading the way.

Who could she be?

She stood out from the audience of maybe a hundred folks during the early afternoon concerts with a bright blue sunbonnet and long flowing dress. I stayed in the audience with my little computer, writing, cruising the Internet and listening to great ol' hillbilly music. The bonnet got lost in all the baseball caps. Most of the audience sported grey hair, potbellies and wayward looks for old friends. This is really a big reunion for most, nothing like a rock concert, just a great chance to visit.

Usually the festival occupies much of the east side of town. Not many places have a community building that can host a folk festival like this. Upstairs a conference room has been devoted, as usual, to a beautiful exhibit of several hundred quilts. Square dancers will be invited to use the gym shortly. Venders peddle crafts with doubtful tradition or use. Kids run around the busy indoor pool. Always unexpected, people and booths seem worthwhile if not fun.

Around 4:00 this afternoon I came out of the theater and spotted that

40. The Sweetest Fiddler in All of Arkansas

same little lady with the bonnet who was in the theater earlier. She sat out in the lobby at the center of an appreciative crowd all listening to her. Perched on the edge of a bench, she was playing her fiddle in a vigorous, rapid-fire style. Like a pixie, she sang with a thin watery tone that attracted me for a couple of tunes. I couldn't hear the words, so I went back into the theater to hear other performers.

Then at 5 p.m., I had an unfortunate run-in with a huge barbecue turkey leg and the Spring Dipper's black walnut ice cream. I finally caught up with Matt Meacham, a former West Plains guy who had played on the main stage earlier today.

"What did you think of Violet?" he asked.

"Who's that?"

"I saw you listening to her out in the lobby. Violet Hensley, she's famous. She's 99 and plays like she's 19."

"She has the sweetest tone I've heard in years. Amazing."

Later my friend Corliss Schaeffer said she heard Violet Hensley had played earlier today.

"I didn't really know who she was," I said. "I hear she's famous."

"Years ago, I used to sell my garlic and herbs at Silver Dollar City," Corliss said. "Violet was active then; she was one of the main acts who was there all the time."

Unfortunately, I've never been to this Ozark theme park. Branson and all its attractions always seemed too far away, too expensive and too contrived. But I've since learned that like the New Jersey shore or California beaches, the Land of a Thousand Smiles has points worth exploring when time allows. At one time three different Elvises appeared in different local music shows.

While listening this evening to the Quebe Sisters, three young Texas beauties who play fiddles as if they could be angels, I learned why Violet Hensley is famous. I logged onto the *Encyclopedia of Arkansas* and there she is.

Now I wish I could come back tomorrow when the weather is supposed to clear up. Ralph Stanley and family will hold forth as the evening's headliners. Bill Oakley, one of the best carpenters and audio technicians in the area, will be at his volunteer job running the beer garden and more. Great folks from all over will be wandering around. And some folks will be looking to see if they can hear Violet Hensley once again.

—West Plains, Missouri, June 2015.

> A quick check of the *Encyclopedia of Arkansas* shows Violet is still fiddling, at 105 years of age.

41

This Is the Ozark Earth

A Conversation with a River Conservationist

For about a decade, Cathy and I focused visits to St. Louis on seeing aged parents. This happened while moving from Rolla during the Great Recession of '08. Both rewarding and traumatic, these trips cemented memories and connections with our beloved hometowns. It was difficult to keep up with friends then.

Luckily, we took time to visit with a personal hero, Jerry Sugerman. He saved the Meramec River from the huge federal Meramec Park Dam project. He didn't do it alone; lots of people helped stop the dam. But he quit a good technical job in the '70s after 14 years at the thriving Monsanto chemical company to devote full-time effort to derailing a questionable project. He took the lead and served the Ozarks heroically.

* * *

A day in St. Louis can leave you spaced out. Visiting diverse haunts once home shows how fast cities change. The Loop in suburban U. City seems continuously reconstructing with and without the guidance of nearby Washington University.

In grad school I lived with Chinese students in a busy apartment building along Delmar. Most Saturdays we spent afternoon hours cooking then cleaning up to feast on spicy dumplings, hot pot and whatever else my friends missed from the Mainland. I introduced them to Pratzels, a local Jewish bakery that opened a back door after midnight Saturdays to sell fresh, warm bagels. A sweet aroma to end the Sabbath. But the family-owned bakery is gone now; at least good Chinese places have sprung up to offer unique aromas of their own.

* * *

Jerry lived in U. City most of his life. He seemed like a total city guy. He loved the St. Louis area, but the Ozarks won his deepest devotion.

41. This Is the Ozark Earth

We visited five or six times in recent years. His words always flowed in a torrent. He had many interests and much enthusiasm for life. It's hard to do his feelings justice. At times Jerry seemed at a loss for words, at others he was articulate and passionate. He explained he had been seeing a specialist to understand his occasional loss of memory. On one of our last visits he told me that he had been diagnosed with early onset Alzheimer's disease and he was continuing to see a specialist. So, this is not an oral history transcript, but a remembrance of Jerry's feelings about Ozark rivers, especially the Meramec.

One of my strongest memories from these visits was the effort Jerry made to remain articulate. He copied passages of Carl Sandburg's *Rootabaga Stories* onto poster board and practiced reading these complicated pieces aloud. I tried reading some of the stanzas myself when visiting his home and got tongue-tied. He said reading helped and was fun. I don't remember him complaining about his situation; he dealt with it directly. When Jerry got tongue-tied, he just slowed down and the thoughts came out eventually.

His wife Darlene works at the Missouri Historical Society, a place I try to visit in the city whenever time allows. Our state has two state historical societies—very confusing. I've done projects for both institutions. The one in St. Louis is older and richer but focused on regional and urban history. Despite having a national reputation for its collections, directors have come and gone. The State Historical Society of Missouri, Columbia, operates closely with our land grant university and has a beautiful new headquarters, The Center for Missouri Studies. It would be great if they developed names clarifying their goals and cooperated a lot more.

Darlene suggested meeting at the museum in Forest Park, locally known as the Jefferson Memorial.

"You've got to see our new exhibit. It's one of the best we've ever done," Darlene said. "Why don't we meet there?"

The exhibit, *A Walk in 1875 St. Louis*, demonstrates the best that museums can offer. Based on the Compton and Dry pictorial atlas, which illustrated every building standing in the city 140 years ago, the show spread into many galleries. One of the largest such urban atlases ever produced, maps showing famous neighborhoods have been blown up on huge screens with supporting photos, objects, films and funny drawings to show how actual individuals lived in the third biggest American city of its day. As a former museum curator, I loved seeing such creative, award-winning work.

The exhibit primed our pump. Past lives in old city neighborhoods on display evoked family stories from long ago. Jerry and I sat on a bench talking while Cath and Darlene looked around the show. Then we heard curator Andrew Wanko give an enthusiastic illustrated talk on how his team put together the exhibit. Finally, we went to Dressel's, Darlene's favorite Welsh hangout, for lunch. More storytelling and tasty vittles from her Welsh heritage.

We also commiserated about Leo Drey, who had passed on a few days earlier. Leo not only helped preserve thousands of acres in state parks and natural areas, but also demonstrated how sustainable practices can be profitable at the Pioneer Forest. He also hired and inspired young people to conserve Ozark wilderness. Leo and his wife Kay supported conservation with passion and generosity. Luckily the generous L.A.D. Foundation will continue this work. We lamented we've reached an age when many of our friends will have difficulties. We're old guys now, we reluctantly realize frequently. We appreciate more now what we tried to do then. We talked about those we remember from the dam fight and good times on the rivers.

We even commiserated about Jim Gamble, an attorney who managed the Meramec Basin Association, in support of the dam proposal. We both knew him a bit and felt his position on the importance of water conservation and flood control made some sense. But big dams aren't the answer, we agreed. Protecting flood plains from inappropriate development benefits everyone, not only taxpayers, in the long run.

"Rivers provide more recreation per acre than impoundments," Jerry said. "The Meramec may get a little crazy with boats on the weekend, but that's mainly kids doing what comes naturally at their age. At least they're out enjoying nature. The rest of the week's always quiet for fishermen and old folks."

I didn't know much about Jerry's background and why he had devoted himself to opposing a dam. Being a dam fighter did not seem like a secure career move. What inspires a nearly 40-year-old guy to combat the U.S. Government?

"When I was growing up in St. Louis," Jerry said, "one of my father's brothers had moved to Los Angeles. Many times we drove west to visit. My family all loved the national parks along the way. I was in awe of the mountains and forests.

"My friends at Monsanto took me floating in the Ozarks and that was a total revelation. We went on many different streams. I loved them all. The Meramec is closest to St. Louis and just as beautiful as any national park."

Jerry was also inspired by a photography book published by the Sierra Club in the 1960s, *This Is the American Earth* by Ansel Adams and Nancy Newhall.

"The photos evoked some feelings I had from the West. I liked the people I met at Sierra Club meetings. Some were trying to protect Ozark rivers through local zoning. Right away I felt these were my kind of people, serious and open-minded. But some Ozark landowners apparently saw planning as a threat. One of our members, Roger Taylor, a science teacher, had his car bombed. I was in favor of publishing a book showing people the beauty of our rivers, but we dropped the whole campaign. It wasn't worth antagonizing people.

"Once we visited Sen. Stuart Symington's office with a Sierra Club group in Washington, D.C," Jerry recalled. "He was supposedly in a meeting, but he came out to speak with us. All he said was, 'We are going to build that dam!' then went back into his private office. He wouldn't talk with us at all."

* * *

Jerry had a great love of trees, as I saw when I visited him a day after our museum trip. In the garden behind his suburban home in University City, Jerry and Darlene have created a tiny Ozark wilderness. A huge oak had fallen in his backyard, but new specimens have filled in: pawpaw, dogwood, ironwood, Japanese maple and others. We went up to his office to talk more on a cool Monday afternoon in early June.

Jerry's inner sanctum may have been a master bedroom for previous occupants but now was a site of personal deliberation. Jerry's mix of memorabilia made me feel at home.

He had a wonderful device he designed and built years ago to help measure customers' feet for an orthopedic custom shoe business he developed after the Meramec Dam was finally deauthorized and his campaign work ended. Now the machine had been converted to hold a digital camera to allow him to photograph various sized documents. Jerry used the pile filing system along with many boxes and a large phonographic record collection. Luckily these are coming back into favor among audiophiles. Some great early Romantic piano music created a calm background for our talk. We're comfortable being old guys.

* * *

John Danforth won Stuart Symington's seat in the U.S. Senate in 1976. Jerry Sugerman was on the newly elected senator's staff to advise on Meramec dam issues. Incumbent Sen. Tom Eagleton announced he would not support further funding for the federal project unless a regional referendum showed wide support. The dam was voted down in a regional election in 1978, then most land returned to private ownership.

We laughed about Jerry's reputation for gourmet meals on the river, complete with poached fish. Ralph Brown was a guy who inspired a degree of mutual awe for his tough common sense. Making a living renting canoes and raising potatoes in a small garden, Ralph often ate his spuds raw in white bread sandwiches because he couldn't take time to cook and miss a phone call from a possible rental customer.

The only monument to these Meramec dam fighters may be two ponds the Corps of Engineers excavated near their proposed dam site at Meramec State Park on the banks of the river. Will floaters and hikers in the future know why these ponds still sit in the flood plain?

The music played on from Jerry's stereo. In one corner of his office a large poster with a photo by *Life* magazine photographer Andreas Feininger depicted a dusty wayside town on Route 66 in Arizona, 1953. It was the opposite of the cool, green Meramec River, but to Jerry just as memorable.

The American earth, both the great West and the humid Ozarks, inspired this city guy as much as his friends had during a crucial time in his community's life.

* * *

Another inspiring visit: Boxing Day '16, with Jerry and Darlene plus her brother Doug, a long-term visitor/refugee from Nebraska. We went to the Missouri Botanical Garden for their Garden Glow winter festival. It was sort of crazy.

Thousands of visitors descended on the place. Tickets were $18 a pop for non-members. That didn't faze the crowds.

But it did turn off our mutual friend David Curtis, who lives and farms along the Meramec River near the venerable town of Bourbon with its famous water tower. David likes coming into the city. He's known Jerry from the campaign against the dam. We had set up that he'd meet us at the Garden. But at 5 p.m., after parking and trying to find us in the crowds, he texted Cathy that he was heading back to the country.

I can't blame him. The usually sedate Garden was mobbed. But the staff had things well organized. Everyone had tickets timed every fifteen minutes. The workers wore flashing star buttons and directed folks towards which long line to join as we neared the visitors' center.

David had arrived a few minutes after 5 p.m. so Jerry and I went back out to the parking lots to try to find him. It made both Jerry and me nervous to be lost in the crowds trying to find a guy neither of us had seen for several years. Our cell phones didn't help us make the connection. It was a sea of people.

Jerry began hollering, "David, David Curtis, where are you?" But people just ignored us as we walked through the crowd. No one knew where David was. A guard let us back into the visitor's center when I got the message that David had become totally frustrated and gone back to the farm.

Both Jerry and I were frustrated too, but amazed at the crowds. We walked through the throngs looking at the faces and wondering if we recognized anyone. We had both grown up in this city, but we didn't run into anyone we knew.

Yet everyone was so polite and patient. There was no pushing or shoving. Lots of families with kids. It was a relatively warm evening, low 50s.

People were in a good mood. Three days of grey cold weather had broken that afternoon.

Venus beamed as an orange sunset flamed over the Garden. We met Cath, Darlene and Doug upstairs to begin our trek through the evening's displays.

Mr. Shaw's white marble tomb glowed with holiday lights out in the

distance. We didn't see everything. We talked and oohed and aahed at the seasonal displays. Darlene and Cathy took cell phone photos; Doug took lengthy videos with his amazing $50 tablet. Jerry and I took it all in with simple joy. Just seeing the bright lights was enough for us old guys.
—June 2015

> Jerry died August 23, 2019, following an accident while riding his bicycle in St. Louis.

Sidebar

Rex Harrel's Best Story

> Rex was a ladies' man, married several times, always with a bright twinkle when Cathy and I visited at his shop. He was probably the most famous traditional craftsman from the Ozarks.
>
> The editor of the late *Ozark Mountaineer* magazine, Clay Anderson, told me to see him when I was organizing the Appalachian-Ozark craft exhibit for the Speed Art Museum in Louisville, 1989. Rex showed a collection of handmade tools made from high quality steel from worn-out implements.
>
> You can see Rex in the 2010 film *Disfarmer*, about the amazing photographer who lived in neighboring Heber Springs. Maybe there's something in Cleburne County water that turns out strong-willed folk. Some of my people settled there too; the little town of Prim is right nearby.
>
> This story came from one of the last times we visited. Rex was in his late 80s, spry and energetic, still living in the farmhouse he had built long ago, uphill from Wilburn, Arkansas. I hope his spirit has found new dwellings high above the Ozarks.

An old neighbor recently got a bad diagnosis from his doctor: terminal cancer. The farmer asked his son to get together a dinner for as many of his old friends as could fit in their church basement.

After the big barbecue dinner, which he and his son cooked for the group, the still healthy-appearing man stood at the head table. He cleared his throat and began.

"I know many of you wonder why I've invited you to dinner this evening. Well, I've had some bad news. The doctors tell me I have an incurable case of AIDS. They have no idea where this may have come from, but they told me to wrap up my business and say good-bye to my friends."

Everyone looked shocked. The room soon cleared after the friends shook hands with their neighbor, the farmer who seemed to be healthy but wasn't apparently.

Sidebar: Rex Harrel's Best Story

After the last guest left, the son asked his father, "Dad, why did you say it's AIDS? The doctors said nothing about that." The man had a slight twinkle in his eye when he replied to his son, "I don't want any of my old friends messing around with your mother."

42

In Search of Commonwealth

In Memory of Doug Wixson

> What does it mean to be an intellectual in our time? Does it mean publishing a lot or being active in important issues of a community? This remembrance was for a collection focused on one man who answered these questions thoroughly.
> More than 30 colleagues wrote pieces for *Douglas Wixson Remembered* that Fred Whitehead, a Kansas City writer, compiled and edited with love and skill in 2019 for John Brown Press. Luckily, Doug left a long paper trail as well as many friends and strong family ties.

* * *

Of all the wondrous times I spent with my Okie buddy, the most memorable may be our fishing trip to the Ouachita River in the wilds of Arkansas in the spring of 2002.

Doug couldn't help being a teacher. He loved to share stuff. He cooked up this trip. I was honored to be his Sancho Panza, perhaps in the same spirit as he insouciantly took up the mantle as my mentor. Our goal, besides adventure and small mouth bass, was to find the physical remains of Commonwealth College, the radical experiment of the late 1920s and early '30s.

He and his life-long companion in educational exceptionalism, Suzanne Chamier, had left the University of Missouri–Rolla for diverse challenges in central Texas.

But we kept in touch by mail, real letters. Both he and Suzanne have been steady correspondents. Having recently finished his biography of the great Missouri worker-writer Jack Conroy, Doug began taking trips into the High Plains to follow Sanora Babb's trek from Oklahoma to Hollywood. Doug may have loved research on the road most of all.

Our plan was to meet at the Queen Wilhelmina State Park lodge for our first night. It's roughly halfway between Georgetown, Texas, and Rolla, Missouri. I barely made it by dark. Doug had taken a warm-up hike and

42. In Search of Commonwealth

had his gear ready for the next day. Even choosing this location was an educational stroke of genius. The name of this lovely site suggests much about early Ozark economic development. Kansas City railway men and Dutch capital developed the resort in the 1890s on Rich Mountain, the second highest in the Ozarks.

As much a scholar as an activist who played a role in our local Peace Issues Group, the Rolla Red Readers, and the anti–Meramec Dam campaign, Doug was also a savvy investor. He was fascinated by the stock market almost with the enthusiasm he had for contemporary literature. Besides giving Cathy and me John Bogle's book on mutual funds, he gave us a binder of notes and photocopies of good financial writing. He was a big fan of laddering treasury notes and the right index funds. Here's what Doug typed as a foreword:

> I hope that you can use some of this, and I encourage you to write your own "notes to yourself," using a loose-leaf binder with dividers.
> That way you don't have to carry this junk (necessary junk) around in your head, and can devote yourself to Blue Bells blooming, gumbo and blessings.
> Please make additions and send me copies. Maybe we could write an investment book for grassroot socialists living under capitalism.

This financial acumen matched Doug's love of aircraft and tools. When Cathy and I visited his new place in Austin, he wanted to show me his closet-sized shop by the garage, tools as tidy as an engineer's kit. This respect for mechanical craft may be part of the reason I was eager to fly with him in a small plane he regularly rented in Rolla.

I'm not sure where we landed—at a public strip somewhere in the Belleview Valley north of the St. Francois Mountains in the eastern Ozarks. My dad had a cabin outside of Caledonia. He met us at the airfield and drove over to his place for lunch with farmers Leonard and Ginny Hall, an author of great Ozark books and a former Broadway dancer. We hiked a bit, took a picture, and flew back to Rolla by sunset.

The next morning my father died of a massive heart attack at home in St. Louis. A few days later Doug sent us a 5 × 7 color print of the group, with Leonard and Timon smiling at each other as if they had just seen Blue Bells blooming along Possum Trot Road.

On our Arkansas expedition Doug had triangulated where Commonwealth College must have been located in hills outside of Mena. He was not hopeful anything would be found. He was right. The site was posted against trespass by political malcontents.

We went into town, got necessary tackle and found where to rent a canoe. That afternoon we put up our tents at the Shirley Creek Float Camp just north of the Hog Jaw community, as it's called on the map.

I can't write that without thinking of Annie Proulx's novel *That Old*

Ace in the Hole, which deals with a Global Pork Rind's field rep trying to buy up farms on the High Plains where the Texas and Oklahoma panhandles define the great beyond. Bob Dollar at first looks at the locals as total rubes and losers. But things change.

Doug was sort of like Bob Dollar. He was a field representative for the commonwealth of Woody Guthrie and Will Rogers, Molly Ivins and Ann Richards. A tough dude who survived illness for years, he kept up his correspondence electronically. Cathy and I visited Doug and Suzanne in his last weeks. We went to museums, favorite local Austin spots and almost to the Broken Spoke. Suzanne and Doug shared a passion for music, but Doug's active dancing and banjo picking days were long gone, though his correspondence seemed as engaged as ever.

Back in '02 Doug and I spent the whole day on the Ouachita River, fishing, swimming, drinking beer, talking, bird watching, napping, etc. If we caught any bass, they were safely returned home.

The only person at our bivouac was a lone Forest Service volunteer campground host with a small trailer for the summer. Doug was fascinated.

Here was a real guy out in nature helping the public. We stayed up late talking by our fire. The next morning, we headed back north and south, to our work like folkloric shadow catchers who had seen truth in flames and on the river. We came out of the Ouachita Mountains renewed.

—Springfield, Missouri, Spring 2018.

> Doug died on May 26, 2017, in Austin. That evening, a beautiful Texas Hill Country sunset filled the western sky.

43

Plonked in Nowheresville

Tristen Russ

> This began simply enough. My 16-year-old foster grandson, Tristen Russ, visited our cabin near the Jacks Fork River several times. Over the years he has graduated from snake hunting to tournament-quality fishing. This suggests what a super young man he became.

The hottest week this summer, and no A/C. But we're hanging out by the river. No problem.

Except last Friday. We decided to check out one of the sweetest spots, Bee Bluff, just upstream from Bay Creek.

The Ozark National Scenic Riverways—a linear park along Current River and its tributary, the Jacks Fork—abounds with gnarly wilds. Driving down to Bay Creek, we pulled over to talk with a ranger.

"Toward Bee Bluff's fine," the man said. "But just a half-mile away the gravel bar gets a little soft because of all the flooding."

Tristen and I drove up, unloaded my canoe near the last camping spot, then paddled our way up to a shady gravel bar for the afternoon.

Higher than a thunderhead, this cliff creates a fishing hole a half-mile long and seemingly as deep. As pure as summer sky, the Jacks Fork remains clear and inviting. Tristen landed a bunch of small-mouth but threw them all back. "It takes five years to grow one a pound," he explained. "I never keep 'em."

I landed a bluegill that would be small in an aquarium, but did catch a great nap.

Finally, afternoon heat was breaking. I paddled Tristen downstream. In fifteen minutes he pulled in a half dozen bass others could legally keep. All on a brown rubber worm.

We loaded up, saying "hi" and "bye" to the folks at that last camp where we parked. We headed up what I thought was a shortcut.

All of a sudden, the track turned soft. "Turn in here, then you can back out," Tristen suggested when we hit loose gravel. Wrong move!

Oops—we got stuck by a big ol' sycamore. Backed up a little, but just dug deeper into river rock.

Near dark, I walked back to that last campsite to see about calling a wrecker. Tristen stayed to try to dig us out with his hands and sticks.

"No cell service, you're way out there," this big ol' boy named Jim said, knowing right where we were stuck. He offered to come have a peak.

"You take care, that's my truck!" his wife exclaimed. Grabbing a 20-foot log chain stowed with his gear, he set aside taters he'd been frying over a fire. "Save me some!" Off we drove up the trail.

Jim explained his family tries to camp here once a year. His dad grew up in a log cabin with a dirt floor not far from the Jacks Fork.

"This ain't nothing," Jim said when he first spotted my old Ford. "If I had my one-ton hay truck we usually bring, I'd had have you out in a minute."

Jim's efforts turned out to be the longest ten minutes of my life. He directed us to place his chain at three different spots on my quarter-ton, then pulled us sideways. Tristen and I kept digging loose gravel out from the tires with sticks.

He finally pulled us away from that monster sycamore. We left a big hole full of branches to warn people.

Be careful! Jim and his family from LaRussell, Missouri, may not be camping to help you get out of that ditch in the middle of Nowheresville. And Tristen will only be there in spirit.

> This collection is dedicated to Tristen, who died in a highway accident in no way typical of his careful nature. But calamity perhaps can be too common for 17-year-olds driving to a job early in the morning.

Memoir

*From China's Skuzziest City—
Teaching Oral History*

Ending this collection with a piece on China may seem a stretch, but the connections between our two regions have lasted a long time. Biogeographers have known eastern North American and eastern Asia as the first and best known disjunct of closely related plants thousands of miles apart. Daniel Boone dug ginseng to sell to the Emperor's buyers. The surprising similarity of some plants in China and the U.S. is one of many aspects that makes travelers in both locations feel at home when overseas (see "Biogeographical Relationships between Temperate Eastern Asia and Temperate Eastern North America," *Annals of the Missouri Botanical Garden*, vol. 70, nos. 3 & 4, 1983.)

* * *

It's nearly 3 a.m. in central China when my dreams drift over to Crawford County, Missouri, USA. Maybe I'm restless from showing *Don't It Feel Like Home*, a film about the Steelville area, to grad students in Shijiazhuang, recently known as China's most polluted, dirty and ugly town. We've found it's hardly a cultural desert anymore, not "nasty" as the Lonely Planet called the city 20 years ago.

This town is the setting for the late director Hu Bo's film, *An Elephant Sitting Still*, recently released in the States to great acclaim. Too bad the director did not live to enjoy this reception.

Critics say it's a dark film, maybe a Chinese equivalent of *Winter's Bone*, the Ozark film portraying Jennifer Lawrence struggling to save her family land. Am I naturally drawn to these kinds of noir scenes? Maybe.

I've made a career staying away from the mainstream, but not by plan. Spending almost a year in Vietnam, when most of my classmates found ruses to beat the draft, changed my trajectory considerably. My career in oral history has become more mainstream in recent decades.

I worked on the 90-minute Steelville film long ago with Tom Shipley, the one-toke guy from Rolla. My host at Hebei University of Science and Technology got a kick out of that song when he found it on the Net a few days ago.

Will Wang loved Death Metal and Kiss as a kid. "One Toke Over the Line" seems like a gentle folk song to him. Drugs have of course been a complex, longtime issue in China.

Our film creates a charming picture of this Ozark resort community. We were hired through a special fund created by the Steelville Telephone Exchange in the '90s to produce a promotional oral history love song for the greater Crawford County area. Unfortunately, not many people have seen it in the U.S. due limited distribution.

It's a gas for me to revisit via video the upper Meramec River country while teaching in China. To see a variety of folks floating down Ozark streams, sunbathing and swimming must seem like an exotic indulgence for students in Shijiazhuang, a village of 500 souls a century ago. Now it's a metropolis of 10 million people. In this lecture hall/classroom for 200, Steelville has become a foreign place for me; China, by contrast, a powerful reality that grows and changes with almost unknowable logic.

I've been dreaming about the Dairy Isle, the hamburger heaven David and Merrill Horner purchased and renovated in Steelville. Their burgers have infiltrated my subconscious. Maybe it's because I've eaten a steady diet of Hebei food for the last two weeks, including a banquet featuring donkey meat. I've loved most treats. Cathy not so much. Too much Chinese food for her.

Maybe hamburgers are a comfort food. I too am a little nervous to be in China. Dreaming of hamburgers in Steelville, Missouri, takes me to a safe place. The international trade talks between our two governments have created a discordant mood. Are we going back to the bad old days when China was seen as the great evil? From graduate work, I know America's perception of Asia runs hot and cold with little logic and almost by whim.

"How do you know they'll let you leave if you say the wrong thing?" my brother-in-law Joe Kovarik commented when I told him about this chance to teach.

I had wondered about that myself in idle moments. Have the Chinese censors been reading my e-mail, and know I am an unreformed capitalist running dog deserving Communist re-education?

* * *

We walked toward the city center to find a McDonalds burger place a few nights ago, to get something unlike what we've had for the last weeks. I had a Sichuan Double Chicken Spicy Burger. Cath had a standard one-paddy burger with fries. Both almost tasteless. Not so the Sichuan chicken, but it had lettuce. I ate it all. No problem. Cath also had no reactions. Just early to bed for us with a sense of wonder after a long walk through the still busy park.

Not a typical evening, but nothing has been expected. We share a kind of apprehension here. We don't know what's next. For me this range of feelings creates a fascination for all that's happening because so much is new. For Cath this trip hasn't been much fun because she worries over details and doesn't share my amazement with China's progress. So my job has been double, as comforter and organizer. Luckily most of the organizing for teaching has fallen to Will.

He's an enthusiastic guy who loves his ideas about the Ozarks. That's why I'm here. This opportunity to teach developed late in the fall. We were visiting Jim Bogan and Mary Bird at their new place outside Rolla. He had just received an email from Professor Wang looking for someone to inspire his English language students. Jim couldn't do it himself—knee surgery.

"Maybe I could give it a try," I offered and gradually over the early weeks of winter most details were worked out via email. I explained how I have a manuscript focused on the rural Ozarks and could focus lectures on oral history methodology. Will said, "Fine, we can work out details later." Unfortunately, since arriving in China, I've lost my email connection because of government restrictions. Luckily, I'm prepared to teach. This lack of a Google connection was our only unexpected problem.

What makes this visit somewhat unusual has been a focus on oral history and the Ozarks. I'm reading portions of my book and showing videos from the Ozarks to kids mildly fascinated with this exotic corner of America. I feel doubly tasked: to build appreciation for America's diverse heritage while encouraging students and Will to consider undertaking the first steps of an oral history project, a new research area for the People's Republic of China (PRC).

Will makes everything easy. He is an unusual scholar, a PhD in literature whose dissertation was on the great English mystic poet William Blake as understood through Chinese Taoism. In a few days we're going to one of the great Taoist sites here, Taishan, a sacred mountain to the east in Shandong province. Will it be a tourist trap as has become common elsewhere?

We've done few such touristy things in three weeks here. I have been focused on teaching, which has been surprisingly easy, partly because Cath has helped with PowerPoints to create teaching visual aids. Will takes care of all arrangements; his girlfriend Willa, other details.

The Hebei Science and Technology U. campus lies a couple of miles south of downtown, but not in a bucolic suburb. Industry and apartment towers surround the gated complex. Built in an international Brutalist style, the campus offered a mix of traditional Chinese landscaping with huge classroom buildings where chilly interiors, clogged plumbing and temperamental internet require constant flexibility from our host. I was adaptable and appreciative of my students' excellent English.

The first group was graduate students with a focus on careers as translators. I read them the story about Aileen Hatch's grandfather's wagon burning, then showed the Steelville film, which led to a discussion of rural vs. urban living. On the second day I read George Lane's moonshine story and showed "Downtown," by Carbon Trace Productions, a friend's project about changing Springfield.

For most of the students Mr. Lane's story had some relevance. Many have recently moved to this fast-growing city with their families, part of PRC planning. They often have grandparents back in rural communities. They understand why grandpa makes moonshine. They picked up on how George's story takes place during Prohibition. Wasn't that an idealistic but poorly implemented scheme during a strange period of American history?

"We also had a government Prohibition period in China," one student held up his hand and explained. "It was during the Song Dynasty. The emperor ruled because of crop failure none of the grain harvested could be used for Biajiao," a form of drinkable grain alcohol. "He helped save many lives from starvation a thousand years ago."

That encouraged one student to recall how her family had suffered during the Great Hunger of the early 1960s. Everyone in the large hall became quiet. It was a hard time in central China. Millions died partly as a result of the Great Leap Forward. They evidently knew personally about famine.

Another student said he had a great-uncle who was a bandit. That changed the atmosphere in the lecture hall. A few students laughed.

"What kind of a bandit? This is very unusual," I asked.

"He didn't have many choices back then."

"Did he have to support a family?"

"He couldn't have a wife or child. He had to support his parents."

"So, how did he make any money as a bandit?"

"He robbed people when they were traveling. He went to prison."

"That's a sad life."

"Eventually he got out and continued to take care of his family."

* * *

Not teaching one Saturday, we took a bus trip to the countryside with Will while Willa tutored as many as 20 children in English. Her usual Saturday gig.

"The money's really good," Will explained. "People know we deeply care about children, learning and literature. Our rate is $70 an hour. There are many families in Shijiazhuang who can easily afford this, but we don't want to take on too many students. We have other projects."

It's almost an hour ride to the Luquan District west of the city. Will did his undergraduate work on the west side of this huge city, which looks just like all the other parts. Huge blocks of 30-story, or higher, apartment buildings gradually give way to ruins of farmhouses and villages under seemingly casual cultivation near the Taihang Mountains. Mostly fruit tree plantings. Few folks ride at mid-morning so Will feels comfortable talking. I model interviewing.

"I was always a reader. That's why I decided to major in English. Even when I was a little boy, I read books like *Jane Eyre*. I was born on August 2, 1977. My father was a factory worker who scared the hell out of me.

"'You'd better do good on the GAO KAO' [standardized college entrance exam], he warned. 'You don't want to be a factory worker where your boss yells at you every day.' So I did okay. I got into Hebei Teachers College then taught high school for three years. I taught textbooks as I was told. So boring!"

Will's dissertation at Beijing's Foreign Language University on William Blake's poetry led to a friendship with Jim Bogan and visits abroad.

"I wanted to be a writer but I've learned I'm lazy. So much better being a college professor than having to write all the time, especially in Shijiazhuang. We don't have pressures like larger, prestigious places. I can work with my students, with younger kids; I can do critical essays; I can read about what I think is important."

Eventually we made our way to the Junlebao Dairy Farm, which features display gardens, an educational center and, today, a cow-walking event, which seems similar to back home charity events attracting well-intentioned crowds raising funds. Will had never been here. It's set up for modern mass tourism, which describes today's crowd.

But the weather changes. A spring shower blows in. Waiting for a bus, I continue interviewing Will so he can see how it's done, encouraging him to tell stories endlessly. I focus on his work.

"I write a lot about popular culture. I like writing short columns, especially for *Guang Ming Daily*, a paper of record for the Communist Party. My latest column is about a family TV show where the wife has to stand up to her husband. I mention Cathy's story about her tuition."

Shortly after she graduated from Saint Louis University, Cathy's mom found out her father expected his two daughters to pay him back their tuition, but not his three sons.

"Girls don't need a job," Cath explained his reasoning. "Our mom just felt it was unfair. Eventually my father gave in."

Big Joe would get a laugh out of that, kudos in a Commie newspaper.

"I've never been a member of the Communist Party," Will said. "Maybe I'm too independent-minded. But I am also not much of a believer in democracy; I have seen how even our local elections are effected by candidates who buy votes. I am for a meritocracy. I think Xi Jin Ping is doing a pretty good job for us now."

* * *

One of the first Ozarkers to trade with China never had a chance to visit the dragon kingdom. Daniel Boone, pioneer hero, spent many hours collecting ginseng from the Missouri backwoods then selling it to brokers. Clipper ships hauled Ozark roots across the Pacific for the Emperor to enjoy.

I've thought often of Squire Boone and our native plants being harvested for sale so long ago. Now ginseng is cultivated in Wisconsin and rare in the Ozarks. Have our values changed? Do we know how to protect what was once common?

* * *

In such a dynamic city, how can Will Wang be attracted to American culture, especially the Ozarks? He's a big fan of *Winter's Bone*, both the film and the novel, and has told his students to at least see the film while I am here.

"Most of the people in Shijiazhuang have roots in our rural areas. For holidays we all go back to the rural countryside to see family," Will says.

A few days before leaving we go back to the Luquan district to visit a new complex, the Western Evergreen Resort, in a mountain valley. Shops like in Breckinridge, Colorado, line a stream. The hotels seem typical of Aspen or Vail. A chairlift takes visitors to a replica of the Great Wall. A greenhouse covering 20 acres is under construction. Local workers replant the landscape. Will regrets we won't have time to visit the large Prague Beer Village.

"I love the Ozarks and Jim's cabin in Moonshine Hollow because I feel so free there," Will explains his attraction to his American colleague. He has visited Rolla and University of Kansas at Lawrence because of his academic interests.

When he gets into a classroom, Will bosses students around like a drill sergeant and gives specific commands for homework and projects.

Most of all: "Practice speaking English! Don't be shy!"

He gets groups to pick a spokesperson. Most kids indeed enjoy trying out their English. They've been studying it since 4th grade. I am jealous; my Mandarin hasn't improved much while here. I'm too busy being overwhelmed by all that's swirling around, keeping Cath happy and consulting with Will while navigating this rural metropolis. Taking buses and walking to Will's favorite restaurants—usually in multistoried shopping centers—we've only seen a few fellow round-eyes. As a working city, Shijiazhuang attracts few international visitors. Now I have some sense how it feels to be a minority, always out of place.

Mainly through reading Joseph Needham's history of Chinese science, I'm in awe how advanced the Middle Kingdom has often been. I wish I knew more about traditional Chinese medicine as well.

A few chilly days bring back my persistent winter cough during classes. Will suggests I try traditional cough medicine, available at a pharmacy near his apartment.

"It's so tasty, I didn't mind having a cold when I was a kid!" he says. Will's right. It reminds me of honey and lemon juice mom used to make. *Nin Jiom Pei Pa Koa* has a few special ingredients, according to the label:

Tendrilleaf Fritillary Bulb
Loquat Leaf
Fourleaf Ladybell Root
Indian Bread
Pummelo Peel
Platycodon Root
Prepared Pinellia Tuber
Chinese Magnoliavine Fruit
Snakegourd Seed
Common Coltsfoot Flower
Thinleaf Milkwort Root
Bitter Apricot Seed
Fresh Ginger
Licorice Root
Almond Extract
Menthol
Honey
Maltose
Syrup

* * *

Two weeks ago I was drinking beer and enjoying hot pot with Feiyue in Beijing as we prepared to leave China. Now I'm back in the Ozarks packing up my all stuff, preparing to sell our house and move. Craziness! Today has meant going through old recordings from oral history projects. A donation of tapes and transcripts to the state historical society is finally in the works!

Two lugs of mail had surprises, including the Winter/Spring 2019 Issue of *The Oral History Review* [https://academic.oup.com/ohr] featuring Alexander Freund's essay on oral history in China, "Long Shadows Over New Beginnings?" For a scholar who may speak less Mandarin than the average Canadian, he presents a fascinating review of how life histories may have become "a tool of mass control" during the Cultural Revolution of the early '70s.

Freund's overview reinforces what I saw while teaching those weeks in Shijiazhuang. Education may be highly localized, just as in the U.S. Each province has its academic superstructure and goals. Whether Will Wang or others develop an oral history project at his university depends on diverse variables. I left him with enough ideas to get started, if he and the bureaucracy want to.

Following my last meeting with freshman English, Will presented me with a bundle of 100 RMB notes, as promised. Cathy was surprised a historian could be generously paid, but she hadn't seen all the logistics ahead of time. It's not a field for quick wealth, but meeting expectations usually yields promised returns, as I have seen in different projects over decades. My career has skimped along barely making expenses, but at least has saved a few Ozark voices and images for Chinese young people and others in the future while paying me subsistence.

Friends had advised me not to worry leaving to go home; teaching on a tourist visa is no problem because no wage was paid, only an honorarium. I felt a magnanimous relief finally to be relaxing in O'Hare Airport despite our flight to Kansas City being delayed for six hours by tornadoes ripping the Great Plains. No special questioning in leaving China. I knew our foster daughter Teresa and her husband Jay would monitor the weather and meet us. I enjoyed walking around the crowded concourse in Chicago to look at books, magazines and newspapers published since I had been in China. So much news. So inconsequential compared to our hours with friends, students and big Buddhas inspiring us from many centuries.

Ambling about the terminal I met a fellow Missourian who was on our flight from Beijing, Reid Millard, president of Parker-Millard Funeral Service and Crematory, Columbia. His son and daughter had joined him in Fujian Provence to buy black granite for memorials.

"Americans have no idea how advanced China has become," Reid said. "They're building a massive university from scratch where we were. Their trains move millions daily on strict schedules. These folks know how to do business!"

A few days earlier I heard a slightly different assessment from another traveling business family. We shared a three-hour dinner at the fancy Shangri-La Hotel in Qufu with a couple consulting on regional transportation infrastructure.

"We grew up in Weimar, which was part of East Germany then," the wife said. "China reminds me of our time under communism. Everyone is subtly spying on everyone else. No one will tell you the truth, what they are really thinking. They know the government is always listening, watching out for who might be disloyal."

Her husband agreed that the surveillance state can feel oppressive. But he was truly impressed by how fast trains keep their schedule. So seafood on this inland buffet was as fresh as Qingdao.

Maybe the Chinese dragon is like India's elephant, the critter who was visited by several blind visitors long ago: one saying this animals is like a snake, another claiming it's more of a whale; did the third think it was solid like a cedar tree?

Memoir: From China's Skuzziest City—Teaching Oral History

Is this what the friends found in the recent Shijiazhuang film *The Elephants Sit Down*? Like the U.S., China is vast and changing. Lots of good stuff, some questionable stuff too, just like the USA. My Chinese friends each had slightly different attitudes to what they're experiencing, but all appreciate the economic progress. This makes China a foil to the Ozarks, which seems unchanging by comparison.

This is part of the reason I study Mandarin, contemporary politics and oral history. Is China setting the future for the whole world? Are they destroying the environment with too rapid development?

I remember a commanding officer from 1968 returning from his tour in Vietnam. "Our next war is going to be with China," he predicted. "Vietnam is just a prelude to The Big One!"

Even then, before setting foot in Saigon, that made me sick. Can a war be inevitable? Fifty years later after a half-dozen trips to Asia, I still wonder if the hot heads will take over.

Opinions seem so diverse among people we know in China now. This trip gave both Cath and me much hope and gratitude. But what governments will do, we can hardly guess.

What is it that makes some people patient and wise, others hot-headed and egocentric? Can't we have differences without fighting?

* * *

> One of my strongest memories from visiting China in 2019 is spending a few days in Qingdao, a seaside city famous for its German-inspired beer. We met the Guo family who had been living in Springfield where Grace was studying literature. Mr. Guo runs a company to buy Ozark hardwood for manufacturers in China. They generously showed us their beautiful city.
>
> One winter day several years ago we had spent an afternoon visiting Ozark lumber yards. Mr. Guo would ask the mill owners to open bundles of boards so he could inspect their quality. Very carefully he examined each board for defects to make sure the quality of the firm's wood met standards his customers would expect.
>
> Ozark forests produce some of the finest oak timber in the world. We have a huge variety of oaks. These forests not only produce lumber, but they also harbor lots of wildlife, make for clear streams and clean up polluted air. Anything we can do to protect and promote our forests will help us, Chinese people who need furniture or flooring, and the world at large, which needs peace and economic progress. No reason we can't have both.

Epilogue

Bedrock, Paradox and Petroforms

Having cultivated these tales, I find a bushel remaining unplanted. So here's one with hints at what's missed.

Luckily one article that cannot be included because of space limitations can be found on the Internet. I wrote about petroforms and friends who first identified them in the Ozarks for the *St. Louis Post-Dispatch* some 22 years ago.

Native Americans made these arrangements of stones hundreds if not thousands of years ago in prehistory. Archaeologists believe they may have multiple functions, as do petroglyphs.

Brian Kridelbaugh and Nancy Bryant first became aware of them while hiking near Rolla in the national forest. Since Brian was a stone mason, he knew sandstone slabs should lie horizontally. These were standing stones. Nancy and Brian mapped dozens of stone arrangements at multiple sites throughout the Ozarks. It gradually became apparent to them certain stone shapes were commonly used.

Carol Diaz-Granados and her husband Jim Duncan from Washington University in St. Louis accepted Brian and Nancy's invitation to visit the initial site to see this discovery for themselves.

On a hot summer day long ago I went with Carol and Jim, authors of *The Petroglyphs and Pictographs of Missouri*,[1] and my Rolla friends to see the standing stones. Carol confirmed these stones were, in fact, petroforms. The first found in Missouri.

It was a bit unnerving. The more you looked at the different arrangements, images started to appear. Maybe it was the shadows. Brian pointed out several buffalo.

"According to my compass, certain stones seem to be directional, you know, the cardinal points, or solstice markers," Brian said. He was so enthusiastic about their discovery. Carol was too, and recalled similar standing stones at other sites she had visited on research trips over the years. It was an immense discovery.

It impressed me these two friends had the curiosity and passion to research this phenomenon. You can read their report in *Missouri Archaeological Society Quarterly* vol. 21, no. 3, July–Sept. 2004. They went on to win an award for the new research in 2003 from the Eastern States Rock Art Research Association. They accepted the award at an ESRARA conference in Huntsville, Alabama, where Brian and Nancy presented slides on their discovery to archaeologists in attendance.

As I write this I think of these friends and others I haven't seen in years. I know glorified pot hunters looking for arrowheads and keeping few records of their digging. This effort was something else—true research. I regret I will never see Brian again because he died in early September 2020. A stonemason's life is tough.

"It's a young man's work," Brian used to say. He was never shy of hard work. He rarely gave up on projects but worked at his own pace and to his own high standards. He inspired me to take time to look deeply into landscape and nature in general.

Brian hauled hundreds of stones to an earth-sheltered house Cathy and I built outside Rolla with help of President Jimmy Carter's solar tax credit. Brian built stone planting beds, laid creek rock pathways, enclosed a well with sandstone. New folks own the house now and maintain the radiant floor the Chiles brothers from Springfield designed and installed long ago. The concrete floor has special plastic pipe connected to solar collectors and the wood stove. The system takes a bit of oversight. Brian's rocks take care of themselves. They're inspiring in their solid simplicity.

* * *

We visited our old place outside Rolla a few months ago and were impressed the new owners have improved on what was left behind. We loved that unique house. We felt we were riding the wave of the future with solar energy. It hasn't quite arrived, but maybe soon we'll all be driving electric vehicles powered in part by sun and wind. That was the hope of many back-to-the-landers who've came to the Ozarks in recent years: grow a garden and heat with a solar greenhouse, or some similar alternative energy arrangement.

All kinds of arrangements are possible. Wood stoves will always be popular for heating in the Ozarks, except for those of us living in town—hard to heat with wood in a city, unfortunately. Sitting around an old potbelly to warm up cannot be beat.

Energy's relevant now because cold weather comes in as I finish this manuscript. Today I made the first gumbo of the season with the last fresh okra from a nearby farmers market.

My first time to try a duck gumbo. Springfield has a great locally owned butcher shop that Cathy likes. Her dad was a butcher. He liked duck too, but Rita would not cook it for him. I can see why. It was a messy, nearly all-day job.

Cooking can be creative if you have time and good veggies. We've been living on salads, pizza and Sichuan noodles during this pandemic time. Not much creative cooking, from me anyway. Cold weather changes that.

"It's stringy. The texture is terrible," Cath comments on testing this gumbo. "The okra makes it gunky." I haven't made one in months. It can be tricky. Ray Brassieur, whose PhD is on Ozark French culture, taught me beaucoup. I remember our habanero vinegar sitting back in a corner. Two tablespoons cut the goop while strengthening the spicy broth. Some crawdad andouille sausage from Horrmann's shop brings it all together.

This collection may be similar. Lots of variety, unfortunately some pieces will not fit in the pot. Perhaps a few of these will get on my blog or whatever takes its place in the digital future.

Already I'm considering another collection, this one focused on deliberate, strong-willed lives in the Ozarks. These amazing folks range from Edna Staples, long-time leader of the Shannon County Historical Society, to Gen. Nathaniel Lyon, martyred at Wilson's Creek. These will be "Ultimate Ozarkers," people who offer continuing inspiration but are often overlooked in standard historic accounts.

Hopefully I will have a chance to deliver a paper on teaching oral history in China at the International Oral History Conference scheduled for Singapore but canceled once already. Cathy and I had hoped to also visit Taiwan where I spent a summer long ago teaching English and studying Mandarin. Can they work out a future for democracy there and elsewhere?

It may seem a bit strange to end a book on oral history in the Ozarks with a visit to China. We have shared many connections over the centuries, including similarities of plants in Eastern America and China first noticed by the Swedish naturalist Carl Linnaeus in the late 1700s. We then go from Daniel Boone digging ginseng for export on to Missouri journalist Edgar Snow buried at Peking University, Beijing. Combined, Arkansas and Missouri sold about $2 billion of various goods in China in 2018.

Isn't Asia as basic to understanding our country as European and other ethnic aspects of national heritage? After all, isn't this how American Indians received their commonly used appellation? When I was in grad school, I lived in Lafayette Square, a neighborhood near downtown Saint Louis, which the Revolutionary War ally and hero, the Marquis de Lafayette, visited in 1825. Near the center of this venerable park, one of the first parks west of the Mississippi, stands an imposing larger-than-life-size bronze statue of Thomas Hart Benton, one of the most formidable senators of his day and great-uncle of the great Ozark artist named in his honor. On the base of this imposing figure, these few words from one of Benton's speeches have been inscribed: "There is the East. There is India."

Where did that come from? This inscription always blew my mind when out for a walk. Why was it chosen for this renowned statue? It's one of the first and greatest pieces by one of the first American women to gain recognition as a sculptor, Harriet Hosmer. Senator Benton stood for the Union on the eve of the Civil War. He wanted our nation to be unified and saw the American West and trade with Asia as a great benefit for all in the future. Benton's hope for a peaceful future remains a vision worth respecting and carrying forward.

Both China and Taiwan reportedly have done a good job controlling the spread of Covid-19. We have lots to learn from them. They have peacefully navigated their differences so far and hopefully will arrive themselves at some harmonious accommodation. It takes time, as we should know from our own civil war still having repercussions.

Harmony above all, in history, in gumbo, in music, in agriculture, in everyday life. People came to the Ozarks because they found harmony with the land and its stone. We still must.
—October 25, 2020

Appendix 1

A Brief Guide to Doing Oral History Interviews

This is based on material I developed for lectures in China. My goal was to inspire students to consider doing family oral histories even if they were never assigned. This procedure follows methods I used with middle and high school students when teaching for state arts councils. The outline can be flexible, but most of these steps should be considered for any kind of interview.

The Oral History Association has a thorough webpage explaining the process, and many excellent guides and examples are available as suggested below.

- Decide on a topic that interests you.
- Choose who to interview.
- Set an appointment that allows ample time for your preparation.
- Do research in developing questions and practice using your recorder.
- Write a release to allow future use of your findings.
- Arrive early.
- Establish rapport.
- Ask questions about early years and relevant biographical details.
- Gradually lead up to your main questions.
- Look for additional information and turning points.
- Inquire about photos, other records, places to visit.
- Remember to request signing the release, either before or after the session.
- Try to do at least one follow-up interview soon after the initial visit.
- Send a thank-you note or call.
- Write a report/summary.
- Archive, and copy recording, maybe transcribe.
- Share your work.

Types of Questions for Oral Histories

- Biographical/family
- Stepping stones vs. turning points
- Open ended vs. yes/no
- Leading questions
- Surprising/unexpected/challenging

Friendly
Deep/searching
Economic, political, social and religious
Suggestions of others to interview

Oral History Release of Information

"I hereby authorize release for whatever literary, scholarly and scientific purposes may be determined, the recordings, transcriptions and contents of interviews between myself and Mr. Primm, the interviewer. I understand that others may listen to this recorded interview and that information from it may be used in documents, newspapers, books and scientific reports in accordance with any restrictions listed below. (The restrictions may include protection of my privacy, ideas and other matters.) This agreement also allows the interviewer to make and use photos, drawings and videotape associated with the interview."

This is the release wording I used on several projects including with Ft. Leonard Wood and the USGS. When printed, the form had blanks for my interviewee and myself to put in our contact information, date and signatures. Below that was a section for any special restrictions. I always had two copies to be able to leave one.

Appendix 2
Oral History Projects and Related Contributions

This list includes projects I worked on while centering my career on oral history. A few related activities deserve mention as well. This overview of one fieldworker's background and livelihood gives a glimpse of career choices.

Because I was a freelancer, I've done a variety of work. These jobs are not included here unless some connection with oral history seems relevant. I've also contracted to do family and business histories, not listed. Recording people's ties to nature has been my focus.

2020: **Oral history consultant**, Carbon Trace Productions, Springfield, Missouri. A team is seeking to revisit *Shannon County*, two films from 1981. After 40 years, this production has become increasingly popular on YouTube, leading Missouri State University's Special Collections to seek funds to produce a follow-up.

2019: **Guest instructor in Oral History**, Hebei University of Science and Technology, Shijiazhuang, Peoples Republic of China. Three weeks of classes and cultural exchanges.

2015–16: **Interviewer**, National Park Service/Missouri State University. Minorities on Rt. 66. Springfield and Greene County offered an African American hotel, restaurant and campground, the only welcoming hospitality between St. Louis and Tulsa in the Jim Crow era. The project will be part of the new National Trail being developed along the historic Mother Road from Chicago to Los Angeles.

2010: **Judge**, Oral History Association. Helped decide Elizabeth Mason Award for regional history. Served on other committees, as explained in text.

2005–08: **Project coordinator**, *Tree Dialogues*, an interactive exhibit based on visitors' stories about trees and a CD based on oral histories from the exhibit and elsewhere. Funded by East Central Community College, Washington, Missouri.

2002–2008: **Presenter and storyteller**, National Park Service, Ozark National Scenic Riverways, Van Buren, Missouri, and a variety of community events and venues. I have developed more stories about Nathaniel "Stub" Borders and other rivermen and their adventures.

1999–2003: **Contractor**, U.S. Army, to do oral history of settlement near Ft. Leonard Wood, Missouri. Edited and contributed to local history of the region, *Made in the Timber* (Champaign, Illinois, 2003.)

1998: **Visiting speaker**, Moberly Area Community College, Jack Conroy Memorial Lecture, "Backwoods people," multi-media performance based on Ozark oral history. This opportunity to present research began my storytelling career. Several programs at the Shiloh Museum, Springdale, Arkansas, and elsewhere.

1997: **Brownlee Grant recipient**, Missouri State Historical Society. Grant awarded for oral history of a destroyer crewed by St. Louis Naval reservists in the South Pacific during World War II.

1997: **Consultant**, Missouri Forest Heritage Center, Winona, Missouri. To help develop the Twin Pines Conservation Center, I wrote articles, gave programs to local groups, and gave tours when the facility was eventually opened.

1991–95: **Grant recipient**, oral history research in Mark Twain Forest, U.S. Forest Service. Focused on projects involving historic uses of the Big Piney River and mining in an historic French community in the eastern Ozarks.

1990–94: **Speaker**, Missouri Humanities Council "American Mirror" speakers bureau. Presented programs on Missouri history and culture to statewide audiences.

Producer and Writer, Oral History of the Ozarks. Worked on four videos on the Ozarks funded by the National Endowment for the Arts and other agencies.

1989–93: **Oral history researcher**, U.S. Geological Survey, Rolla, Missouri, for project with Ozark National Scenic Riverways. Resulted in lengthy technical report and article.

1987: **Board member**, Traditional Arts Apprenticeship Program. I helped choose craftspeople to receive grants to teach others and evaluated these partnerships.

1987–88: **Guest curator**, Appalachia/Ozark Tradition, exhibit, J.B. Speed Art Museum, Louisville, Kentucky. Collected folk material in Arkansas and Missouri for this museum.

1983–98: **Visiting Artist**, Young Audiences. I taught oral history and writing workshops in approximately 40 primarily rural schools in Arkansas and Missouri.

1983–88: **Curator**, Ozark Agricultural Museum at Maramec Spring Park, St. James. Responsibilities included assembling objects for exhibit, cataloging the museum's collection, oral histories, acquiring historic equipment for display and use, etc.

1982: **Scholarship to attend Rural Conservation Short Course** sponsored by the National Trust for Historic Preservation, Cazenovia, New York, on community and landscape conservation. Inspiring to see how small towns can thrive.

1981–83: **Grant recipient**, Missouri Humanities Council. Grant to carry out the Ozark Rivers Oral History Project while doing public relations at the Meramec Regional Planning Commission, Rolla, Missouri.

1975–77: **Project interviewer**, Religious Society of Friends and Social Activism in greater Philadelphia, Pennsylvania. A self-funded oral history with limited results while working for newspapers in the Delaware valley and freelancing.

1970–72: **Regional coordinator**,

Vietnam Veterans Against the War. Worked with national committee to plan veterans march on Washington, D.C., in April 1971. Also finished MA in Political Science from Saint Louis University.

1969–70: **Community organizer,** The Block Partnership Inc., St. Louis. I worked with white suburban churches and synagogues to pair with African American groups in the inner city to work on projects identified by urban residents. Some fifty partnerships were developed, but the United Fund decided not to continue necessary funding.

1969 **Summer school student, Stanford University, Palo Alto, California.** Studied sociolinguistics with Joshua Fishman on release from active duty in Vietnam. I had signed up for intensive Mandarin but arrived two days after this language program began; fortunate to find inspiring class with a master scholar.

1968 **Newspaper series writer,** for the *Beckley Post-Herald*. freelanced articles on the federal "War on Poverty" in West Virginia and focused on the structure and outcomes of government funding. Was stationed here before going to Vietnam.

1967: **Draftee, editor of military newspaper**, *The Vietnam Review.* After graduation from Washington University in St. Louis, was trained at the Defense Information School, Ft. Harrison, Indianapolis. Initially stationed in support of Recruiting Main Station, Beckley, West Virginia, then assigned to HQ, First Logistic Command, Long Binh, South Vietnam, September 1968 to June 1969.

Appendix 3

Oral and Community History Bibliography

In each list I include my 10 top choices. In all cases more studies could have been selected. I want to focus on my personal top picks, maybe not the latest scholarship but these are works which have inspired me.

1. Examples of Written Oral Histories

Agee, James. *Let Us Now Praise Famous Men* (Boston: Houghton Mifflin, 1941). This may be more an example of documentary lyricism, yet it offers many voices accurately.

Armitage, Sue and Laurie Mercier. *Speaking History: Oral Histories of the American Past, 1865—Present* (New York: Palgrave Macmillan, 2009). This anthology presents a wide range of speakers culled from an equally diverse selection of archives.

Banks, Ann. *First-Person America* (New York: Random House, 1981). Anthology of interviews gathered from the Federal Writers Project, 1938–42, by Depression-era authors who conducted some of the first oral histories done in this country.

Ball, Edward. *Slaves in the Family* (New York: Ballantine, 1998). An amazing search to reconstruct one family's history of owning 4,000 slaves in the American South. After winning the National Book Award and appearing on *Oprah*, the author has written additional compelling explorations of America's deleterious racism.

Ching, Frank. *Ancestors: 900 Years in the Life of a Chinese Family* (New York: Morrow, 1988, 2009). While not strictly an oral history, this epic family history inspired the Hong Kong–based attorney to have a son to carry on his lineage.

Hurston, Zora Neale. *Mules and Men* (New York: Harper 1935, 1990). More of an anthropological participant-observer account, these visits to the author's hometown with local storytellers shows how narrative prose can recreate the feelings of folklore.

Portelli, Alessandro. *The Order Has Been Carried Out: History, Memory, and Meaning of a Nazi Massacre in Rome* (New York: Palgrave Macmillan, 2003). A dense, multi-level history of a partisan attack, the Nazi revenge and continuing conflicted memories.

Rosengarten, Theodore. *All God's Dangers: The Life of Nate Shaw* (New York: Knopf, 1974). An oral biography of tenant farmer, former prisoner, union organizer and one of the greatest natural storytellers ever recorded.

Stacewicz, Richard. *Winter Soldiers: An Oral History of the Vietnam Veterans Against the War*, foreword by Donald Ritchie, Series Editor (New York: Twayne, 1997, 2008). At 450 pages this well edited collection shows the struggle to be relevant; an accurate assessment as I was a regional organizer and knew some of the subjects.

Terkel, Studs. *Working: People Talk About*

What They Do All Day and How They Feel About What They Do (New York: Pantheon, 1974). Of the pre-eminent oral historians, many books and recordings over his 96 years, this was the first to grab me.

2. Plays, Films, and Television Emphasizing Oral History

This lists a dozen works, more than the print bibliography, because movies can be deeply inspiring for anyone starting out in oral history. My friend Davey Dunsteader advised, partly based on his experience with the True/False Documentary Film Festival in Columbia, Missouri.

Circo, 2010. 75 Min. Written and directed with Cinematography by Aaron Schock (1960–), of Hecho-A-Mano Films. Originally a public policy academic, Schock is now pursuing his documentary passions. *Circo* follows Tito Ponce, his wife, children, elders, and menagerie as they crisscross Central and Western Mexico. *Circo* has been shown in numerous festivals and on PBS, HBO, and Showtime.

The Fog of War: Eleven Lessons from the Life of Robert McNamara, 2003. 107 Min. Directed by Errol Morris. Sony Picture Classic (theater), Columbia Tri-Star Home video (DVD Purchase), Amazon Prime Rental. A film by Errol Morris centered around interviews with Robert McNamara, former Secretary of Defense. Film includes his involvement in conflicts from World War II, including McNamara weeping about mistakes he made carrying out the Vietnam War. All the while, Errol Morris masterfully merges media, music, and McNamara.

Garlic Is as Good as Ten Mothers, 1980. 51 Min. Directed and produced by Les Blank (1935–2013), who specialized in capturing scenes of having fun while exploring the fringes of American culture. This film focuses on the Gilroy, California, Garlic Fest and sifts through commentators, customs, and cooking, all the while reveling in the greater glories of garlic. You're left with an appreciation of garlic as the common thread through the cuisines of different cultures.

High School, 1969. 75 Min. Directed and produced by Frank Wiseman (1930–). Zipporah Films. Wiseman's second of more than 40 films. Shot over five weeks at Northeast High School in Philadelphia, Pennsylvania, and edited for immersion into a typical school day. In recent years Wiseman has produced a documentary a year for the Public Broadcasting System.

I Am Not Your Negro, 2016. 95 Min. Written and directed by Raoul Peck (1953–). A film based on 30 pages of James Baldwin's (1924–1987) notes and an accompanying preliminary outline that he started in 1979. At age 24, Baldwin, disliking the racial treatment in New York City, self-exiled to Paris. Baldwin was an accomplished essayist and novelist who sketched out a tribute to and personal recollections of Malcolm X, Medgar Evers, and Martin Luther King, Jr. The film is a revelatory prophecy that brings out the unfilled promise of the American Dream. Six years after release, it frequently streams on Prime, Hulu and Netflix.

The Laramie Project, 2002. 97 Min. In the early 1990s, Moisés Kaufman (Playwright, Scriptwriter/Director) with the NYC Tectonic Theatre, developed techniques that capture and script "Moments." Then in the mid-90s, a murder of a gay University of Wyoming student occurred, and five troupe members spent a year in Laramie capturing "Moments." In 2001, HBO assembled an all-star cast and Kaufman directed the made-for-TV-film (97 min.). In January 2002, the star-laden film premiered at the Sundance Film Festival as an audience favorite. Tectonics was simulcast to 150 theatres and used the one-time opportunity to capture, reflect and share local "moments." Years later, *The Laramie Project* still streams on HBO(Max) "carrying on" this emotional issue.

Latcho Drom (Safe Journey), 1993. 103 Min. Written and directed by Tony Gatlif (1948–), a French director who also concurrently serves as Professor at the French National Film School, this film demonstrates how ethnicity matters. Gatlif, who is of Romany and Algerian descent, in the face of the predominate documentary approach (Cinéma Vérité), used counterintuitive techniques. These including music in lieu of narration, caravanning across the diaspora, and staging, rehearsing, and retaking musical performances. This Celluloid lightning is a greatest-hits tour de force of Gypsy Music.

The Midwife's Tale, *American Experience* (series), PBS, directed by Richard P. Rogers, Season 10 episode 8 (aired January 19, 1998). 90 Min. DVD from PBS and Amazon. An 18th-century rural healer's life is discovered through the work of a 20th-century historian, Laurel Thatcher Ulrich. Her book is based directly on a Maine midwife's journal she found in a little-used archive. Select academic and public libraries offer streaming through Kanopy.

Reds, 1981. 195 Min. Actor, Writer, Director and Producer—Warren Beatty. Nine nominations with three Academy wins. Beatty spent 10 years researching and fundraising and 18 months of production. *Reds* script is based on *10 Days That Shook the World*, a book by John Reed, *Reds* main character and real-life embedded reporter in the Russian Revolution. Historic Bolshevik framework as well as details surrounding Reed's love life are added to give *Reds* the Hollywood "epic" sweep. Oral history interview clips peppered throughout with unidentified "real" commentators make *Reds* one-of-a-kind. These direct observers in Moscow, Paris, and New York lend a documentary sheen to a "blockbuster." The Sondheim soundtrack is sublime.

Shoah, 1985. 570 Min. Claude Lanzmann (1925–2018). *Shoah* was 12 years in the making and a 9½-hour life's work that documented the Holocaust. Lanzmann was a French new-wave director and intellectual associated with Jean-Paul Sartre and Simone de Beauvoir. The power of *Shoah* is in its subtle and intentional triggering of the imagination. Exacting and comprehensive, the first-person testimony is the only narrative. Lanzmann released 6 more *Shoah*-related films over the next 30+ years.

Super-Size Me, 2004. 100 min. Morgan Spurlock, (1970–). A wacky reality TV film that follows the star, writer, director, and producer, Morgan Spurlock, as he eats only McDonalds for a month while chronicling the effects on his body. Spurlock's films are "edutainment" that intersperse pop culture with storytelling.

Up film series, 1964–. Grenada/ITV. Michael Apted—Research Assistant, Writer, Director, and Producer. In 1963, Apted, a young British ITV researcher, received specific instructions to find fourteen photogenic seven-year-olds, navigate bureaucracy for permission to film at the London Zoo, and arrange follow-on home and school interviews. This led to Apted scripting and arranging *7 plus 7* in 1970. When adolescent angst proved the importance of social classes, again the UK audience loved it. That's when ITV locked in Apted and the series. Over the next 50 years, Michael Apted went on to a storied career with critical acclaim for directing and producing over 40 dramatic films. He made 7 more *Up* films with *28 Up* making several "All Time Best Lists." Only occasionally does the *Up Series* seem like a sophomoric sociology when Apted, as well as a couple of the now-adult interviewees, created a few paparazzi moments.

3. Some of the Best Guides to Help Do Oral History Right

Coles, Robert. *Doing Documentary Work* (New York: Oxford University Press, 1997). This wide-ranging meditation describes researching diverse communities.

Dexter, Lewis Anthony. *Elite and Specialized Interviewing* (Evanston: Northwestern University Press, 1970). With roots in economic history, this study by an eminent political scientist reprints an essay by Charlie Morrissey, one of the pioneers of freelance oral history.

Evans, George Ewart. *Spoken History* (London: Faber and Faber Limited, 1987). This memoir describes the early work of a BBC interviewer who specialized in documenting rural life.

Kidder, Tracy. *Old Friends* (New York: Houghton Mifflin, 1993). This literary account shows an empathetic interviewer at work within a special community, as does the earlier classic *House*.

McNeil, W.K., edited by William M. Clements. *An Arkansas Folklore Sourcebook*. (Fayetteville: University of Arkansas Press, 1992). This guide explains a variety of resources available to understanding traditional culture in a state that takes pride in its complex heritage.

Morton, David. *Recording in America* (New Brunswick: Rutgers University Press, 2000). This fascinating chronicle includes the early days of oral history and ends with a chapter entitled, "The Tape Recorder, Home Entertainment, and the Roots of American Recording Culture."

Neuenschwander, John. *A Guide to Oral History and the Law* (New York: Oxford University Press, 2009). The standard resource on details of intellectual property issues in oral histories.

Ritchie, Donald A., editor. *The Oxford Handbook of Oral History* (New York: Oxford University Press, 2012). Detailed essays on important considerations in doing oral history.

Schama, Simon. *Landscape and Memory* (New York: Knopf, 1995). This wide-ranging study suggests the importance of environments in creating communal memory.

Yow, Valerie Raleigh. *Recording Oral History: A Guide for the Humanities and Social Sciences* (Lanham, MD: Altamira Press, 2005). This handbook is both thorough and readable.

4. Choices in Rural Oral History

Caudill, Harry. *Night Comes to the Cumberlands: A Biography of a Depressed Area* (Boston: Little, Brown, 1963). This classic describes the environmental effects of regional exploitation.

Ferris, William. *You Live and Learn. Then You Die and Forget It All: Ray Lum's Tales of Horses, Mules and Men*, with Foreword by Eudora Welty (New York: Anchor 1992). This long transcript with many notes and photographs offers insight into Southern storytelling and farming.

Galvin, James. *The Meadow* (New York: Holt, 1993). A non-fiction novel based on a family's struggle to maintain ownership of their ranch.

Gaventa, John. *Power and Powerlessness: Quiescence and Rebellion in an Appalachian Valley* (Champaign: University of Illinois,1980). This study helped create a new "bottom up" understanding of rural community, which in part led to a MacArthur "genius grant" for the author.

Glassie, Henry. *Vernacular Architecture* (Bloomington: Indiana University Press, 2000). "The American landscape says that people chose to exchange the confidence of communal life for the excitement of the pursuit for wealth," page 113, gives a taste of the breadth and depth of this intriguing study by a great folklorist/historian.

Harper, Douglas. *Changing Works: Visions of a Lost Agriculture* (Chicago: University of Chicago Press, 2001). This beautifully designed study uses oral history to support a selection from the largest non-governmental documentary project in the history of photography, sponsored by Standard Oil of New Jersey in the 1940s and now housed at the University of Louisville.

Hurston, Zora Neale. *Mules and Men* (New York: Harper, 1935, 1990). This folklore classic shares stories of Southern and voodoo customs.

McPherson, Robert S. *The Journey of Navajo Oshley* (Logan: Utah State University Press, 2000). This narrative uses a son's oral history to tell the story of a worker who traveled the West during a time of uncertainty.

Pike, Robert E. *Tall Trees, Tough Men* (New York: Norton, 1967). This classic oral history, mainly based on anecdotes and local lore, manages to capture a period of New England forest history somewhat typical of timber operations in the Ozarks and elsewhere.

Rouverol, Alicia and Stephen A. Cole, photography by Cedric N. Chatterley. *I Was Content and Not Content: The Story of Linda Lord and the Closing of Penobscot*

Poultry (Carbondale: Southern Illinois University Press, 1999). How does a woman survive the end of a job she's had for more than 20 years?

5. Classic Ozark Accounts

Beckham, O.L. *Ozark Night Call* (Joplin, MO: World of Printing, no date). This is one of several collections involving coon hounds, fabulous characters from the backwoods and living close to the bone. A rare item, but worth the search.

Broadfoot, Lennis Leonard, illustrated by the author. *Pioneers of the Ozarks* (Claxton, ID: Fourth Printing, 1972). Begun during the Depression, this collection centers on short interviews and portraits of the earliest settlers that Mr. Broadfoot was able to visit. The largest collection of his drawings is now being preserved at the Harlan Museum, West Plains, Missouri.

Harington, Donald. *Let Us Build Us a City: Eleven Lost Towns* (New York: Harcourt, Brace and Jovanovich, 1986). Inspired in part by James Agee's travels in the South, this elegant Arkansas author traveled his state to celebrate special people, places and his wife Kim.

Marbut, Curtis F, translator (from German to English). *The Great Soil Groups of the World and Their Development* by Konstantin Dmitrievich Glinka (1927). Born near Cassville, Marbut taught geology at the University of Missouri. He became director of the U.S. Department of Agriculture's Soil Survey Division until his untimely death consulting in China in 1935.

Randolph, Vance. *Pissing in the Snow and Other Ozark Folktales* (Champaign: University of Illinois Press, 1976). All of Vance's Ozark books are fun to read, but this may be the easiest entry into essential storytelling.

Scully, Julia. *Mike Disfarmer: Heber Springs Portraits, 1939–1946* (Santa Fe, NM: Twin Palms Publishers, 1996). This collection of 180 contact prints includes an essay by an editor who helped publish these photos in the 1970s. Much of Disfarmer's work is now housed at the Arkansas Art Center, Little Rock.

Sisco, Marideth. *Winter's Bone: Music from the Motion Picture* (CD, 2010, 15 songs, also available for streaming online.) Marideth's friends, who make up the Blackberry Winter Band, added to the film version of the Daniel Woodrell novel. Her other writings and music also deserve attention.

Staples, Edna. *Wolf Over the Ridge...Games We Used to Play* (Birch Tree, MO: Open Book Publishing, 2003). Ms. Staples wrote much of the Current River's history and taught at one-room schools nearby. This book explains 150 games used in these primary schools along with more than 20 songs for play parties and other musical gatherings.

Van Ravenswaay, Charles. *The Arts and Architecture of German Settlements in Missouri: A Survey of a Vanishing Culture* (Columbia: University of Missouri Press, 1977). This huge collection by a Boonville native has incredible photographs of unexpectedly fascinating objects, large to small.

Wallis, Michael. *Way Down Yonder in the Indian Nation: Writings from America's Heartland* (New York: St. Martin's Press, 1993). An enjoyable travelogue of essays, especially on Rt. 66.

6. Additional Ozark Writers and Musicians

As the Ozarks attracts diverse wordsmiths, I must mention a few more, who may not appear elsewhere in this book, to give a sense of treasures to find. Though many others could be mentioned, these are some who have inspired me over the years:

C.D. Albin; Gloria Attoun and Michael Bauermeister; Walter Bargen; David Benac; James Bogan; Loring Bullard; Johnny Cash; Neil Compton; Larry Dablemont; Bob and Sharon Dyer; Tim Ernst; G.W. Featherstonhaugh; Mike Fraser and Tenley Hansen; Susan Flader; Emily Higgins; Charles Wayman Hogue; Phillip Howerton; Sue Hubbell; Paulette Jiles; Gary R. Kremer; Don and Kathy

Love; Dave Malone; Howard Marshall; Margot Ford McMillen; Harry Middleton; Lester Mondale; Lynn Morrow; John Mort; Thomas Nuttall; Leland and Crystal Payton; Milton D. Rafferty; Carter Revard (Nompewatheh); Roy Reed; Quinta Scott; Frank Stanford; Bonnie Stepenoff; Fred Tompkins; Eric and Amelia Tumminia; Lucinda Williams; Miller Williams; Steve Wiegenstein; Larry Wood; W. Raymond Wood; C.D. Wright; Steve Yates.

Appendix 4

Schedule of Questions: Oral History of Land Use in the Ozarks

These questions were developed in consultation with Dr. Robb Jacobson of the USGS to examine traditional farming along the Current River. They were later adopted by Dr. Paul Albertson for a project he started at Ft. Leonard Wood in October 1997.

This is an example of an interview schedule, which is usually developed as research on a project begins. This helped to make sure I covered all topics when I was at a loss for words.

Ft. Leonard Wood Geomorphologic History Project

Introduction

These questions are designed to provide additional information about the historic context of settlement in the Ft. Wood area until the development of the base. The resulting interviews should provide the Fort archaeologist with significant details in interpreting potential historic sites in federal ownership.

Interview question schedule

Main topic: Find out different land uses. Where were the farms and how were they worked? How did the families cope with the Depression and social change, especially changes that can still be seen on the land. The questions marked with a "=" are of most importance to geological aspects of land use and should be answered as clearly as possible.

Is it possible to get a sketch of the farmstead, and any historic photos or related material?

LIVESTOCK
 - What areas were used for open range during what periods?
 - Where did the livestock stay during which seasons?
 - How were different livestock managed?
 = In what areas did livestock have the most environmental effects?

= Did any livestock seem to cause more gullying?
- What was livestock's effect on riparian vegetation?

CROPS
- How similar to slash & burn agriculture?
- What different kinds grown?
- What grown on uplands, what on bottoms?
- Why would locations of cropland be changed: gullying vs. loss of fertility?
= Did chert deposits prevent gullying in any fields?
- Were new crops tried? Rotation?
= Effects of plowing: gullying? What kind of tillage used, how often?
- Draft animals kept after/if tractors came into use? Threshing machines?
- How does diversification of land use vary thru time?
- Has stream networking increased in upper reaches of the watershed?
- Has there been a change in the amount of runoff?
- What sequence has led to gullying? [cutting; livestock: erosion]
- Is the gravel being pushed down or pulled up?
= Did gullies form on the upland or down by the larger creeks?

BURNING
- What time of year did burning take place?

= How long did it take for the bare soil to be covered with new growth?
- Effects on gullying?

LOGGING
- When were the forests cleared? Cleared completely? Allowed to grow back?
- What kind of cutting was done locally?
- How was timber skidded?
- What were the desired results: regrowth or fields?
- Were cattle, etc., grazed in the timber?
= Any gullying associated cutting; building new roads?
- Any tie slides in the area used a long time?
= Did tie rafts tear up river banks?
- Were log jams in/alongside streams frequently burned?
= What did the rivers look like? Did a lot of trees fall into the stream channel?
- Was there an effort to remove these trees?
- Did modern power sources create any kind of effect on the use of timber?
- Were orchards planted/replanted as a major resource?

SEDIMENTATION
= Was mud, sand and/or gravel regularly deposited in the big streams or small tributaries?
= Were attempts made to prevent gullying?

LIFESTYLES
- Did most people own their places? Many tenants?
- What important services were nearby: mail, school, church, stories?
- Was the Depression a major factor in the area?
- How did people feel about public assistance?
- Any memories of towns: Bailey, Cookville, Dundas, Moab, Tribune, Wharton, Wildwood
- Any agricultural organizations, other groups important in community?
- What churches were prominent?
- Any Native American families or other ethnic groups in the area? How did people get along?
- Differences in child-rearing, education, marriage?
- Did people think of themselves as living in the Ozarks? What does this mean?
- Any problem with lawlessness, fighting, crime, over-hunting?
- Folk beliefs, superstitions, use of wild plants, culinary habits, gardening?
- Stories, folk history, arts, memories of the Civil War or other crucial events?
- What did people do for health care?
- Did anyone make a lot of money when the Army came in?
- Have people in this area changed much in recent years?
- Comment: "I have never seen people so satisfied with themselves…." "The Ozark people are so connected with living that they don't care to bother with earning money while the rest of us are too busy earning money to live." Are these observations from the '40s true?

TRANSPORTATION
- When and why were roads and fences built?
- Did the railroads mean much to your family?
- When did the family first get a car?
- Did tourism affect the uplands?

WORK
- Who was the biggest tie hacker in the area? When was the last raft run, what were markets?
- Tomato canning, sawmills, factories; any other income possibilities?
- What was the biggest business?
- Were there people thought to be rich? How did they get along?
- Was there any mining done? Any unusual occupations?
- Did people stay a long time or was there a lot of resettlement, coming and going?

Chapter Notes

Part I

1. Linda Maple, *Breaking Ground: The Lower Elwha Tribe and the Unearthing of Tse-whit-zen Village* (Seattle: University of Washington Press, 2009).

Part II

1. H.P. Lovecraft, *Supernatural Horror in Literature* (New York: Ben Abramson Publisher, 1945), p. 12.
2. Alexander Freund, "'Confessing Animals': Toward a *Longue Durée* History of the Oral History Interview," *Oral History Review*, vol. 41, issue 1 (Spring 2014), p. 5. This fascinating essay ranges from Medieval handbooks of penance to Oprah Winfrey.
3. This was on the USS *Schley*, a World War I destroyer crewed largely by Missouri naval reservists called to duty a year before the attack on Pearl Harbor. The materials are at the State Historical Society of Missouri archive, in Columbia.
4. Valerie Raleigh Yow, *Recording Oral History*, 2nd ed. (Lanham, MD: AltaMira Press, 2005), p. 68.

Chapter 4

1. This article was written after I completed a series of interviews for the project. Summaries of the interviews were given to staff archaeologist at the Potosi ranger station along with the signed releases from each person interviewed. How this material is used and archived is a responsibility of the agency but is important to the interviewer too. It's necessary to know your work will be protected and possibly useful in the future.

Sidebar: Alford Forest

1. David wrote an email on Nov. 20, 2020 to clarify the size of the project, which is located near the popular Rockbridge Trout and Game Ranch, helping to protect its water quality, "I think it's important to state the original size of the Alford Forest as purchased in the '40s was 4300 acres, and remained owned in its entirety by Ella until she donated the 3200 acres to OLT, leaving the remaining 1100 acres to her heirs, but still protecting that 1100 acres under conservation easements with OLT, so the full 4300 is now under OLT protection. Indeed with the 4300 acres as land protected (though not owned) under a single entity (OLT), the AF is larger than the Shannondale Forest."

Memoir: Adirondack and Ozark Ancient Forests

1. Other projects for the Forest Service were centered on the Big Piney River as part of Challenge Cost-Share Agreement No. C9-05-83-029. This work was summarized in the magazine of the Missouri Historical Society, St. Louis, *Gateway Heritage*, vol. 19, no. 3 (Winter 1998–99), p. 19–27.

Part III

1. Yow, *Recording Oral History*, p. 97.
2. Daniel L. Schacter, *Searching for Memory: The Brain, The Mind and the Past* (New York: Basic, 1999), p.56.

Memoir: Almost a Great Job for an Oral Historian

1. Much of the history of the iron works and the modern park are in James D. Norris, *Frontier Iron: The Maramec Iron Works 1826–1876* (Madison: State Historical Society of Wisconsin, 1964) and Barbara L. Green, "Slave Labor at the Maramec Iron Works, 1828–1850," *Missouri Historical Review*, vol. 70, no. 2 (Spring 1979), p. 150–164.

Part IV

1. Ft. Leonard Wood, Maneuver Support Center. ERDC/CERL Special Report 03-5 (Champaign, IL, July 2003).

Chapter 11

1. Published by BookMasters, Inc., Ashland, Ohio, 1992.
2. *Letterman: The Last Giant of Late Night* (New York: Harper, 2017), p. 148.

Memoir: Dancing with the Spirit of Vietnam

1. John Dower, *War Without Mercy* (New York: Pantheon, 1986), p. 146.

Chapter 17

1. First edition (New York: Harcourt Brace, Jovanovich 1986), reprinted editions available, as well as new posthumous works and critical studies.

Memoir: Holding the Feather

1. For more information on this community, see Michael I. Niman, *People of the Rainbow: A Nomadic Utopia* (Knoxville: University of Tennessee Press, 1997).

Part VI

1. Some debate exactly where Booger County is, believing it's just hilly Douglas County and its one incorporated town, Ava. Sandy Ray Chapin focused a whole book in 2002, now a collector's item, on the subject: *Searching for Booger County: Ozark Folk Histories* (West Plains, MO: Elder Mountain Press, 2002) which focuses on detailed bicycle tours of the region.

Chapter 24

1. This article is based on a book review of Abraitys' *The Backyard Wilderness: From the Canadian Maritimes to the Florida Keys* (Frenchtown, NJ: Columbia Publishing, 1975), a sweet collection of his nature-based newspaper columns.

Chapter 25

1. *John T. Woodruff* is available at Springfield's new History Museum on the Square, at the nearby historic Rail Haven Motel, or directly from the publisher, Pie Supper Press, 2338 S. Maryland, Springfield Missouri 65807.

Memoir: Hillbillies and Black Helicopters

1. *A Connecticut Yankee in the Frontier Ozarks: The Writings of Theodore Pease Russell* (Columbia: University of Missouri Press, 1988).

Chapter 31

1. Michael Wiegers, ed., *What About This: Collected Poems of Frank Stanford* (Port Townsend, WA: Copper Canyon Press, 2015).

Chapter 33

1. *The New Yorker*, December 16, 2019.
2. This operation became one of the most successful protests by VVAW. Some 50 veterans from around the country met at

the American Civil Liberties Union headquarters in Manhattan to plan a week of creative protest in Washington, D.C., for spring 1971. John Kerry emerged as our leader to give one of the most famous testimonies before the Senate Foreign Relations Committee, saying, "How do you ask a man to be the last man to die in Vietnam? How do you ask a man to be the last man to die for a mistake?"

Chapter 35

1. Roy Reed, *Faubus: The Life and Times of an American Prodigal* (Fayetteville, AR: University of Arkansas Press, 1997), p. 17. This biography is unequalled for its writing and research into Ozark political culture.

Memoir: Portrait of My Father

1. Leonard Hall, Timon and colleagues had been members of Friends of the Land, a 1950s agricultural and conservation organization active in the Midwest. See Stephen Heyman, *The Planter of Modern Life: Louis Bromfield and the Seeds of a Food Revolution* (New York: Norton, 2020) p. 192.

Part VIII

1. Bruce Jackson, *Fieldwork* (Urbana: University of Illinois Press, 1987), p. 70.
2. Alex Primm, "Carrying on an Ozark Legacy: An Oral History of the Carnahans in Missouri Public Life," *Gateway Heritage, Missouri Historical Society*, vol. 22, no. 1 (Fall 2001): pp. 6–17.
3. Interview with Aileen Hatch, May 21, 1998, now in State Historical Society of Missouri, Author: Ozark Rivers Oral History Collection. See also Steven D. Smith, *Made in the Timber: A Settlement History of the Fort Leonard Wood Region*, ERDC/CERL Special Report 03-5; July 2003; Maneuver Support Center, Ft. Leonard Wood.
4. Olaf Blanke, et. al. *Leaving Body and Life Behind: Out-of-Body and Near-Death Experience*, in *The Neurology of Consciousness*. Second Edition, edited by Steven Laureys, et. al. (Cambridge, MA: Academic Press, 2015), pp. 323–347.
5. Michael Frisch, "From a Shared Authority to the Digital Kitchen, and Back," in *Letting Go? Sharing Historical Authority in a User-Generated World*, edited by Bill Adair et.al. (Philadelphia: The Pew Center for Arts & Heritage, 2011), p. 132.
6. Lewis Anthony Dexter, *Elite and Specialized Interviewing* (Northwestern University Press, 1970), p. 137.
7. Interview with Bud Massey, September 6, 1996, now in State Historical Society of Missouri, Author Rapport, rural, Ozarks, magical thinking, post-traumatic stress disorder: Ozark Rivers Oral History Collection.
8. Wendell Berry, "A Promise Made in Love, Awe, and Fear," in *Moral Ground: Ethical Action for a Planet in Peril* (San Antonio: Trinity University Press, 2010), p. 389.
9. Jane Smiley, "Say It Ain't So, Huck: Second Thoughts on Mark Twain's Masterpiece," *Harper's Magazine*, January 1996.
10. A classic study in rural sociology remains Arthur J. Vidich and Joseph Bensman, *Small Town in Mass Society: Class, Power and Religion in a Rural Community* (Princeton University Press, 1968). See also Catherine McNicol Stock, *Rural Radicals: Righteous Rage in the American Grain* (Ithaca: Cornell University Press, 1996).

Epilogue

1. Montgomery: University of Alabama Press, 2000.

Index

Numbers in ***bold italics*** indicate pages with illustrations

Adams, Mr. and Mrs. Earl 123–125
Adirondack Mountains, N.Y. 65–68, 196
African-American Ozark Heritage 49, 67, 167–171
Alford, Ella 62; Forest 62–64
Angel, Gerald 56
Apperson, Phoebe 91
archaeology 12, 67, 277
archives 8, 12, 24, 64, 70, 88, 91, 118, 122, 170–171, 281, 286
Arkansas 7, 63, 76, 88, 92, 100–101, 126, 136, 165, 189–190, 198, 212–213, 215, 232, 252, 260, 263, 279
Arkansas Outdoor Hall of Fame 100
The Arkansas Traveler 193

back-to-land movement 63, 73–78
Bacon, Basil 126–129
Bailey, Wendell 160
Banta, Zelma 49
barite (tiff) mining 5
Barker, Nobel Sr. 63
Bass Pro 126; *see also* fishing; sports and hiking
Battle of the Bulge 140
Beaulne, Kent 157
Beckley, W.Va. 67
Belgrade Church 48
Bellevue Valley 48
Benton, Thomas Hart 279–280
Berger, Kay 70–78, 145–151
Berger, Ted 70–78, 145–151
Big Dry Fork Creek (Phelps Co.), Mo. 30
Big Piney River, Mo. 96, 172, 210
Big Smith (band) 75
biosphere reserves (United Nations' program) 190–195
Birch Tree, Mo. 142
Black River, Mo. 54, 177

Blunt, Dollye Cole 48
Bogan, James 181, 210, 269
Boone, Daniel 272, 279
Borders, Nathaniel "Stub" 172
Boston Mountains, Ark. 215
Botkins, Gary 177
bridge, low-water (hog trough) 19, 21, 206
Brinktown, Mo. 113
Brinley, Bert 33–35
Brinley, Cody 33–35
Broadfoot, Lennis L. 101, 187–189, ***188***, 290
Brooks, Carolyn 18, 134
Brown, Ralph "Treehouse" 15–23, ***16***, 31, 178–183, 251, 257
Brown, Rose 206
Bryant, Nancy 277
Bryant Creek, Mo. 62
Buffalo River, Ark. 191
Buffalo Trace (bourbon) 66
Bunker, Mo. 54, 60

Caldonia, Mo. 48
California Air Resources Board 62
campaigns for elective office 8, 18, 191, 244
carbon sequestration 62, 81, 270
Cardetti, Leo 91
Carey, Ken 219–226
Carnahan, Mel 244, 297
catfish 32, 38, 40, 249; *see also* fishing
Cavender, Richard 19, 87
charcoal production 22, 56, 58
Cherokee tribe 7–8, 208
China 118, 254, 267–275
climate change 77, 81, 195, 242
Codemo, Mary 174–176, ***175***
Compton, Gladys 49,
Council Bluff Church 48
Council Bluff Dam 34
Courtois Creek 48

299

Index

Courtois Hills 50
Courtois, Mo. 49
Craine, Roundy 32
Crocker, Oliver 51
Crystal Bridges Museum of American Art 213
Cuba, Mo. 134
Culler, S.L. Lumber Co. 50–51, 55
Current River, Mo. 2, 99, 180, 192

deer 15, 92, 96, 242
Depression 21, 48, 50, 67, 191, 207, 215
Devil's Elbow, Mo. 96
Dexhimer, Alva Gene 187
Diaz-Granadoz, Carol 227
Disfarmer, Mike 260
Doe Run Co. 54
Dogpatch, Ark. 232
Doniphan, Mo. 99
Douglas County, Mo. xii, 164, 296
Drey, Leo 256
Dubie, Chief Wana 145
Duncan, Jim 227
Dylan, Bob 65

Echols, Bill 83, 225
Echols, Nancy 83, 225
education 35, 48, 58, 75, 88, 101, 115–121, 155, 228, 290
Elgin, Robert L 91
Encyclopedia of Arkansas (online) 136
Enlow, Elaine 232–234
Enlow, Howard 232–234
Enough, Mo. 48
Eureka Springs, Ark. 165, 198–204

farming 71, 79–81, 90
Faubus, Doyle 215–218
Faubus, Orval 8, 233
fens 54–57, 177
fishing 85, 98, 265; gigging for river fish 109; *see also* Bass Pro; catfish
floating 16, 20–22, 97, 105, **180**, 210, 256, 268
forests 63, 65–68, 79–81, 84, 173, 225
Ft. Leonard Wood 94, 107, 113, 248
foster parents 123–125, 202
fox 60–61, 141
Frankclay, Mo. 49
French Ozark heritage 2–3, 35, 46, 79, 157–159, 190

Gasconade River, Mo. 24, 32, 97, 172
German Ozark heritage 24–31, 157, 207–209; Missouri Rhineland 24, 43
ghosts 46, 52
Glassie, Henry 1, 289

Grand Ole Opry 39
Grasshopper Hollow 53–59
gravel bars 69, 85
Greenwood Forest Land Trust 223

Haenke, David 62, 73
Haffer, Ray 92–93
Halbert, Ada 181
Halbert, Britz 48
Halbert, Earl 181
Hall, Leonard 235
Hall, Virginia 235
Harington, Donald 101, 136
Harmony, Barbara 198–204, **199**
Harrel, Rex 260
Hatch, Aileen 5, 101–108, 245
Hazel Creek, Mo. 49–50
Hearst, George 91
Hearst, Patty 91
Hearst, William Randolph 91
Hebai University of Science and Technology 269
Hensley, Violet 252
Hildebrand, Homer 97
historic preservation 95, 134
Historical Land-use Changes and Potential Effects (report) 69–72
Hobbs State Park, Ark. 100
hogs (domestic and wild) 73, 88, 92, 96
Holt, Bob 163
Horner, David 206
Horner, Merrill 206
Howard, Jesse 187
Hughes, Ford 89
Hughes, J.W. 50
hunting 2, 5, 33, 35, 50, 53–61 97, 100, 191–193, 217, 223, 240, 265
Huzzah Creek, Mo. 15, 181

Italian-Ozark heritage 174

Jacks Fork River, Mo. 2, 82–86, 265
Jacobson, Anne 205
Jacobson, Robb 2, 30, 70, 80
James, Lucy Wortham 87–93
James Foundation 87–90
Jeffers, Dr. Joseph 136
Jones, Ronnie 145, 148
Joseph Chapel 48
Jouharian, Richard 212

Kansas City, Mo. 274
karst topography 77, 203
King, the Rev. Cecil 79–81
Korean War 21
Kridelbaugh, Brian 277

Index

Lake of the Ozarks 127
Lane, George 107, 270
Langenberg, George 24–31, **25**
Leake, Dorothy 341
Lebanon, Mo. 167
Lederer, Katherine 169
Leong, Wing Yin "David" 170
Letterman, David 101–108
Licking, Mo. 101
Little Piney River, Mo. 2, 79–81

Mace, Marvin 109–111, **109**
Made in the Timber 95
Mammoth Springs, Ark. 79
Maramec Spring 48; Agricultural Museum 71; Park 87–93
Marbut, Curtis 190
Mark Twain National Forest 45, 48, 147, 284; *see also* US Forest Service
Martin, Amel 56, 60–61
McGinnis, Leroy 134–135
McGinnis, Ovia Marie 134–135
memory 3, 71
Meramec Basin Association 256
Meramec Regional Planning Commission 19, 22
Meramec River, Mo. 18, 179–183, 205, 254, 268
Mihalevich, Norma Lea 112–114
mills 12–13, 21, 63, 80, 93, 100, 184, 206, 239, 275,
mining 49–51, 91
Missouri Arts Council 180
Missouri Botanical Garden 240
Missouri Cultural Heritage Center 3, 190
Missouri Department of Conservation 54, 83, 85, 178, 192
Missouri Historical Society 255; *see also* State Historical Society of Missouri
Missouri Humanities Council (formerly Committee for the Humanities) 22
Missouri Park and Recreation Assoc. 90
Moondog (Louis Thomas Hardin) 211
moonshine whiskey 48, 107, 272
Moore, Louis 130–133
Moore, Randy 147–149
Morrin, Peter 18, 134
Mount Ida, Ark. 213
Mountain View, Mo. 9, 83, 222
music 120, 39; Grand Ole Opry 39; Someone Still Loves You Boris Yeltsin 120

National Endowment for the Arts 181
National Heritage Region 194
National Water Council (Eureka Springs, Ark.) 198–201

Native American artifacts 11, 27, 30, 91, 146, 277
The Nature Conservancy *see* TNC
Niangua River, Mo. 38–42
Nickel, T.J. Preserve, Okla. 53

oak barrels 39, 135
Oklahoma 7, 53, 150, 167–168, 170, 262, 267
Oral History Association 63, 168
oral history, methodology 43–46, 54, 243–251, 269, 281, 288–289
Oral History of the Ozarks Project 179
Oral History Review 11, 70, 243, 273
Ouachita River, Ark. 262–264
Ozark Area Community Congress 63
Ozark Land Trust 62
Ozark Mountain Daredevils 75
Ozark National Scenic Riverways 190, 222
Ozark Property Rights Council 194
Ozark Rivers Oral History Project 19
The Ozark Society 191

Paddy Creek Wilderness Area 97
Palmer, Mo. 46–52
Pattie, James Ohio 97
pine timber 50–52, 84
Potosi, Mo. 48–49, 51
Primm, Cathy 125; Timon & Nancy 235–242, 263
Primm, Nancy 235–242, 263
Primm, Timon 235–242, 263
Pryor, Roger 76
Purinton, Wayne 118
Puxico, Mo. 227

Quakers 48, 75, 155, 197, 211
Queen Wilhelmina State Park, Ark. 262

rafting cross-ties downstream; 48, 96, 97–100, 140
railroads, Frisco 205 215, **216**
Rainbow Family 145–152, **146**
Ramsey, Napoleon B. 97–100
Randolph, Vance 8, 290
rapport 71, 82, 105, 202, 244, 247–251, 281
recording (analog cassette) 9, 45; digital 44, 82, 90, 122, 247
Reed, Bill 139–142
Reed, Roy 8
Reed, Trudy 139–142
Rockbridge, Mo. 62
Rolla, Mo. 5, 18, 24, 32, 75, 79, 112, 124, 145, 152, 169, 179, 201, 244, 278
Rolla Daily News 18, 122–133, 154
Rolling Heath School 98, 113
Rosebud, Mo. 26,

Index

Roubidoux Creek, Mo. 7
Route 66 (historic highway) 15, 40, 96, 167
Runner, Bob 50
Russ, Tristen 265

St. Francois Mountains, Mo. 35, 263
Ste. Genevieve, Mo. 33, 46, 157, 182
St. James, Mo. 19, 36, 88, 90, 137
St. Joseph, Mo. 49
St. Louis, Mo. 5, 18, 76, 157, 167, 168, 212, 240, 255–259, 263, 271, 277, 279
The St. Louis Post-Dispatch 65, 239, 277
Sauer, Carl 1–2
sawmills 12, 55
Schoolcraft, Henry Rowe 75
schoolteachers 49, 113; *see also* education
Schweke, Alexa 170
Schweke, John 170
Scotia, Mo. 17, 21, 179, 206
Scots-Irish Ozark Heritage 79, 191
Scudder, Gini Webb 160
sediment, in rivers 80, 84, 293
Seed Tick School 50
Shannondale, Mission of the United Church of Christ 63, 295
Shaw, Tony 116–118
Shelton, Virgil M. 96–97
Shipley, Tom 179, 268
Shirley, Mo. 48
Silver Dollar City 234
Sligo, Mo. 47
Smallwood, Alma 36, **37**
Smallwood, River Charlie 36, **37**
Snelson, Walter 89
Snow, Edgar 279
sodium arsenite 65
Someone Still Loves You Boris Yeltsin 120
Sowers, Steve 145
Speculator, N.Y. 66
sports and hiking 76, 161, 228; *see also* Bass Pro
Springer, James 184–186
Springfield, Mo. 169, 230, 278
springs, natural fresh water 62, 77, 79, 87, 110, 160, 198–204
Stanford, Frank 201, 296
State Historical Society of Missouri (Columbia) xii, 64, 91; *see also* Missouri Historical Society
Steelville, Mo. 206, 268
Sugerman, Darlene 254–259
Sugerman, Jerry 254–259
Sutterfield, Floyd 55–56, 248–249

Tahlequah, Okla. 53
Thich Nhat Hanh 120–121

Thomasville, Mo. 149, 151
ticks (wood, deer) 7, 15, 75, 168, 224
TNC (The Nature Conservancy) 54, 100, 177, 193, 238, 241
Toll, Jack 82–86
Toll, Marty 82–86
Trail of Tears 48, 208
Trammel, Clint 63
transcripts 102, 82, 170, 249, 273
trapping 60; fish traps 32–33
Tree Dialogues 44, 283
Treehouse, an Ozark Story (video) 93, 181
Trump, Donald 232, 251

US Army 87
US Army Corps of Engineers 22, 27, 34, 127, 191
US Forest Service 46, 54, 66, 145, 161; *see also* Mark Twain National Forest
US Geological Survey, Water Resources Division 24, 69–72, 83
US National Park Service 69, 83, 180, 191–194, 256, 283

vegetables 36, 73–78, 175, 249
Veterans Vietnam Restoration Project 115–121
Viburnum, Mo. 48
Vienna, Mo. 19, 24, 208
Vietnam 7, 18, 77, 115–121, 141, 194, 196, 201, 211, 237, 275

Walker, Flossie 50
Walmart 190, 213
Wang, Will 267–275
Wang, Willa 267–275
War of 1812 7
Washington County, Mo. 48–49
Welker, Steve 50, 51
West Plains, Mo. 112, 152, 189, 252
West Plains Gazette 155, 160
whippoorwills 42
White River Trace 48, 172
Wiggins, Charlotte 149
wildlife: deer 15, 92, 96, 242; fox 60–61, 141
Winter's Bone (Daniel Woodrell) 7, 250, 272
Wiseheart, Susan 64
Wixson, Doug 44, 262–264
Wonders of Wildlife Museum; Springfield, Mo. 129
World War II 21, 44,

Yancy Mill 79–80
Yeary, Frances "Nana" 205–209
Yow, Valerie 44, 70, 289, 296

www.ingramcontent.com/pod-product-compliance
Ingram Content Group UK Ltd.
Pitfield, Milton Keynes, MK11 3LW, UK
UKHW041925140426
5217IPUK00014B/315